ALSO BY JOHN GIORNO

Subduing Demons in America: Selected Poems, 1962–2007

Everyone Gets Lighter

You Got to Burn to Shine

Grasping at Emptiness

Suicide Sutra

Shit, Piss, Blood, Pus, & Brains

Cancer in My Left Ball

CUM

Cunt

Balling Buddha

Johnny Guitar

Poems by John Giorno

The American Book of the Dead

GREAT DEMON KINGS

FARRAR, STRAUS AND GIROUX   NEW YORK

GREAT DEMON KINGS

A MEMOIR OF POETRY, SEX, ART, DEATH, AND ENLIGHTENMENT

JOHN GIORNO

Farrar, Straus and Giroux
120 Broadway, New York 10271

Printed in the United States of America
First edition, 2020

Owing to limitations of space, illustration credits can be found on pages 349–51.

Library of Congress Cataloging-in-Publication Data
Names: Giorno, John, author.
Title: Great demon kings : a memoir of poetry, sex, art, death, and
    enlightenment / John Giorno.
Description: First edition. | New York : Farrar, Straus and Giroux, 2020.
Identifiers: LCCN 2020003414 | ISBN 9780374166304 (hardcover)
Subjects: LCSH: Giorno, John. | Poets, American—20th century—Biography. |
    Performance artists—United States—20th century—Biography.
Classification: LCC PS3557.I53 Z46 2020 | DDC 811/.54 [B]—dc23
LC record available at https://lccn.loc.gov/2020003414

Designed by Gretchen Achilles

Our books may be purchased in bulk for promotional, educational,
or business use. Please contact your local bookseller or the Macmillan
Corporate and Premium Sales Department at 1-800-221-7945,
extension 5442, or by e-mail at MacmillanSpecialMarkets@macmillan.com.

www.fsgbooks.com
www.twitter.com/fsgbooks • www.facebook.com/fsgbooks

10   9   8   7   6   5   4   3   2   1

CONTENTS

John Giorno had been working on *Great Demon Kings* for more than twenty-five years, and he finished it the week before his death.

"John Giorno, a precious, luminous primordial palace, gleaming and blazing with majesty, was the center of my life."

—UGO RONDINONE

GREAT
DEMON
KINGS

PROLOGUE

In 1951, after a few weeks studying poetry, my sophomore high school English teacher said, "Homework is to write a poem. Go home, write a poem, and bring it in next Tuesday."

I was shocked. Write a poem, not possible! It was like flying through the air like Superman, or being an opera singer, something I couldn't do. The 1940s and '50s were still medieval times in America. There were no day care centers where poetry was taught to prekindergarten kids. As the deadline loomed, on Monday I sat at the desk in my room and wrote a poem. I didn't know how to do it, but looking back, I already knew that you couldn't just imitate a poem. I stumbled onto something, inventing a poetic technique. Words arose in my mind, first as sound, the sound of wisdom or the sound of what they meant. I tried to focus on them, to see them clearly, and wrote them by hand on a piece of paper, and later typed them on the portable Royal typewriter. The poem is lost, and I am sure it was bad, but I was like a baby Olympic athlete going over the high bar for the first time, and crashing down to the ground. When I finished, I felt very happy—a bright white feeling, a brief moment of bliss. From which comes the words *follow your heart*.

I handed in my homework, and on the following Tuesday, Miss Glick said, "I have read your poems, and I have liked them all. There are three that I like best, and I am going to read them to you."

She read the first poem, and then the second. The third poem was mine. I got a rush, holy smoke, wow! She looked at me, and said, "John, very good."

And I really liked doing it. I said to myself, I'm going to write more poems, and I did. And it was what everybody was supposed to do, *follow your heart*, seeing the bright feeling in your heart-mind, believing in it, and continuing with great diligence; the bright clarity being a reflection of one's true nature. At that moment, I became a poet.

The author's house on Old Brick Road

THE NEXT SCHOOL YEAR, my English teacher, Deborah Tannenbaum, said to me, "John, you should go see Dylan Thomas at the YMHA. He's great. You will love him." We had studied *A Child's Christmas in Wales*. Hearing her read the story, I experienced a slight rush of energy, and a warm, clear, happy feeling. She explained his innovations with voice and performance.

I took the train in from Long Island by myself to the YMHA on Lexington and Ninety-Second Street, and saw the world premiere full-cast reading of Dylan Thomas's play for voices *Under Milk Wood*. He sat center stage with five performers, each on a wooden stool. His magnificent voice and the five other voices seemed to me like a great musical composition, like Bach. He smoked cigarettes and was drunk, sweat pouring from his face. The cast was composed of brilliant actors, cult figures in New York theater: Dion Allen, Al Collins, Roy Poole, Sada Stewart Thompson, and Nancy Wickwire. I was struck by lightning.

Two weeks later, Dylan Thomas again performed *Under Milk Wood* at the Ninety-Second Street Y. I got a seat front row center.

It was too close, and I developed a pain in my neck from looking directly up. Thomas towered over me on the stage, and the cast of performers and bright white lights were overwhelming. But it was still a great performance. His breath and internal winds created heat, and as he perspired, sweat ran in droplets. When he threw his arms around, drops of his sweat swirled about, and some flew out into the audience: one hit me. A blessing, holy communion, I was anointed. He was the most amazing thing I had ever seen. Not only were the poem and the performance great, he *was* poetry.

This experience changed my life. It resonated with the boundless possibilities of what poetry could be. I was a poet, and developed as a performer over the next fifty years, empowered first by Dylan Thomas.

After the performance, I bought two albums of Thomas's poetry, released by Caedmon Records. I played them endlessly in my bedroom, fascinated and obsessed, trying to understand and absorb something. All the other poetry I knew was archaic. This was before Burroughs, Ginsberg, and the Beats. I was imprisoned in the stone age of the early 1950s.

In the fall of 1953, Dylan Thomas returned for yet another performance of *Under Milk Wood* at the Ninety-Second Street Y. I got fifth row center seats, and took my girlfriend, Marion Eisenberg. By now, I was becoming an expert in the subtleties of Dylan Thomas's performances.

During the intermission, we were in the lobby smoking cigarettes and ran into friends from the High School for the Performing Arts, where Marion was studying acting. One of her classmates was Suzanne Pleshette, who very shortly would become a famous movie star. We were all sixteen years old.

"It's very well produced," said Marion confidently.

"The flow is extraordinary," said Suzanne. They were both being modest professionals.

"It's so amazing," I said. "I've seen it twice before, but each time it is so shocking! It's dazzling poetry."

When the lights blinked, I had to go to the toilet and ran as fast as I could. I didn't want to miss anything. I pulled the bathroom door open at full speed, lurched forward, and collided with a man. My face hit his fat face, my chest against his chest, cheek to cheek for an instant. It was Dylan Thomas. I froze, wide-eyed and speechless. I stepped back, bowed shyly, and said in a tight, little voice, "Hello!"

Dylan Thomas gave a small, wonderful smile, and said hello softly in return. He continued on to the backstage door. I went back to my seat, transfixed. I felt he had reluctantly kissed me. I was blessed with a touch of his skin. The rest of the performance was like listening to great music, and I sat there in bliss.

Thomas died two weeks later.

As a teenager, I received all my spiritual training from reading great novels and poetry. I read Hemingway, F. Scott Fitzgerald, Beckett, Jean Genet, Proust, Dostoyevsky, Tolstoy, Virginia Woolf, Joseph Conrad, Emily Dickinson, Faulkner, Walt Whitman, Gertrude Stein, and T. S. Eliot. They said, in a nutshell, that one was doomed in a world bound by ignorance, and the only way to liberation was through love and sex, pure transcendent desire, and that always ended in disaster. Everything ended in suffering.

I received a full transmission of worldly knowledge by the time I was seventeen, and what I learned when I later studied at Columbia was redundant. There, I read Plato and Aristotle through to Thomas Aquinas and Machiavelli, Locke and Hume and Burke, Darwin and Marx, Nietzsche and Thomas Dewey. None of it did any good. Nothing solved the problem. I studied Buddhist philosophy, Asian literature, and oriental art, discursive and intellectual thought, and we had endless discussions. I liked it, but it did not solve anything either. Many years later, Dudjom Rinpoche, the greatest Buddhist scholar of his time, would say, "No one becomes enlightened reading a book."

I would have to wait my time. In my Oriental Art class at Barnard, we saw a slide show of the history of religious art and architecture across Asia over four thousand years, but it was the professor's own recent slides of stupas and temples that I was most drawn to. During our studies of Hinayana and Mahayana Buddhism, professors hinted that another form of Buddhism, tantric or Vajrayana Buddhism, had survived in remote Tibet. "We don't know much about it," I remember the professor saying. "What remains is in Tibet with the lamas." It was there that I would eventually find home.

IN APRIL 1956, during the Easter break of my sophomore year, my friend Peter Zimels, who went to the University of Michigan at Ann Arbor, came to visit. My large single room on the top floor of Livingston Hall overlooked the grandiose Georgian campus on Broadway and 116th Street. We were nineteen years old, poets. We drank a lot. Our present and future seemed pretty dismal and hopeless. It was a joke to fathom what we were supposed to do with the rest of our lives.

"The reason I dislike Columbia," I said to Peter, "is that everyone is here to become lawyers, doctors, businessmen, and professors. Their aspiration is to get some horrible job making money to support a wife and children, a bourgeois life imprisoned in suburbia. Peter, are we supposed to do that? Get jobs, and be gainfully employed! I would rather die." We screamed with laughter. "I think not!"

Although it was unspoken, the highest pinnacle of what we had learned in high school and college was that a transcendent mind, noble aspirations, enlightenment—the highest human achievement—was the most difficult state to attain. It was a path beyond making money and wasting life at a mundane job. "But besides being poets, how do we fit practically into life?" I asked.

"There is no solution, no way out," said Peter, which was both completely true and really funny.

Our answer was to drink more bourbon and smoke more Camels. Short-circuiting our nervous systems, coupled with our adolescent energy, gave rise to a clarity and bliss, which we recognized as the ultimate and absolute true nature. Occasionally, Peter had pills, Benzedrine, "Bennys" as they were called, and pot, or reefer. We drove around visiting friends, and hung out with Marcia Stillman, Peter's girlfriend, in her mother's apartment on Park Avenue. Peter and I usually ended up back at my place, drinking Jack Daniel's straight up.

One night, Peter said, "I have something that is going to blow your mind," taking a book from his pocket. "A book of poems by Allen Ginsberg, called *Howl*. Have you heard about it?"

I hadn't.

"I thought not. It's so cool! Just published this February by City Lights in San Francisco." He handed me the book, which had a black-and-white cover. "And here's something to go with it." He gave me three joints.

I was tired of reading—poetry or anything else. I had spent my whole life reading, and every day meant massive amounts of more required reading. All that reading had not solved the problems, only made them worse, and made my awareness of the troubles with the world more acute. "Poems don't solve anything, poems don't change anything."

"John, trust me! This is a very special poem. I thought of you when I first read it," Peter insisted.

"For good or bad, better or worse, I just want to live life, not read about it." But seeing Peter's display of love, I had to be polite. I respectfully skimmed through the pages, looking at a few lines, flipping through it several times like a fan making wind. "Thanks. I'll read it later." I put the reefer and the book first on my desk, and later in the bottom drawer.

One night about two weeks later, I had a hangover and a headache, and I remembered the three joints. In the mid-1950s, drugs were not easy to come by. I smoked a joint, and after a while looked at the book that Peter had given me.

I opened the black-and-white cover. I read *Howl* and was shocked. It was a traumatic experience, like falling down the stairs and seeing stars. Great exaltation! I felt my life being changed, a veil or caul of ignorance lifted from my eyes. I had never read anything like it before. It was a reflection of my heart-mind. I had a propensity for being unhappy, not for any one reason, but for every reason, as a marginalized, gay poet. But *Howl* contained gay images; for the first time, gay pornographic images that were not archaic or in literary disguise, *street porn* that was unbelievably beautiful. Dylan Thomas had shown me the possibility of poetry, but for the very first time, a poem struck deep into my heart. I started weeping.

It didn't seem possible that someone could write such a poem. What Ginsberg did for me, he had also done for countless other people, for every gay man or hip person of my generation. I was filled with awe at his accomplishment, his great compassion.

At that point in contemporary literature, Samuel Beckett was the only really cutting-edge writer—difficult, boring, and great. There was no one else. I really liked T. S. Eliot, *The Waste Land* and *The Love Song of J. Alfred Prufrock*, which I had read every year since I was fourteen. Perhaps they were my first understanding of the nature of emptiness and suffering, and indicated an early attraction in the direction of Buddhist teachings. There was Auden, Whitman, Baudelaire and Rimbaud, and countless other wonderful poets, but they were from another century or another time, not *now*. None of them had ever touched my heart and mind as Allen Ginsberg did so miraculously.

Sitting in room 803 in Livingston Hall, I had to get out or burst. I tucked *Howl* under my white T-shirt and belt, so nobody would see this sacred book, and grabbed the two remaining joints and my cigarettes. I ran down the stairs and fled campus, crossed Broadway, and ran down 115th into Riverside Park. The weather had just changed to spring. The air was suddenly warm and delicious, and tiny chartreuse-green leaves had burst out on the trees for the first time that day.

I held *Howl* in my hand and I wanted to scream, to explode, to do something drastic with all the energy flowing. I ran along the park paths yelling with glee, leaping into the air and shouting, running as fast as I could, jumping as high as I could, again and again. Underneath the surface of so much elation, I knew that this was archetypal behavior. I felt as if I was the embodiment of James Joyce's *Portrait of the Artist as a Young Man.* There was the awareness of the sheer joy of swimming in vastness.

"Yahoo! Ha! Ha! Ha! Ho!" I yelled. The sound moved in the wind of my breath. Clear light and absolute bliss rang in my heart, radiating out and filling the universes beyond the vast dome of black sky. I realized what I was doing—howling! "Yahoo! *Howl.*"

I ran a little too fast, skidded, and fell on the stone pavement. I got up and kept running, and dancing, jumping as high as I could, almost pirouetting, the liberation of Nijinsky, and falling with a crash. I skipped on with a charley horse. I felt a dampness running down my face. I had scraped and gashed my head and face on the pavement, and blood poured down my cheeks. I had torn my jeans, cut my knees, and blood ran down my leg. A blood sacrifice, and a blood offering!

I sat down, smoked a joint, and read the poem again in the dim light from the lamppost. It was really true. It said those words. I was crying and shaking uncontrollably, having a nervous break-down. Then, energy propelled me through space. I held *Howl,* waving it over my head, weeping tears of joy. I sailed down the broad promenade into the humid, briny breeze that blew in from the ocean and up the Hudson River. It was revolutionary and miraculous that someone had written such a poem.

I was a part of the generation liberated by Allen Ginsberg's *Howl.* When I tell this story to young people now, sixty years later, they say, "It's great it did it for you and it's a nice poem, but it doesn't do it for me." Now, *Howl* is a fixture of the academic curriculum, required reading in every poetry class. It has become a part of the museum of great poems, like Yeats's "Sailing to Byzantium," which are wonderful but no longer have the power to liberate. Their cultural moment has passed. Dylan Thomas had set me on a path, but Allen Ginsberg was my first living hero poet; he radicalized me, changing my poetry by showing me my mind.

The first edition of
Howl and Other Poems

BEFORE *HOWL,* **I** had read Jack Kerouac's *Subterraneans* and *Dharma Bums,* and my friends and I discussed Kerouac endlessly. I trusted his understanding of the world, maybe reluctantly at first, as the only possible true way of viewing and being. He was my high aspiration, the mirror in which my aspiration saw itself. It was delusional, but Kerouac became the vehicle for me to see myself. And so, throughout college, whenever I had a problem or didn't know what to do, I said to myself, "What would Jack Kerouac do? What would Kerouac think?" Kerouac wouldn't sit still for a music class or pose for a yearbook photo, and so neither did I.

Kerouac was known to drink at a working-class bar on the Lower East Side called Sammy's Bowery Follies, and so there I went (not knowing that I was just a block north of what would become my lifelong home). The stars here were the heavily made-up women singers, in their fifties and sixties, but ravaged by age and hard living, looking decades older. In velvet and satin gowns, pearls and lots of big fake jewels, and wide-brimmed hats with ostrich feathers, they bellowed out the classics with shaky voices: "Sweet Rosie O'Grady," "You Made Me Love You," "Silver Threads Among the Gold"—the same songs they had sung as beautiful young girls. I was a poet and was fascinated, inspired, by these fabulous creatures, that they could do such a thing with their voices, breath, and bodies.

Kerouac had worked on ships, and so for my summer vacation of 1955, I joined the merchant marines. On a ship to Greenland, I worked in the galley as a mess man. During rough seas, I had fun serving food and coffee as we were rocked by the waves; the other sailors and I became children, playing a game in an amusement park. At night, the ship banged into small icebergs that the lookout couldn't see. I lay in my bunk bed, delighting as ice hit the heaving iron hull like great songs. The next summer, I took a job as a deckhand on a cargo ship carrying grain to Israel, then heading to Brazil for sugarcane, then carrying oil back up to Savannah.

Back in New York, I continued in Kerouac's footsteps and partied across New York with my friend Alice Dignan. We went to Smalls Paradise in Harlem, drank in the crowded black bar, and listened to the great music and danced. In the noisy, smoke-filled Cedar Tavern, we drank with Pollock and Rothko, and in the White Horse Tavern, we drank where Dylan Thomas had. At Kettle of Fish, a bar with a gay subtext, I actually twice spotted Jack Kerouac himself, though I was too scared to approach.

The White Horse Tavern

FINALLY, ON MAY 31, 1958, a Saturday night at about nine o'clock at a party in New York, I met him. It was like being struck by lightning, a shock similar to the one I experienced reading *Howl*, one from a book and one from real life. In the bleak cultural years of the 1950s, Kerouac and Ginsberg were the only living voices of truth, shining angels who touched my heart, the only ones who showed there was the possibility of change, and a clear perception of reality. I thought of them as great poets, living gods, and had imagined knowing them would be like having a relationship free of negative emotions, ideal. But that was before I got to know them. Everyone was a complete disappointment.

I was twenty-one years old, just finishing college at Columbia. As usual, I was with Alice. We disdained parties, but Alice had heard from the sculptor Carl Andre that a cool party was happening on 108th Street and West End Avenue. As usual, we were drunk on vodka martinis.

I was young and beautiful and that got me what I wanted and all I wanted was sex. I had all the money I needed; my parents gave me an allowance and paid my bills. Alice and I were a famous couple among a certain set of cool people at Columbia and at the West End Bar, small consolation for our suffering; our egos were all that we had. We were obnoxious.

We arrived at the party as dysfunctional royalty. Alice was wearing a black cocktail dress, and I, a rumpled white linen suit. We walked through the hot, crowded party with the arrogant scorn of cats, scanning everything, but not looking at anything, because nothing was worthy. It was a humid night, and the dense cigarette smoke and sweat made a stinking fog. We nodded occasionally and headed toward the kitchen, where the bar was. We ran into someone we knew and were very relieved to have someone to talk to. We moved on and stood dumbly in a dim, crowded hallway, drinking red wine and smoking Camels.

"There's Allen Ginsberg," said Alice. I didn't understand.

"John, darling, there is Allen Ginsberg . . . The one you really like . . . who wrote that poem . . . *Howl!*"

"Where?" I said, surprised, looking around and not seeing. Ginsberg was standing behind me with his shoulder poking into my back, talking to someone. I was stunned. My hero poet, who existed only in myth, was touching me. I was speechless.

"Hello, Allen," said Alice, extending her hand grandly. He bowed and kissed it, like a gentleman. "My name is Alice Dignan . . . And this is John Giorno." She was obviously deferring to me. "He's a poet."

Allen got interested. "You're a poet? Who are your teachers?"

My youthful bravado banished my nerves. "I had them all. And they weren't all that good," I said, cheerfully confident. Columbia had world-renowned professors, but their effect on me was less than I had hoped. "They were wonderful, but a big waste of time or a small waste of time."

"Huh?"

What I meant was that I had spent my whole life reading and studying, and I had received the most important teachings, and an understanding of literature, from two great high school English teachers, Deborah Tannenbaum and Philip Rodman, who had introduced me to everything. At Columbia, I studied with all the illustrious professors, but it was only a refinement of what I already knew. There was no breakthrough knowledge, with the exception of Buddhist philosophy. I did not understand much more than what I knew between the ages of fourteen and seventeen.

This was not what Allen wanted to hear. "How can you say that!" he said disapprovingly. I was surprised at Allen being so straight. But I wanted him to like me. I would have done anything. "They are great!" I said enthusiastically. "And I've had them all. Mark Van Doren, Lionel Trilling, Eric Bentley. They are all totally great. They changed my life."

"Good!" said Allen, smiling.

I was shameless. "I am editor of the *Columbia Review*," I said boldly. "Or was." It was the undergraduate literary magazine, where I was poetry editor. "Impermanence." I laughed gently.

"Wow! You are?" He seemed predictably impressed with what I thought of as these bourgeois credentials and conventions, not what I would have expected of the enlightened revolutionary.

"I love Mark Van Doren. He was my poetry teacher for two years."

"I had a meeting with him two years ago. He was delightful."

"But that's all finished. I'm at the moment of being liberated. Just now, this coming Tuesday, I graduate. I've always been a student, going endlessly to classes. Now, I'm a free man, finally, a *free man.*"

Allen seemed charmed. Someone came up and asked him something, distracting him.

"You're in luck," Alice whispered. I didn't understand. "He likes boys. You are in luck, John, darling!"

Allen turned his attention back to me. "What are your plans?"

"I just want to write and continue working on poems," I said, and he nodded approvingly. "I go to Europe for the summer. In the fall, I have a fellowship to attend the Iowa Writers' Workshop."

"Wow! Congratulations!" Allen radiated appreciation. In the 1950s, the Iowa Writers' Workshop was the most prestigious literary school in America. Someone else interrupted and Allen turned away.

Alice laughed. "You've done very well," she said.

"Why not!"

I looked around us and to the left saw a skinny kid bouncing up and down, and in a flash I remembered some photographs of the Beats, and recognized Peter Orlovsky, and next to him was Gregory Corso. Even though 1958 was pretty early, they were already icons.

I looked to my right, and between Alice and me, and there was the head of Jack Kerouac. I was stunned. Jack Kerouac had been listening to what I had said to Alice and Allen. Jack Kerouac was standing behind me, leaning his head forward, his chin touching my shoulder, trying to listen to us through the loud din of the party. It was incomprehensible! Jack Kerouac existed only in myth, like a movie star or a Greek god. He was touching me and listening to my words.

Jack! I got a little dizzy; I felt a blissful rush in my head and my heart. For an instant, I was speechless, dumbstruck, without thoughts, in a god world, just there in the moment. I hadn't yet realized that that was the most important state to be in.

After a while, I managed to say something to Allen. "What year were you here at Columbia?"

"Nineteen forty-eight," said Allen, being fussily exact, which was his personality.

"This is fifty-eight," I managed, in a constricted voice.

"And Jack was nineteen forty-four. At our first meeting, Jack offered me a beer over breakfast, and when I said, 'No, no. Discretion is the better part of valor,' Jack barked back, 'Aw, where's my food!'"

We all laughed a little awkwardly. The story was lame, but everyone deferred with kindness to Allen. I realized that Allen was different from his public image of the personification of hip and cool; he was embarrassing, a little nerdy, dumb because he was too smart. He had the imprint of an old-fashioned style, which made him seem a little like what we were rebelling against. But it was also startlingly clear that Allen was the leader of a movement, the spokesperson, the one who usurped or claimed the job. He was the person on whom everyone focuses their trust and devotion, as a symbol for their own aspiration.

Jack Kerouac smiled warmly at Allen. Jack was so beautiful. He was wearing a short-sleeve shirt, and I could see his muscles, and he had an amazingly handsome face. We looked in each other's eyes in the dimness, and his body and being were magnetizing. Just seeing him fulfilled something in me.

"Oh, you went to school here too?" I said daringly, leaning my right shoulder toward Jack. I had to say something. I loved him.

"I just finished, now. I have been a student prisoner all my life. Being released from the suffering of school!"

Jack Kerouac smiled, leaned forward with his thumb stuck in his belt, and touched the back of my hand with his other hand. An electric shock passed between us. "You're lucky," said Jack.

"I guess so!" I was thrilled. I couldn't believe he said those words, a rush of joy. "Yes!"

Jack tilted in again and said something else. It was very noisy and I couldn't hear him. A moment of panic: how could I not hear what Jack Kerouac was saying to me! "I can't hear you." He came even closer and his lips touched my ear and I could hear sound, but I couldn't understand the words. For an instant, we looked again into each other's eyes. My heart was hooked together with his. We were without discursive thoughts, resting in one another, a simple feeling of clarity.

I asked him something stupid, just to continue our connection. He couldn't hear me, so he put his ear to my mouth, and we touched again, my moving lips pressed against his upper earlobe. I was drunk and so was he, and we staggered, our cheeks brushed against each other. We could have kissed, stuck our tongues in each other's mouths, rubbed our dicks, and hugged our hearts together, but there were so many people around.

I said something else stupid and he smiled, and responded. He was so incredibly beautiful. I was in love with his smell, and the heat coming from his body, and the compassion radiating from his heart. And what pushed it over the top was that it seemed mutual.

"Why are we here?" asked Jack.

What did he mean? A moment of panic, where? On earth? At this party? Something more complicated like karma? "I don't know." Looking in his eyes, I felt dumb and frightened, but it seemed like the right answer, because defeat included all the possibilities, including that all answers are delusion, and the ultimate truth of being here and not being here. All those thoughts whizzed through my mind in an instant.

Gregory Corso said something loudly. He handed a joint to Jack, who took a puff and passed it to me. I inhaled long and deep, held it in my lungs, and passed the joint back to Jack. I was ecstatic, smoking marijuana with Jack Kerouac. It was a very hot night. I was hyperventilating and sweat poured from me in sheets. My clothes were soaked and the air was thick and wet with humidity. I was underwater.

Allen Ginsberg was watching us, taking it all in, and I could see the sharp disapproval on his face. He stepped forward, pushed between Jack and me, and separated us, moved deliberately in, and cut us off. "You two know each other!" he said, slightly peeved.

"Oh!" Catastrophe. Allen swam in like a great white shark and killed. Something inside me screamed. He destroyed love through jealousy and possessiveness. He ended something that in its purity could and would never ever happen again.

"Gregory said let's get out of here," said Allen, frowning. "Jack, let's go."

Allen led Jack away, through the door into the other rooms. They all walked out, moved on, and it was over. They vanished, but I was happy beyond belief at such an amazing occurrence. "John, darling, do you feel empty, now that they're gone?" said Alice, puffing on a cigarette.

"I feel totally great! Exhilarated! I can't believe that just happened!" It struck me as a good omen, an auspicious sign, meeting these guys at the moment of the beginning of the rest of my life.

Jack Kerouac

AS A BOY, when I first heard blues singers like Bessie Smith and Billie Holiday, or Judy Garland, I understood something, and got a warm feeling in my heart. All my life, during both the good and bad times, on the outside I appeared to be a happy, good-looking, and good-natured guy. But the truth was, I suffered with severe depression, and was in complete denial, because I didn't know there was such a thing. In the 1940s and '50s, nobody acknowledged it, unless the person was nuts, a schizoid, manic-depressive and nonfunctional. I saw that friends who went to psychiatrists were not successfully treated. In fact, seeking medical help seemed to make things worse. I had no interest in heavy medication: lithium that made you fat and brain-dead, or electric shock treatment that killed the mind. I would hold on to this bias my whole life. Not fully acknowledging my depression was the only way to endure it.

Suicide became a lifelong obsession. Rarely did a day pass when I didn't think of suicide, the happy possibility of it, and on those days when I didn't think temptingly about it, I noted I hadn't thought about it. I always had the gut feeling of wanting to do it.

After graduating Columbia, the darkness followed me to Europe during the summer of 1958. At first, I had little trouble keeping it at bay. I was young and insatiable, and I cruised and made love with countless men, day and night. In Paris, I was so sex-obsessed that I blew off an old friend's invitation to check in with her to the famous Beat Hotel, to meet "this weird guy" William Burroughs, who was writing *Naked Lunch*. One night in Zurich, a beautiful pale architecture student led me into a cemetery, where we tore open our clothes, caked ourselves in mud and cum, kissed and shivered all night, atop what we later realized was the tomb of Ulrich Zwingli, the Swiss leader of the Protestant Reformation, denier of all mortal pleasure. Leaping over tombstones the next morning, I laughed: "We got out alive!"

But by the time I reached Italy, between ecstatic bursts of great art and great sex, the depression caught up with me. In Rome, I staggered through a debauched, star-studded underworld, the same scene and the same summer that was inspiring Fellini's next big movie. Late one night at the famous nightclub Bricktop's, I even met Fellini in person, but couldn't make an effort to talk. Sensing my sadness, Bricktop took me under her wing, and at the end of another night, on her penthouse terrace overlooking the Tiber, she said to me: "John, I worry about you." I tried to laugh her off, but she persisted. "I've seen boys like you."

In September 1958, I drove in a green Mercury from New York to Iowa City. I had received a graduate fellowship for poetry to the University of Iowa's Writers' Workshop, run by Paul Engle. No other universities offered writing degrees. I was taking the next right step, being a poet. And I had had a poem, "Portrait of a Boy," published in the winter 1957 issue of the *Arizona Quarterly*, at the University of Arizona, and other poems in several small magazines, which made me feel good, because I thought it was the real world.

In Iowa, a small group of poets met in a World War II Quonset hut classroom and discussed one another's poems. My work was not like theirs and I didn't share their literary concerns, but I felt I learned a lot from the discussions and interaction. I was an outsider, a loner and a bit lonely, and, of course, depressed. What had I gotten myself into?

I wasn't happy with my own poems, which weren't developing the way I wanted. I didn't know what I wanted to do with them. I was young, and felt stuck. I had great admiration for Allen Ginsberg and Jack Kerouac, but I did not know how to let that influence change my work. It became very depressing, but I had to stick it out. I couldn't quit; because it was poetry, it was as though I had made a sacred vow.

I drank in Kelley's every night, a cool bar owned by a woman named Irene. We really liked each other and she had natural wisdom and great kindness. We got close enough for her to reissue Bricktop's warning from a few months earlier: "I worry about you."

In early 1959, Tibet's battle for independence from Communist China was met with sustained, brutal reprisal. The Dalai Lama fled Tibet, as did several hundred thousand lamas, monks, and nuns, and other Tibetans. I was horrified when I first heard the news on the radio. Every day, the first thing I did when I came home from classes was to turn on the radio and wait for the in-depth coverage of the tragic story on the six o'clock news. Accompanied by forty noble families and two hundred soldiers, the Dalai Lama struggled over the Himalayas toward India, as the Chinese bombarded monasteries, looted and destroyed temples, knocked down statues of the Buddhas, and burned books. It was a great catastrophe, and it resonated in my heart as the most powerful experience of the day. Going to school, reading, and writing bad poems seemed inconsequential.

I was deeply, overwhelmingly moved by the destruction of Buddhism in Tibet. Inexplicable grief took over my consciousness. Depressed and dissatisfied with my poetry, I took the Tibetan Buddhists' exile as a sign that I had to leave this world, too. Suicide seemed like the only viable solution. I didn't want anything from the world, and only wanted out. I wanted to go home to the purity of my true nature.

On February 23, after days and weeks of extreme depression, a voice inside me—my voice but slightly, malevolently different—said, "Tonight is the night. Tonight, I'll do it." I was a little shocked by the words. Tonight was the night of my suicide. I had to follow my heart. Down came the rain.

I pulled a straight razor across my wrist, and did it again and again. Blood rushed out from the long slices. I dug the razor into the cuts and pulled it across them, deeper and deeper. Blood gushed out. I did it again and again. It was a grand canyon. If you're going to do it, you might as well do it right.

I must have passed out, and when I awoke, the bloody mess

had coagulated. I got the razor, slippery with syrupy blood, cut into the liverlike mess, slivering ribbons of flesh. I opened it up and it started bleeding again. I thought maybe it would coagulate again and I cut four more slits. My hand and arms were shaking and trembling. Sinking slowly, I fell off into a deep sleep.

I was going back, as Emily Dickinson said on her tombstone, *"Called Back."* I was beginning a long voyage. There were musical crescendos, like for the gods in Wagner or the doomed royalty of Puccini. I visualized the radio news reports of the Dalai Lama fleeing Tibet for India, I saw him being carried in a sedan chair by his monks. I cried big tears for the Dalai Lama. I heard the sound of the deep resonance of the mantras being chanted and the rumble of the earthquake of the end of the world. My mind flip-flopped and I was the Dalai Lama and my monks and attendants were carrying me home. I lay on a big, ornate, brocade throne litter, moving over the rugged mountain paths, up and down valleys, to another world. I was going to the pure land of the Buddhas. The hallucination changed into an Egyptian royal barge surrounded by large retinues: Egyptian attendants and Nubian slaves. I was descending on a black river into the underworld. And everything became peaceful and nice, a soft glowing light, cool as camphor.

When I was dead, I would be dissolved into the primordial space of bliss and light, returning to a basic ground. And I longed to stay there. In the late night, I half awoke several times from thirst, each time more intense. My lips were parched and cracked, my mouth bone dry. There was the faint light of early morning. It must come really soon, I kept telling myself. How long does it take? I pushed myself back to sleep. Then, I woke up and it was bright daylight. The white bedsheets were a mess, drenched with vivid, red blood, and my arm was gashes of gnarled meat. I looked at the clock and it was 7:00 a.m. How was it possible? I tried to kill myself eleven hours ago and I was still alive. What was I going to do? I was so thirsty, it was excruciating. I wanted a glass of water before I died. I managed to get up and stagger to the bathroom. I drank some water and it didn't do any good. I was still thirsty. I collapsed on the floor, and went to sleep.

There was a lot of noise and screaming. My landlady had found me on the bathroom floor and was talking excitedly with her daughter. "I'll be okay," I said. I was conscious, in a painless daze, as I was carried down the stairs strapped in a stretcher, into an ambulance, which was soon speeding down the streets to the hospital. It was only when I heard the shrieking siren blaring directly over my head that the severity of the situation sank in.

"Oh, no! Now, I'm really in trouble!" And there loomed the nightmare of how I was going to explain it, squiggle past it, get on with it. I was obviously going to live.

I had lost five pints of blood. The body holds eight pints. I had thirty-two stitches. I recovered and was out of the hospital in three days. I couldn't go back to my rented room. They had burned my mattress in the backyard. I wanted to check in to a motel, but a classmate and his wife insisted I stay with them. I didn't want to, but they refused to drive me to a hotel, or let me take a taxi. They took me to their house and I slept on the couch in the living room. I was tired, but felt good, given that life goes on.

Paul Engle visited me in the hospital and was pleasant and concerned. The morning after I was released, I had a meeting with him in his office. "John, this is very serious."

"Yes, I know! But I'm okay! As you can see!" I said, laughing and being positive. "Sorry to cause so much trouble."

"I am calling your mother and father, but I wanted to tell you first that I was going to do it."

"Oh, no! Please, let me call them first, and explain, and then you call them." He looked disapproving. "Please, give me twenty-four hours."

I called my father, whom I loved, and who was good-natured with a gentlemanly grace. I didn't want to cause him or my mother any trouble. I told him I tried to commit suicide, lightheartedly, making the words soft and melodious, trying to defuse their meaning. "And I'm fine. I'm in really good shape."

After Paul Engle called him with the truth, my father called back, very concerned. He and Mother were flying out to Iowa City, to take me home.

I WAS BACK on Old Brick Road in suburban Roslyn Heights, trying to figure out what to do next. The house was 1949 modern, and had walls of windows looking onto the gardens and flowers and lawn. The three-hundred-year-old oaks, with their autumn leaves, always meant sadness, and then it was the desolate winter. Spring arrived with fourteen dogwood trees coming into bloom, and when the fifty bushes of peonies flowered, it was the peony pavilion. I worked a little on poems, without much enthusiasm or success. Since I didn't know what to do, I was waiting to see what would happen next, what opportunity or direction might appear. I was prepared to just allow something to happen.

I went into New York often and saw my friends, including my friend Peter's girlfriend, Marcia Stillman. Her mother had just rented her an apartment in a brownstone around the corner from their home on the Upper East Side, to use as a studio. Marcia gave me a key and invited me to use the small spare room anytime. Diana Barrymore, the daughter of John Barrymore, lived in the apartment next door. She was a flamboyant, alcoholic actress who committed suicide there a year later.

One evening in November 1959, my father and I were at home sitting in front of the fireplace with a roaring fire, having a drink before dinner. My mother was in the kitchen cooking. "John, I have something to say to you, and I mean it with the best intentions," said my father kindly. "You should get a job. Some work you like to do. It will be good for your health. Some gainful employment!" We both laughed. "It will be good for you."

"Yes. I know what you mean."

"Something you enjoy doing."

After struggling and failing in various ventures, my father had inherited a reweaving business from his father. He did what he had to. My mother, the family's driving force, was a talented and successful fashion designer, and created lines for legends Hattie Carnegie, Elizabeth Arden, and Arnold Scaasi. She did what she loved.

My parents were concerned about my well-being, stability, and good health. They were very generous, but I had to join repugnant life, and get an ordinary job, and work to make money to pay for what I didn't want.

"Yes," I replied. I knew instantly the time had come, and I had to bite the bullet.

After much thought, I decided to go work on Wall Street, as a stockbroker or customer representative, which seemed an easy, acceptable compromise. In those years, Wall Street was genteel, not the cutthroat jungle that it would become.

I got an apartment on East Seventy-Fourth Street, between Second and Third Avenues. It was a two-story, former stable/carriage house with a big skylight. I furnished it elegantly and sparsely, mostly with antiques from my parents' basement. I bought a classic sports car, a 1954 MG TD, pale yellow.

I went to work on Wall Street for Fahnestock & Co., an old-guard brokerage firm, as a customer representative. It was very easy, as the firm was still a gentlemen's club of sorts. The New York Stock Exchange opened at ten in the morning and closed at three in the afternoon, and everyone took two hours for lunch. By four o'clock, I was back on the Upper East Side in bed, taking a nap.

For about a year, I had a daily routine, working at the firm during the day, and reading about Tibet in my free time. The reading inspired a melancholy for a place I did not yet know, an affinity and again a sadness. Why hadn't I been born in a place like Tibet? Could I go into a monastery, practice meditation as a monk, become enlightened? But that Tibet, I knew, was no longer. I often found myself sleepwalking through life for weeks at a time in a numb depression.

The one thing that broke me out, at least usually, was sex. In the golden age of promiscuity, I cruised all the time, had fabulous anonymous sex, and found that I could have almost anybody. I went to the Everard and St. Mark's baths for ten hours at a time. Given the ups and downs, hangovers, and depressions, I had a reasonably good time.

By good fortune, I met a lot of artists living downtown, which developed into many interlocking friendships. It was what could be called the early New York art world. I met Hans Kline, a painter who introduced me to the painter Wynn Chamberlain, who became my regular companion at gallery openings, the Judson Dance Theater, and various artworks called Happenings. I met artists and dancers, composers and musicians, and poets, an extended group of more than one hundred people, and we all became friends. I began to see a life outside my brokerage firm, a life I wanted to be part of. Among the people I met, most significantly, was Andy Warhol.

PART ONE

ART WITH ANDY

I loved art before I loved poetry. At P.S. 222 in Brooklyn, before my family moved out to Long Island, I had covered the classroom walls with collage and assemblage. For three years, I went to Pratt Institute every Saturday morning to study drawing, painting, and art history. In high school, when I had nothing to do, I went to the Museum of Modern Art, and stood in front of Picasso's *Guernica*. It was the first time my mind connected to a work of art in some profound way. In 1951, I reveled in MoMA's big exhibition of Abstract Expressionists, finally seeing the full picture of the movement. While I was at Columbia, the museums on Fifth Avenue were always a source of refuge. And so from there, it was a logical step to the galleries of Fifty-Seventh Street.

I first saw Andy Warhol at openings at Dick Bellamy's Green Gallery and at the Pop Art show at the Sidney Janis Gallery on October 31, 1962. It was the very first show of the original seven Pop artists—Warhol, Lichtenstein, Rosenquist, Segal, Wesselmann, Dine, and Indiana—and it so outraged and offended the old-guard Abstract Expressionists (de Kooning, Rothko, Motherwell, etc.) that they all resigned from the Janis Gallery in protest. It was the Halloween that changed art history.

Andy Warhol

SEVERAL DAYS LATER, I went with my new friend Wynn to the opening of Andy Warhol's first one-man show, at the Stable Gallery. It was right after the Cuban Missile Crisis, and everyone believed a nuclear war could actually happen at any moment. The atmosphere added to the electricity of the show. *Gold Marilyn Monroe* hung on the wall as you entered. This was it! *Troy Donahue*, *Red Elvis*, serial paintings of Campbell's soup cans, Coke bottles, and dollar bills. I had an instinctive flash that this was one of the moments that change history. Everyone in the art world was there.

I stood in the very crowded gallery, a little dazed. I knew it was better not to have complicated thoughts about the art, but to simply be with it. Experience it beyond concepts, in the very noisy room. We walked up to Andy, and Wynn said, "What do you think?"

Andy wrinkled his brow. "I don't know what it means!"

"I'd like to introduce a young poet, Giorno."

I took hold of Andy's soft hand, which dangled from his wrist, and squeezed it. We looked in each other's eyes. Something happened, a spark.

"Ohhh!" hummed Andy. I dropped his hand.

"I love the show," said Wynn. Andy was pleased.

Over the next few months, I ran into Andy at art openings, parties, and Happenings. On November 10, at the opening of Lee Bontecou's show at the Leo Castelli Gallery on East Seventy-Seventh Street, I saw Andy across the room, but I didn't go up right away, because I thought it too pushy.

I said hello to Lee, whom I was coming to know and like. We were both shy, often standing back against the wall at parties and making small talk, watching the superstar artists, Bob Rauschenberg, Jasper Johns, and others, play out the great drama.

And I loved Lee's work. Her sculptures were big paintings made of welded steel frames stretched with heavy-duty canvas from old mailbags found on the street, sewed with fine copper wire, painted with rabbit-skin glue and black soot, and collaged with found material: saw blades, velveteen cloth, rope, pipe fittings, spools, washers, and grommets. Her work was a hybrid of surrealism, Abstract Expressionism, and Pop Art. It was incredibly powerful. The sculptures looked like sawed-off turbojet engines, elegant, dormant volcanoes with teeth.

In the crowd, I saw the art critic David Bourdon and offered my take. "Black holes. They're volcano pussies."

David smiled, and said a little prissily, "Barbara Rose calls them vagina dentata."

"Vagina dentata!" I said, bursting with laughter. "That's so great!"

I said hi to Andy, but there was almost no interaction. He left soon after.

In January 1963, at the opening of Jasper Johns's show at Castelli, Andy left before I could even say hello. Jasper's show was collage, Abstract Expressionist paintings. There were stencils of alphabet letters and the words "red" and "yellow" painted not in their colors. It seemed brilliantly revolutionary. Jasper was young, pencil-thin, handsome, charming, but a little sharp-minded. And I couldn't help but notice he had a big basket hung in his khaki pants. Every time I saw him at openings or parties, my heart beat a little faster.

That spring, at the opening of Salvatore Scarpitta's show at Castelli (paintings of abused, found objects sunk into brownish, grayish paint), Wynn said to Andy, "Come to dinner tomorrow night. John and I are going to see Yvonne Rainer at Judson Church and we can all go together."

"Oh, yes," said Andy. I was surprised, as Andy and Wynn didn't really know each other.

Yvonne Rainer premiered her new dance piece *Terrain* at the Judson Dance Theater. Beforehand, Wynn was having this small dinner in his loft on the top floor of 222 Bowery. He invited Bobo

Keely, an Upper East Side friend, Andy Warhol, and me. Wynn cooked a wonderful dinner of coq au vin. We drank wine—I more glasses than anyone, and Andy almost none—and had a good time. Andy and I were getting to know each other.

The four of us rushed to Judson for the 8:30 performance. Yvonne danced her brilliant new work. Andy and I sat next to each other and it felt wonderful.

Afterward, saying goodbye, I said, "Good night, it's so great being with you. We should get together?"

"What about tomorrow night?" said Andy. "There's the premiere of Jack Smith's *Flaming Creatures*."

I was a little surprised at Andy's enthusiasm. Jack had already been screening *Flaming Creatures* in people's lofts and everyone, including me, had seen it many times. It was already a cult classic. But this was the premiere, as in Hollywood premiere, which excited Andy. So of course, I agreed.

"Here's my telephone. Do you have a piece of paper?" Andy scribbled his number on a matchbook cover. AT9-1298. AT stood for Atwater.

The next night, Andy and I went to the midnight premiere of Jack Smith's *Flaming Creatures* at the Bleecker Street Cinema. Also on the bill was Ken Jacobs's *Blonde Cobra*, a portrait of Jack Smith.

"It's so beautiful." Andy Warhol was really interested in Jack Smith. Jack was a genius and a mess, and always fucked everything up for himself. Andy was able to take many important ideas from Jack, which then went into the making of "Andy Warhol." Among them, Jack coined the term "superstar."

At a party afterward, Jack Smith leaned into me and said, "You look like Dick Tracy."

"Cool!" I said graciously, but I was a little offended. What did that mean? I looked like a tough-guy cop, an Italian American stereotype? I didn't tell Andy. Jack said it several times that year, which made me keep my distance.

The poster for
Flaming Creatures

AFTER *FLAMING CREATURES*, Andy and I started going out all the time, cultivating and embracing our own peculiar vision of New York culture. It was the year that everything happened. More pivotal things occurred in 1963 than any other year, except 1968, which was the end of the '60s. In 1962, all the Pop artists had had their first one-person shows, and in 1963, they were having their second shows and becoming more established. The Judson Dance Theater happened every Wednesday night. Happenings occurred sporadically, and there were countless dance and music events.

On Friday night, May 3, 1963, we went with the curator/critic Henry Geldzahler to see the Ronettes and the Shirelles perform. They were pop stars, rock goddesses at the peak of their careers. It was a chilly night, after a day that had been the first burst of spring. We took a taxi over the Manhattan Bridge to the Brooklyn Fox Theatre on Flatbush Avenue, an ornate 1920s movie palace. We were in the twentieth row and got semi-VIP treatment, as Henry worked for the New York City Office of Cultural Affairs. A sea of screaming teenage girls and boys surrounded us. By chance, I was smack in the middle of something extraordinary.

The Ronettes were pretty girls with huge beehives, slim figures, and tight-fitting pink dresses with slits right up the center. They sang, swayed, and shimmied, and when they dipped their knees, the slits opened up, and the audience screamed. The Ronettes were very different from the demure innocence of other girl groups, and the first to sing sexually charged songs. When they played their hit song "Be My Baby," the high-pitched shrieks from the crowd were almost louder than the rock 'n' roll music.

"It's the best song I ever heard," I said in awe.

Andy was frightened, and kept saying, "Ohhh!" Every time the kids screamed, he looked worried.

"They were created by Phil Spector," instructed Henry. "And he created the sound, too." It was called the wall of sound, a combination of sensual intimate girl voices and full blasting orchestration. It was fabulously strong.

A couple of days later, Andy and I went to a concert by the composers Karlheinz Stockhausen and Morton Feldman. It was Stockhausen's first concert in New York—in fact, his American premiere. He was already legendary, the most cutting-edge in avant-garde experimental music. We arrived late at NYU's Loeb Student Center. It was crowded and we sat down in an aisle on the left side near the stage. Morton Feldman went on first, with a heavy, serious, and great composition. Then he came and sat next to us on the floor in the aisle to listen to Stockhausen. The art world had very much anticipated Stockhausen. He was a pre-approved genius. And he came through, giving a powerful, brilliant performance of an electronic composition.

Everyone from the art scene and music circles was there, including John Cage, Terry Riley, David Tudor, La Monte Young, Steve Reich, Philip Glass, and Max Neuhaus. It was boring atonal music, not the rock 'n' roll that Andy and I loved, but it was important to be there, and be seen. For me, despite not loving the music itself, I basked in the brilliant energy of a seminal moment in music history.

"What do you think?" I asked Andy.

"Oh, it's great," he replied unexpectedly.

Andy and I saw each other almost every night. We spoke on the telephone every morning and made a plan. I picked him up at his town house on Lexington Avenue and East Ninety-First Street, and we went together to openings, Happenings, underground movies, and parties. There were so many things going on. It was the beginning of Pop Art, its freshest, strongest time, and it was changing art history. I did not quite realize this, but my intuition told me to go with it. It was a sweet earthquake.

I still had my job on Wall Street during the day, but it soon felt like the most important part of my life was Andy. Sexually speaking, we fell into an odd pattern: when I was drunk enough, he would blow me. Or when I was still in bed hungover, he would call, ask me what I was wearing, and then show up. It didn't happen that often (I was going to the baths and hooking up with other people), but there was a flow of sexual energy between us.

One night, we crammed ourselves into a small basement theater on Fourteenth Street to see the Living Theatre's production of *The Brig*, a play by Kenneth Brown, which everybody had been talking about. The play was semiautobiographical, based on Brown's experience in a Marine Corps brig in Japan, and to Andy and me, it felt a little like actually being in prison. On stage was a chain-link-fence cage and double-decker beds. The cast was twelve men—prisoners numbered one to eight, and four guards—and Judith Malina dressed in a khaki jacket and pants and holding a riding crop. It was directed strictly according to the U.S. Marine Corps manual. Judith put the prisoners through the paces.

The men with crew cuts and dog tags, wearing fatigues and T-shirts, made small talk about home, girlfriends, and getting laid in Tokyo. Did you get any tail? Andy kept saying, "Ohhh . . ."

"It's so boring."

"I know it's so boring."

"It opened last night, got a review today in *The New York Times*, and there are nine paying people in the audience and thirteen people on stage."

"It's so dumb," said Andy.

Even though the play itself wasn't that good, the production, directed by Julian Beck, was brilliant. "At least they're trying," I said. "Theater is so hopeless." I had a hangover, and couldn't wait for it to be over.

Later, Judith Malina said, "Valerie Solanas was in the audience and came up afterward, and said, 'How wonderful it is the way you treat men. You know how to treat men. You are the toughest, hardest chick that ever was. You whip those men to obedience.'"

Five years later, in 1968, Valerie Solanas shot Andy, critically wounding him.

A still from Jonas Mekas's 1964 film version of *The Brig*

IN EARLY '63, Andy showed me his new studio on East Eighty-Seventh Street, between Lexington and Third Avenues. The building was a late-nineteenth-century firehouse, red brick with black wooden trim, that looked like an abandoned garage. Over the front doors, a sign read NO. 13 HOOK & LADDER. "It's the witch's house," I said.

"I know, isn't it great!"

"It's *rough trade* and a historic building."

The ground floor was big enough for several fire trucks, and the upstairs, where Andy silk-screened his paintings, was enormous, divided into what was formerly the dormitory and the locker room. It was difficult to heat. The big old gas blower that hung from the ceiling kept breaking down. The roof leaked badly. Rainwater ruined Andy's first *Silver Elvis* paintings, among others.

He made the *Mona Lisa* and *Merce Cunningham Dancing with a Chair* paintings there. And after doing most of his work in small cluttered rooms, the large, open firehouse allowed him to go big. Andy made all the *Death* paintings here. *Silver Car Crash* and *Gangster Funeral. Ambulance Disaster* depicted a car crash with a dead body hanging out of an ambulance window. *White* was from a *Life* magazine photograph of a girl who jumped from the Empire State Building onto a car, crushing it. That April, he did the *Electric Chairs*. The landlord was trying to get Andy to buy the building, but the roof was leaking so badly, Andy was more interested in finding a way out of the lease.

One day, when reports of poison tuna fish made headlines in newspapers and on TV, I said, "You should do tuna fish cans . . . It's all poison."

"I already have!" Andy showed me a painting of two tuna fish cans that he had silk-screened that day.

"Brilliant!"

After a painting was silk-screened and dried, Andy rolled it up and carried it to his house on Lexington Avenue, where he stapled it on the wall of a back room for people to see. "Let me show you," he would say, as he unfurled it. Everyone always said, "Ahhhh!" Sometimes, he stapled four or five canvases on top of one another, unfurling each one. The art itself was vibrant and brilliant, and his theatrical-magician-like way of revealing the work made it all the more exciting.

ON APRIL 23, I went over to Andy's house, as I did almost every night, to take part in whatever was going to happen. At seven, the art curator John Richardson and the art dealer Robert Fraser came to visit. In the back room, we looked at Andy's new paintings, among them *Orange Disaster*: an overturned car crash with dead bodies scattered about. "As if it were a picnic," said Richardson.

More people showed up, including the artists Marisol, Ruth Kligman, and Naomi Levine. The hot day had become a wonderfully warm evening, full of exhilarating vitality. Naomi said, "Let's go to Coney Island." It was a strange idea to go to Coney Island on a Tuesday night in April, but given the weather, why not? Andy said yes, and we all went. Wynn had a car, and John, Robert, Andy, and I went with him, while the others took taxis. We parked the car in front of Steeplechase Amusement Park, and walked to Nathan's, where we rendezvoused.

There was a noisy crowd in front of Nathan's waiting to buy their famous sizzling frankfurters. Andy and I stood at the curb as the others pushed their way to the front. We waited a long time until someone brought us hot dogs with mustard and sauerkraut. The night had turned chilly with the wind from the Atlantic Ocean. I wore only a sport shirt, and was cold. We stood shivering.

We ate the hot dogs, dripping grease and delicious, and drank beer. Down a maze of alleys were bright lights and painted signs— red, yellow, green, pink, blue—and the cotton candy and carnival concessions, and the rides. The legendary Cyclone was down the street, the giant Ferris wheel to the right. Most were closed, because it was too early in the season.

"Under the boardwalk here in the summer, the kids fuck like crazy," said Wynn. "Boy and girls, and boy and boys. I've seen it. Fourteen-year-old girls giving blow jobs to these thugs. It's wild!'"

Rakishly handsome John Richardson and young Robert Fraser, both dressed in dark blue suits and neckties, stood in the alley alongside Nathan's, and cruised the black, Hispanic, and Italian boys. Beautiful street kids wandered around in small groups, bursting with sexual energy. Robert walked off by himself. "Robert is so outrageous," said John. "Once we were out on the town, and Robert pointed to a piece of trade, and said,

'I'm going to get him. I'm going to force him to fuck me.' And he did!"

"Ohhh!" said Andy. We were all laughing. "How does he do it?"

John and Robert were charming, but they had the power and control of the upper-class British, with an arrogance that intimidated everyone around them. Nathan's was the deep sea of the lower middle classes. I was reminded of a famous story of the King and Queen of England enjoying the common thrill of hot dogs during their state visit with the Roosevelts in 1939.

"This is for you." Andy slipped me a yellow plaster-cast corn. "Naomi walked away with it from the corn-on-the-cob place. She said she paid him for a corn and took this." The plaster corn, roughly painted yellow, looked like a cock.

"Andy, thank you. Nine inches." I walked around the rest of the night with the corn in my hand, like a swagger stick.

Nathan's on Coney Island

THE NEXT MONTH, Andy and I were downtown to see a benefit exhibition at the Judson gallery in the parish house behind Judson Memorial Church on Washington Square South. Andy had given a small black etching for the show. We walked around the gallery, looking at the art and saying hello to a few people as we passed.

"What do you think?" I said.

Andy frowned, and said, "It's so terrible."

"Studio scraps and bad art," I said, looking at a meager Claes Oldenburg drawing on paper. "What do you think of the Al Hansen?" It was a small collage painting with Hershey wrappers.

"Uh, Al Hansen is so great," said Andy.

"And Ray Johnson?" I asked. We were looking at his painting, a collage on paper of a geranium in a flowerpot.

"Uh, Ray Johnson is so great," said Andy.

Andy saw the brilliance in the work, and it was a joy to be there and experience it with him. When I was seeing it through his eyes, the art radiated.

As we were leaving, Ray Johnson appeared, and we stood in the sunlight. Ray had fair skin, which was red from an early-in-the-season sunburn. He was young and open, quite beautiful and sexy, wearing khaki pants that showed the outline of his dick, and a pink shirt. Ray said to Andy exuberantly, "I heard what you said!"

Andy laughed, and said, "Ray Johnson is the best-known unknown artist in New York City."

"Thank you!" said Ray, extremely happy.

"A pink shirt!" said Andy, making Ray happier. We all laughed, and Andy and I moved on.

Even though their work was really great, Al and Ray had some fatal flaw that made them failures. They were not the seven Pop artists, or Bob Rauschenberg, or Jasper Johns, and would never be, but why?

ONE NIGHT IN the middle of May, Andy, Ruth Kligman, and I were walking down Third Avenue near Cooper Union. Andy said, "Ruth, I have something to tell you, and you are really going to like it."

"What?" said Ruth.

"I made a *Liz Taylor*, and it looks like you," said Andy. We all laughed. "It does. It really looks like you."

"I can't wait to see it!" said Ruth, smiling and excited. Ruth had been Jackson Pollock's lover, and had survived the car crash that killed him. She had also been the lover of Willem de Kooning, among others. She filled the job description of artist's muse, whatever that was.

She was the same shape as Elizabeth Taylor, always wore a black cocktail dress, and had the same coiffed black hair, red lips, and eye makeup. But Liz Taylor was Anglo-Saxon with violet eyes, and Ruth was Mediterranean Jewish.

The next day at 7:00 p.m., Ruth came to Andy's house. There was the new color *Liz* painting hanging unstretched on the back wall. A monochrome canvas of gorgeous Liz, her pink skin glowing lusciously, vivid turquoise eye shadow highlighting her brow, bloodred lips bleeding their outline, dark and unyielding; she was a goddess, if there ever was one.

Andy, by mistake, had made the shadow on Liz's right cheek a

little broader, the triangle of flesh color a little wider, making Liz look slightly porky; and she looked like Ruth.

"Andy!" screamed Ruth. "It does, it does, it does!" She jumped up and down happily.

"It really does," I said. "Congratulations to both of you!"

"I don't know how that happened," said Andy.

Ruth Kligman

IN 1963, Andy was thinking of shooting a movie called *Kiss* and wasn't sure he wanted to use Naomi Levine for the tight head shot kissing ten guys. I said, "Why don't you have two men kissing?" Andy turned slightly away and deemed it not worthy of an answer. A half hour later, I asked the question again. I thought it was a great idea, pushing the envelope, over-the-top. I was a poet from the world of William Burroughs and Allen Ginsberg, and we were concerned with the sexual freedom of gay men and lesbians. "Why don't you have two guys kissing, but like Doris Day and Rock Hudson?" Andy was silent and scornful. "Or two women?" Andy said, "Ewww!" A week later, I asked again, and Andy sighed, "Oh, John!" which meant, Don't you get it?

Eight years earlier, in 1955, the Bonwit Teller department store in New York had commissioned artists to create displays in its front windows on Fifth Avenue. By chance, Andy's window was next to the window of Bob Rauschenberg and Jasper Johns; they installed them on the same night. In his design, Andy used a photograph of a gorgeous transvestite posed as a fashion model, who passed to the public as a woman.

"Bob and Jasper came and looked at what I was doing," Andy recalled, "and laughed at me. They pointed their fingers and laughed. They were so mean!"

The old-guard Abstract Expressionists had been (and still were) notoriously homophobic. Only straight guys, like themselves, were great painters. Queers, like the friends of their faghag wives, were not eligible. Inheriting and internalizing that loathing, gay artists like Rauschenberg and Johns didn't talk about their sexuality, and shunned homoerotic imagery in their work.

Against this, Andy was a gay man, undeniably swish, his work openly homoerotic. In the 1950s, this was daring and heroic. Andy made drawings for private view—a man's foot and a male head with a licking tongue, and a hard dick hanging from half-opened jeans. And those made for the public were full of innuendo—portraits of drag queens, fetishistic outline drawings of sexy male feet.

Then, in 1958, he was nominated for the Tanager Gallery, an artists' cooperative, but was turned down, rejected because he was too fey. Andy got the message and realized that being a gay artist was the kiss of death. Gay was a subculture, and a dead end; Andy wanted popular culture. To access a large commercial audience, he got rid of the gay content. In his most famous work, the homoerotic would be subverted and hidden.

A WEEK OR SO after Andy had unveiled his *Liz* painting, I picked him up at his house at about six, and we took a taxi to the Museum of Modern Art for an opening. "Why are we going there? I forgot," I said. "What's opening?"

"'Americans 1963,' curated by Dorothy Miller," said Andy sourly. "Claes Oldenburg, Jim Rosenquist, Marisol. Even Bob Indiana, Richard Anuskiewicz, and Ad Reinhardt."

"They're so mean!" I said. "Did Frank O'Hara have anything to do with Dorothy not including you?" Frank O'Hara worked at MoMA and I could just imagine him disparaging Andy's work to Dorothy.

Andy didn't answer.

"They're so mean!" I said again.

In Andy's silence, I found another topic to chew over: news that the Museum of Modern Art was preparing to take over the boxy little building behind it, home of the Whitney Museum of American Art since 1954. The Whitney was outgrowing its space and looking for a bigger site anyway, but MoMA's real estate rapacity was an easy target. "It's so weird," I said, "the Whitney should go through the trouble of building a modernist building in the backyard of the Museum of Modern Art, and not expect to be taken over by the big bully. Their rears are adjoining, how could they not expect to get fucked?"

We got out of the cab and Andy paid the driver. It was exceptionally warm for May. The heat, with my hangover from the night before, made me feel brain-dead.

At the museum entrance, there was a crowd, a big semicircle of people waiting to get in. Andy and I stood on the street at the edge of the crowd and waited.

Someone famous arrived in a taxi. An invisible energy rippled through the mass of people. "It's like royalty arriving," I said, "or a movie star. Who?"

"Duchamp!" said Andy.

"Have you met?"

"No!" Andy became very excited, overwrought. His forehead sweated and he started shaking; his hands and body trembled. He pushed his way through the crowd, and pushed faster, carving a path, bumping into people who gave him dirty looks. I held on with two fingers to the sleeve of Andy's loose sport shirt and got swept along with him. I understood the expression "holding on to somebody's coattails." I didn't know what was happening, but I was not going to get left behind. It was like waterskiing, or surfing—we were going so fast I could feel the wind. It was the only time I ever saw Andy do anything physically aggressive. We forged through the crowd and landed at the curb directly in front of the museum entrance.

Duchamp, exiting the taxi, walked straight into Andy, and since David Whitney (who worked at MoMA; no relation to the museum Whitneys) was also standing there to receive Duchamp, it came naturally for him to introduce the two. Perfectly timed!

"Ohhh!" Andy said. Duchamp and Andy shook hands. Duchamp looked into Andy's eyes, and nodded his head imperceptibly. In that instant, he acknowledged Andy, knew his work, and approved. They had a great, nonverbal moment of communication, one beyond thought.

Duchamp's approval of Andy was like fiesta musicians bursting into play. David introduced Andy to Duchamp's wife, Teeny. We stood there, and it was electrifying. Andy tried to extend the moment, no matter how briefly. "Oh, and this is a young poet, John Giorno."

I shook Marcel Duchamp's hand, which was cold, and said hello. I shook Teeny's little hand and smiled. I was stunned. Duchamp was a mythical creature, who had appeared, unexpectedly, from the heavens. He was at least a demigod, and maybe a god.

Duchamp and Teeny passed into the museum, and the crowd closed in behind them.

"Hollywood biblical," I said, "like the sea in Egypt closing behind Moses." We moved slowly, happily, into the museum. "Andy, thank you! That was amazing!"

"I know!" drawled Andy, very pleased with himself.

"Did you notice that his hand was cold?" I said. "In this heat, like a zombie."

"Yes, I did," Andy replied with a laugh.

"Duchamp's dyed black hair and pasty white skin," I said, "makes him look like one of his own readymades, something other than it is."

Marcel and Teeny Duchamp

SLEEP

In June and July 1963, Andy and I made "Andy Warhol Interviewed by a Poet," a parody or fake interview, about nothing and for nothing, stupid and trashy and dumb. It was a response to the serious, self-serving art world interview. We did it in taxis, when Andy came by my place or I went to his, in the firehouse, and anywhere. Whenever Andy said something that sounded like it could fit in an interview, I scribbled down the words. I made up questions to go with the answers. They were typed up separately. The idea was a dysfunctional interview, in the style of a Tennessee Williams play.

"Oh, just put it together any way," said Andy. "It doesn't matter."

I typed it up and showed it to Andy. He liked it but wanted me to delete several parts, including one about Bob Rauschenberg. The interview was never published. We had a good time doing it, laughing and loving and resting in the play of our minds. There was no bad or good, everything was totally great.

In 1999, Matt Wrbican, curator of the Andy Warhol Museum in Pittsburgh, discovered the original, unedited interview in one of Andy's time capsules.

ANDY WARHOL INTERVIEWED BY A POET
Place: The former locker room of the old No. 13 Hook & Ladder.

POET: (winningly) How long have you been a painter?

ANDY: When I was nine years old I had St. Vitus Dance. I painted a picture of Hedy Lamarr from a Maybelline ad. It was no good and I threw it away. I realized I couldn't paint.

POET: That is revealing. Your first picture was a movie star. What is your capacity? Are you a fast worker?

ANDY: I can make a picture in five minutes, but sometimes

I run into so much trouble. The screens don't print and I have to do them over and over. Or I don't have enough turpentine and everything is sticky . . . I did fifty Elvises in one day. Half my California show. The roof of the firehouse leaked and they were all ruined. I had to get busy and do them all over again.

POET: How come you weren't in the Modern Museum show this year?

ANDY: I was crushed. But it doesn't matter.

POET: How come?

ANDY: (coughing) They had Marisol and Bob Indiana, and I guess they thought three from one gallery would be too much. I was so hurt.

POET: Do you think you paint better than Bob Indiana?

ANDY: (coyly) Aaaaaaa.

POET: What do you think of Abstract Expressionism?

ANDY: Art is dead.

POET: Why is Art dead?

ANDY: Nobody thinks. Nobody uses imagination. Imagination is dead.

POET: What do you think of Larry?

ANDY: He's the daddy of "Pop Art." He's so chic.

POET: What is Pop Art?

ANDY: "Pop Art" . . . is . . . use . . . of . . . the . . . popular . . . image.

POET: Is "Pop Art" a fade [sic].

ANDY: Yes. "Pop Art" is a fade [sic]. I am a "Pop Artist."

POET: Would you like to go with Marlborough?

ANDY: Oh, yes. They are international, and I hear they give you a private secretary. That would be good for my career.

POET: Did you get any free soup from the Campbell Soup people?

ANDY: No! Not even a word. Isn't that amazing? If it had been Heinz, Dru Heinz would have sent me cases of soup every week.

POET: What do you think of the nude figure in American painting?

ANDY: Oh, art is too hard.

POET: What's that can of paint on the floor? It looks like house paint.

ANDY: It is. I mean it's the black paint I use.

POET: Don't you use tubes like other artists?

ANDY: (crossly) Ohhh, no.

POET: What pigments do you use?

ANDY: A silver spray can, plastic paint . . . and varnoline.

POET: What's varnoline?

ANDY: I clean my screens and brushes with it. I am having so much trouble. I am allergic to varnoline. I break out in red blotches and vile sores. I think I'm going to have to stop painting.

POET: Did you just become allergic to it?

ANDY: Yes, in the last two or three weeks.

POET: And you have been using varnoline for two years?

ANDY: Yes.

POET: Don't you think it is psychosomatic?

ANDY: No . . . Yes . . . I don't know.

POET: Well, if you weren't allergic to it for two years, I think it is caused by a mental disorder.

ANDY: (confused) I guess so. It gets in your blood. Varnoline is poisonous. That's what causes the . . .

POET: Where do you have your silk screens made?

ANDY: Mr. Golden.

POET: Is that where Bob Rauschenberg has his made?

ANDY: (huffily) Yes . . . Oh, don't put that in your interview.

POET: Tell me what you do when you're not painting?

ANDY: I believe in living. I didn't before. I spent Fourth of July in the country, and I had forgotten about living. It was so beautiful. I started doing Sari Ronny's Health Club on Broadway and West 73rd Street, every day for four hours. I get massaged, lift weights, box, swim underwater . . . I want to be pencil thin . . . I want to like myself . . . What else? I am making a movie about sleep.

POET: Sleep. What about sleep?

ANDY: A movie of John Giorno sleeping for eight hours.

POET: How fascinating. Could you be more explicit?

ANDY: It's just John sleeping for eight hours. His nose and mouth, his chest breathing, occasionally he moves, his face. Oh, it's so beautiful.

POET: When can I see it?

ANDY: I don't know.

POET: Tell me more about your painting?

ANDY: I am going to stop painting. I want my paintings to sell for $25,000.

POET: What a good idea. What are you working on now?

ANDY: Death.

POET: (transfixed) Hmmm.

ANDY: The girl who jumped off the Empire State Building, a girl who jumped out of a window of Bellevue, the electric chair, car crashes, race riots.

POET: Where do you get the photographs?

ANDY: My friends clip them out of newspapers for me.

POET: Do you think Marisol has affairs with men?

ANDY: Nobody knows.

POET: When can I see the death pictures?

ANDY: In November, I'm having a show in Paris. (with despair) I haven't done them yet! I will have to do all the pictures in a day. Tomorrow . . . I don't know why I'm having a Paris show. I don't believe in Europe.

POET: How do you think Claes Oldenburg compares to Marisol?

ANDY: (impatiently) Ohhh, you can't ask me questions like that.

POET: Would you like to meet Elizabeth Taylor?

ANDY: (ecstatically) Ohhh, Elizabeth Taylor, ohhh. She's so glamorous . . . I want to be born a big diamond on the finger of Elizabeth Taylor.

POET: Tell me more about your painting?

ANDY: It's magic. It's magic that makes them.

The End

THAT YEAR, Jonas Mekas coined the term and invented the phenomenon called underground cinema. He pulled together a generation of young filmmakers by giving them venues and writing about them in his magazine *Film Culture*. He rented small, run-down theaters around the city that happened to be empty for the night: the Jewel, Gramercy Arts, the Symphony, Bleecker Street Cinema. Sometimes Jonas presented programs at two or three different theaters a week, sometimes with no publicity, but through word of mouth everyone came. Jonas screened four or five films each night.

Andy and I went to the movies once, twice, or three times a week, every week for a year. There was Jack Smith's *Flaming Creatures*, Ron Rice's *Chumlum*, Kenneth Anger's *Scorpio Rising*, pieces of Ken Jacobs's *Star Spangled to Death*, a rough cut of Taylor Mead's *Queen of Sheba Meets the Atom Man*, and Taylor in *The Flower Thief* by Ron Rice. We saw them many times, as Jonas replayed them in different combinations, always putting the new film last, so we had to see the others over and over again. Andy and I saw *Flaming Creatures* at least thirty times. These films had an enormous impact on Andy. It was where he got the idea to make movies. He saw what film was, what it could be.

I loved them, but because everyone's work was home movies and really crude, I had lingering doubts about whether it was great art, or just naïve and primitive, or *arte brute*. I doubted but also believed that it was the very beginning of a great period in filmmaking.

The Symphony on Broadway and Ninety-Fifth Street was a big run-down movie house. One night, Andy and I arrived and the theater was dark and padlocked. There were about fifty people milling about and everyone was asking what was happening. Jonas Mekas climbed on the hood of a car parked in front and explained to everyone why the film showing was canceled. Jonas was Lithuanian and had a thick accent, so he sounded like a Bolshevik revolutionary. He stood on the car, towering over everyone, wearing a red plaid flannel shirt, with his right arm raised, telling the complicated reasons for the cancellation, something about city fire code violations.

"Andy, it's a revolution," I whispered seductively in his ear. "A Marxist revolution! Look, he's wearing a red shirt."

"Oh!" Andy frowned.

"He's a Trotskyite. He's so funny!" I was enthralled with Jonas's performance. His energy had a childlike innocence, and the people truly believed that it was, indeed, a revolution. "The film revolution!" Jonas had the young, pure motivation and zeal of a heroic revolutionary. And underground movies went on to change the world.

Another night at the Symphony, we saw a part of Stan Brakhage's *Dog Star Man*. "Oh, it's so beautiful," said Andy, a little disapprovingly, as only Andy could.

There were also lots of bad films. "They're so terrible," said Andy, during a change of reels at the Bleecker Street. We stayed in our seats. "Why doesn't somebody make a beautiful movie? There are so many beautiful things!"

A few days later, Andy bought a 16mm Bolex movie camera. He didn't know how to use it. He asked everyone lots of questions. "How do I focus it?"

ON A LONG WEEKEND in late May 1963, Andy, Bob Indiana, Marisol, and I went up by train to Old Lyme, Connecticut, and visited Wynn Chamberlain. He had rented a farmhouse for the summer.

Eleanor Ward, owner of the Stable Gallery, who showed Andy, Bob, and Marisol in New York, rented an old stone icehouse on the same property. Wynn cooked a wonderful dinner and we drank lots of wine. After dinner, Wynn served 140-proof black rum and I drank a lot. We said good night at about two o'clock.

Andy and I slept in a bedroom, in the same bed, but we didn't have sex. My brain was fried by the rum. I just dropped my clothes, fell naked onto the bed, and passed out.

I woke up about four-thirty to take a piss. In the faint traces of early morning light, Andy was next to me, his head resting on his hand and elbow, wide-awake, looking at me. I went to the bathroom, bleary-eyed, and then back to bed.

I woke up two hours later, and Andy was still looking, his eyes open wide. "What are you doing?" I was still drunk, and confused.

"Watching you."

I took another piss and went back to sleep. I woke after a while and he was still doing it. "What are you doing?" I had a rubber tongue.

"Watching you sleep," said Andy sweetly.

As it became lighter, I saw him more clearly. Fifteen minutes later, I turned and he was looking at me with Bette Davis eyes. I kissed him on the cheek. "Are you okay?"

"Yes."

"Are you sure? Take off your shirt. It's so hot." He declined. I tried to take it off and he giggled. Andy was wearing limp Jockey underwear. "And take off your underwear." His skin was very white and soft, and he had hairless, beautiful boy's legs. It was sweltering. I was wet from sweating in my sleep, so there was no thought of cuddling. I kept my eyes shut, but knew he was still looking.

I woke two hours later and he wasn't next to me. In the bright morning, he was dressed, sitting in a chair at the foot of the bed, still staring at me. "Why are you watching me?"

"Wouldn't you like to know!"

I had a horrible hangover and headache. I took a piss, stumbled back and gave his shoulder a squeeze, and dove back to sleep. It was not my problem that he wanted to look.

The next time I woke and looked, Andy was in bed with his clothes on, his head sunk in the pillow, drowsily looking at me. He was keeping himself up. It was 11:30 a.m. and sunlight came sharply into a corner of the room, heating it up to a tropical rain forest. Sweat poured from my body.

When I woke up at one-thirty, Andy was gone. He was on amphetamines and had watched me sleep for eight hours. That night, Andy got the idea for the movie *Sleep*.

We went back to New York early on Monday afternoon. At the crowded Old Lyme railroad station, we waited interminably for the delayed Boston–New York train. Andy talked, as he often did, about making a movie, what he wanted to do, the kind of movie.

"I want to make a movie," said Andy. "Do you want to be the star?"

"Yes! I do!" Snuggling close, I pressed up against him like a cat. "What do I have to do? I do everything."

"I want to make a movie of you sleeping."

I was a bit surprised. "Great!"

"Just you sleeping."

"I can do it."

"I'm sure you can."

"I want to be a movie star!" I said. It was the American dream. Andy Warhol had asked me to star in his first movie and be his first superstar. I pronounced the words clearly with a downbeat. "I want to be a movie star!"

"I know you do!" said Andy.

"I want to be like Marilyn Monroe." This was before Marilyn became the legend, before she entered the realm of myth. She had committed suicide only nine months earlier, on August 5, 1962. Her career was tottering, and she was the failed superstar, the union of the divine and the profane. Andy had captured that in his first *Marilyn* paintings, done right after her death.

And I wanted that for myself. I was drawn to her suicide and her stardom.

"Oh, John!" said Andy happily.

In the overcrowded, rattling train, everybody was unattractive and sweating. Andy said, "When was the first time you wanted to be a movie star?

"When I was nine years old in the Hotel Pierre!"

"What?"

"You remember, I told you."

In October 1946, when I was nine years old, I had an eye operation. There had been a tumor in my left eye, between the optic nerve and the brain. For about a year and a half, my teachers had noticed that I had difficulty reading, and problems with my sight. I had double vision and the blurring in one eye got worse.

My surgeon, Dr. Algernon Reese, was a world-renowned eye specialist, famous for several innovative operations. His genius was that he adapted surgical technology developed during World War II to modern eye surgery. Previously, my operation would have entailed cutting the optic nerve, removing the eye through the eye socket, and cutting out the tumor, resulting in blindness and a glass eye. Instead, Dr. Reese used electric knives to precisely cut away my brow bone from my skull, then removed the tumor, and put the bone back. It worked: my sight was saved. I was the first patient to have this procedure, and my parents were brave to allow it.

The tumor was benign. After a three-hour operation and a six-week recovery in the hospital, I was taken to several medical conferences, photographed for *The New England Journal of Medicine*, and showed off, like a prize. In 1946, at an American Medical Association meeting at the Hotel Pierre, Dr. Reese presented me. My damaged eye was behind a black eye patch, which was taken off to reveal that my eye looked like a rotting mushroom.

Afterward, at the press conference, they led me into a room, and there were two dozen photographers with big old-fashioned Hollywood flashbulb cameras. In the blinding light, I had the joyous feeling that this was what it was like to be a movie star, Rita Hayworth, Judy Garland, Betty Grable. In the waves of flashbulb light, I said to myself, I want to be a movie star. I liked the feeling. It was scary, but I felt at home.

Then they led me out of the room.

"And then," I told Andy again, "I was back to being alone with a sick eye."

IN JUNE, Andy talked a lot about shooting *Sleep*. One night after a party, he came by my place to check out my bed, to see what it would look like on camera. He examined the electrical outlets and figured out where he would set up the tripod.

I was sitting in a chair in the living room and we were talking. Andy came over, sat down on the floor, and put his arm on my knee and his hand on my foot, and we continued talking and laughing. With both hands, he ran his fingers over my shoes. I was talking and not paying attention. All of a sudden, Andy's face went down to the floor, and he was licking my shoes. He pressed his cheek to the leather and licked with his little pink tongue. Totally astonishing!

He had a secret reputation as a shoe fetishist; for years he'd designed shoe ads for Bergdorf Goodman, I. Miller, and Bonwit Teller. There was Andy Warhol on his hands and knees, licking my Abercrombie & Fitch loafers. He wiggled his tongue around and smelled. My shoes were covered with saliva. It was a turn-on.

I got some poppers to make it better, but Andy declined. I took off my shoes and socks and Andy licked my feet and shrimped my toes. It wasn't as erotic as it was deeply moving that he had allowed himself to do this. His sad, timid little tongue went around each toe. He seemed delicate and fragile.

Every once in a while, I went down and hugged him lovingly and kissed his face. Andy was trembling, and his heart was beating a mile a minute. I squeezed his hard dick in his black jeans, but he grabbed my wrist and pulled it away, while he sucked. Several times I slipped my hand down and gently took hold of his dick, but he pushed my hand away. He did not want to allow any-thing reciprocal, maybe it frightened him.

I decided to cum and put him out of his misery. I sucked on the poppers and jerked off; and he sniffed my crotch and licked my balls. Then, Andy licked the big gobs of thick white cum from my hand and stomach. "Oh, you cum so much!"

I reached for his hard dick and tried to unbutton his jeans. "Do you want to cum?"

Andy took my hand away with both his hands, laughed, and said, "I'll take care of it."

A WEEK OR SO LATER, Andy made his initial portrait of the collec-tor Ethel Scull—the first in a series of portraits he went on making for the rest of his life. He took Ethel to Broadway and Forty-Second Street and photographed her in a booth where, for twenty-five cents, you got a strip of five photos. Out of three hundred different photos, he picked thirty-five, enlarged them, and silk-screened them on a large canvas. It was his first commissioned portrait, and the photos were overly posed and didn't quite work. (In 1968, he would add another picture of Ethel to make it thirty-six.)

His second portrait, of Holly Solomon, was one photo enlarged and silk-screened black on silver. In his third portrait, of Lita Hornick, he figured it out, one photo enlarged and re-peated nine times in multi-ple colors on a large square canvas. Lita's was the first of the classic Andy por-traits.

The author and
Lita Hornick in 1989

JOHN GIORNO LITA HORNICK
APRIL 19, 1989
MARK MICHAELSON

IN MID-JUNE, ANDY SAID, "I want to take your picture in that Forty-Second Street place. Do you want to?"

"Yes, of course!" I said. There was a small burst of joy that Andy wanted to make another work of art with me. And there was the delicious sexual undertone.

Andy mentioned it several times, and a week later, after I'd returned from the beach with a very deep suntan, he said, "Let's do it tonight."

We took a taxi to Forty-Second Street and Broadway. The penny arcade, with its pinball machines and blinking lights, was filthy. In the dismal sweating humidity, a few hustlers, pimps, and prostitutes hung out. We really liked the gypsy fortune-telling machine, her head nodding and her hands moving over the cards. I put in a nickel and pushed the button, but nothing came out. "It figures."

There were two photo booths and one was broken. I sat on the stool of the other one. "Are you ready for your close-up?" Andy asked, parodying the line in *Sunset Boulevard*, and pulled the curtain closed.

He put a quarter in the machine. The camera popped five times. We shot some straight on, looking into the camera, and Andy said, "Close your eyes."

"Boring, like sleeping standing up." It took a long time for them to roll out, and when they were developed, they were boring.

"Oh, act like a star!" The words jolted me. I was doing something wrong. Suddenly, I was afraid that Andy would get rid of me. I started camping, throwing back my head, looking over

Photo booth

my shoulder, smoking a cigarette, putting on dark glasses, getting close enough to kiss the camera. A little embarrassing, but it didn't matter.

Andy took several dozen strips, five photos each.

"They're kind of funny with the suntan," he said.

LATER THAT MONTH, on a sweltering hot Thursday evening around seven, I picked up Andy at the firehouse before we went downtown to a party. That morning on the telephone, he had said, "And I want you to see my new pictures." He was silk-screening the *Silver Elvis* paintings.

We went upstairs. On the floor was a huge canvas with eight life-sized Elvis Presleys with gun in hand, holster, and knife in belt. Andy had painted the silver background the day before and silk-screened the black Elvis images that day. They were magnificent, glittering like diamonds on the bleak cement floor. I was shocked, seeing something truly great for the first time, completely new, above mere intellectual understanding.

Lit by bare lightbulbs hung from the high black ceiling, we walked, laughing, around the edge of the big canvas. The repetition of the shining silver and black Elvises danced on the floor before us. We circled around, Andy following me, and I danced from leg to leg, making exclamations of joy. The painting was beyond words.

"They're a breakthrough!" I had to say something.

"I know, they're so beautiful!" Andy glowed.

"Gun in hand, and the holster on his leg looks like a dick in his pants," I said. "It's so sexy!"

"I know," said Andy. "I'm really happy the way they turned out."

"Elvis giving it to you straight," I said. "They radiate sex. That's a great accomplishment, a painting that's hot."

The air was silken and sensuous. There was a sharp clarity in the space. Sex and death and emptiness. Andy had done it again.

The black Elvis and gun floated on silver and radiated power. The deity Elvis perfectly arisen and the deity Andy perfectly arisen, both standing there. Two gods had taken form.

"They need a lot of work done on them," said Andy, modest and serious. "And they'll probably hate them."

"Don't be silly, a great painting is a great painting, and it doesn't matter."

Andy had taken the Elvis image from a postcard he had received from the painter Harold Stevenson, which was signed by a number of people, including Charles Henri Ford. It was always interesting how Andy found images.

We talked for a while about the important information we had heard that day, not just gossip—politics and the intrigues of the art world. And often, I leaned forward and kissed Andy, pressed my cheek to his cheek, rubbed my forehead against his like a cat, as an expression of love, celebrating the moment of his great accomplishment.

We were late for the party. As we got ready to leave, there was another burst of enthusiasm about the *Elvises*. Andy put out all the lights, except the staircase light. We walked to the stairs, talking, leaning against each other, pressing the edges of our shoulder blades together, laughing. At the top of the stairs, we paused, and hugged each other. We hugged every part of our bodies that could touch, and pressed our hearts together. I stuck my leg between Andy's legs, and lifted him up a little, and let his body lie on my leg and body.

I lost my balance, and we fell backward down the stairs.

My first thought was that the worst had happened. In red alert, I tried to protect Andy. I absorbed my blow as I hit each step, then simultaneously, I swung and flipped him on top of me and absorbed his blow. At the same time I knew that the antidote to catastrophe was to relax and roll like a rag doll.

Hugging each other, we bounced down from step to step. It was totally wonderful. We were Mayan gods thrown from the pyramid to the lower realms. We hit the stone steps, and bounced off into a soup of dark green rainbow light, and hit again. We were the offerings in a blood sacrifice.

I wasn't getting hurt, and didn't feel any pain, and was trying to keep Andy from getting hurt. We landed at the bottom in a pile.

There was nothing but very bright white light, beyond time and space. A rare moment, when in a state of shock caused by physical harm and severe trauma, the mind closes down for an instant, the brain short-circuits, and the consciousness has a glimpse of great luminosity and bliss.

We sat up, started laughing, and struggled to our feet. We said simultaneously, *"What happened?"*

"Are you okay?" I managed to get the words out, not quite knowing what they meant.

"I don't know . . . Let me think," said Andy sweetly.

"Hold on to me." I tried to take charge and stabilize the situation. I was relieved he wasn't angry, and that neither of us was hurt. "Are you okay?" I asked again.

"Yes."

"You didn't break any bones?" I felt Andy up and down, his ribs and hips and thighs and knees, to make sure nothing was broken. "You didn't get hurt?"

"I don't think so," said Andy. "Did you?"

"I have thick bones, they never break." We hugged each other.

What a relief, not a disaster. We relaxed and were stupefied. There was nothing to do but laugh uproariously. "You didn't crack your head!"

"Oh, John!"

"Well, that's wonderful!"

Andy looked serious, and frowned. "I don't know . . . You could have killed me!"

"Andy, don't be silly, I kept getting under you to take your falls. When you're young, your body never gets damaged."

"You tried to kill me!"

"Don't be silly!" Now there was damage control.

"You're dangerous to be with!"

We calmed down, got our equilibrium, and walked out dazed into the sunset. We took a taxi downtown. On arriving at the party, the first person we met was Bea Feitler, the brilliant young new editor of *Harper's Bazaar* and a good friend of ours. The first thing Andy said, loudly with alarm, was "John tried to kill me. He pushed me down the stairs!"

"What happened?" asked Bea as she kissed me. She was so beautiful.

"John tried to kill me." Andy was worked up.

My feelings were very hurt. I was betrayed. "Andy, how can you say such a thing! It was a mistake and a profound moment. It was the most important moment in your life."

"I have to be careful with you." He narrowed his eyes in distrust. "I have to watch out for you."

The huge canvas of *Elvis*es was rolled and shipped to Los Angeles for Andy's first one-man show at the Ferus Gallery in September. Gallery owner Irving Blum cut the canvas into eight pieces, which became the eight famous *Silver Elvis* paintings.

In 1977, in an interview in *High Times*, the journalist Glenn O'Brien asked Andy, "What was your first big break?"

His answer? "When John Giorno pushed me down the stairs!"

ON JULY FOURTH, Andy and I went back up to Wynn's Old Lyme farmhouse with Marisol and Bob Indiana. Wynn was giving Eleanor Ward a birthday party.

The party was in the barn, which was Wynn's studio, and we all had to make Eleanor presents. The best was Marisol's: she picked wildflowers from the meadow and hung them upside down, one foot apart, on two long strings strung across the barn room. I decorated the birthday cake, which Wynn helped me bake. Andy made her a pencil drawing.

Andy also brought along his new 16mm Bolex. Because of the holiday, the Peerless film store had been closed when we left the city, so he had brought only a couple of rolls of black-and-white film. By chance, Wynn had some color film. So that weekend, Andy shot a lot in color, which he didn't normally do. On Saturday, he shot color portraits of Marisol, Bob Indiana, and me. He filmed Wynn and me flying a kite, and me lying in the grass. He used the film camera as if it were a still camera, which he knew how to use.

The day of the party was a hot, lazy day. We were all bored and annoyed at having to prepare for Eleanor's birthday. I lay in a rope hammock between two trees, with my eyes closed, trying to take a nap, dazed from a hangover and the 95 degree heat. Sunlight flickered red and white on my closed eyelids, which somehow made me high. Andy was filming me from different angles. I was very comfortable with him and didn't pay attention. It was also five days before we planned to begin shooting *Sleep*, and I assumed he was rehearsing what he would do.

The footage of me sleeping in the hammock was beautiful— loving, very gay, the classic Greek and Roman god, male beauty. Everything that Andy would make sure not to include in the final cut of *Sleep*, which was about light and shadow. Gay was the kiss of death, and Andy was not political. It was the one time that he could indulge himself with the pure pleasure of love. He filmed inches from my skin.

Fifty-one years later, I would see that weekend's raw footage for the very first time. For four hours in a MoMA screening room, the original film played on a hand-turned movie viewer. In addition to the film from Old Lyme, there was other footage from New York. There were some sections that went out of focus for two minutes, came into focus for a minute, and then went out again.

"Is that Jasper Johns?" asked a MoMA curator, about another figure who briefly is in the frame. "Jasper denies it is."

"Of course it's Jasper," I said. "That's what he looked like back then."

I remember Jasper in the summer of 1963. He had a deep suntan, was thin and incredibly good-looking. And I remember Andy mentioning that Jasper had come by. It was an early, innocent time—Jasper still went out and regularly saw friends. A few years later, he withdrew from most people.

The curators gushed over the shadows of the leaves as they moved with the wind on my skin, an abstract painting. But I got a different rush. It felt like Andy was kissing or licking my skin with the camera, which is what he liked to do. Andy was making love to me with the camera while I slept!

Still from Warhol's hammock film

ANDY SHOT *SLEEP* in July, August, and October 1963. He had talked about it for a month, had already received some publicity, and it seemed like a great conceptual idea. But it was necessary for Andy to actually make the movie. He was still learning to use the Bolex, his first movie camera. He had shot Bob Indiana eating a mushroom—what could be more perfect? He shot the dancer Freddie Herko giving a haircut and dancing—what could be more perfect? And he had lovingly documented our July Fourth weekend. But *Sleep* was more complicated.

On a Tuesday morning in early July, Andy called and said, "Oh, can we do it tomorrow night?" We were both still knocked out from our weekend in Old Lyme.

"Yes, of course," I said happily.

We began shooting Wednesday, July 10. We had just come from a screening at the Bleecker Street Cinema and a loft party downtown. We stopped by Andy's house and picked up the camera and lights. We got to my place and began shooting about one o'clock. I was a little drunk, and made myself a vodka and soda. I took off my clothes, dropping them on the floor. Andy did the setup: two 150-watt aluminum reflector clip-on lights, tripod and Bolex camera, light meter and film. He was awkward and his hands trembled. He had never done it before. It was his first big film.

"Okay, let's shoot!" I said.

Andy paused, turned to me, and said, "Are you ready for your close-up?"

"Yes!" I laughed, remembering that he had used the same line in the Times Square photo booth. I gave him a big hug with my naked body and pressed my soft dick into his leg.

I lay down on the bed, sank into a soft pillow, put an arm up over my head, and closed my eyes. I liked sleeping more than anything else. The movie was Andy's problem. I let my mind rest and fell asleep immediately.

The next morning when I woke up, I saw the apartment lights were still on, and the floor was littered with dozens of crushed yellow Kodak boxes and scraps of film. Andy and the equipment were gone. And I had a hangover.

"It's done!" A slight warm feeling arose in my chest about *Sleep*.

Andy shot again two nights later, and then a handful more times over the next two weeks. If our schedules were different, I left the front door unlocked, and Andy came and did it while I slept. The process had an empty and caressing quality. He'd shoot for three or four hours, until about five o'clock, when the first trace of daylight came. Andy was on speed, amphetamines, when he worked—high and wide-awake. In the dead of night, everything was crystal clear.

The Bolex was an early model. It used rolls of film that had to be reloaded every three minutes, and manually rewound every twenty seconds. Andy sent Gerard Malanga, who had just started working for him, with the many rolls to a west-side Manhattan lab to have them developed. It took a week to get the film back.

We looked at it on an old-fashioned, hand-cranked movie viewer with big reels, and then on an old rickety 16mm projector. The footage was beautiful, but there was a big problem: every twenty seconds the film jerked, caused by the rewinding. "Oh, no!" Two weeks of shooting was unusable, and we had to begin again.

Andy had never made a film, had never been to film school, and knew almost nothing about the process. He asked a lot of simple questions to anyone he thought knew anything: Jack Smith, Al Leslie, Robert Frank, and other downtown filmmakers.

One night at a party, Andy told the filmmaker Bud Wirtschafter about the problem of the image jerking every twenty seconds from the rewinding. "What do I do?"

"There is a rewind device that attaches to the camera, and plugs into an electrical outlet, and rewinds automatically," said Bud with a big smile. "You can buy it at Peerless."

Andy bought the device and we started over again in August, shooting *Sleep* for another ten days. We looked at the film on the hand-cranked movie viewer and the clacking 16mm projector. "Oh, they're so beautiful!" said Andy. It had worked. Everything Andy did was a great work of art.

There were thousands of rolls of film, and Andy didn't know what to do with them. Every roll was from a slightly different camera angle, or had a slightly different frame or light. Andy duplicated some shots that he liked, and placed them after each other and in between other shots. He was familiar with repetition from his paintings, but this repetition was out of necessity. Andy couldn't figure out how to make the shots into a movie.

In mid-September, Jonas Mekas came to Andy's house. There were about six people there, and we watched several three-minute rolls of *Sleep* on the clacking projector. Jonas was very impressed. He didn't stay long, but I knew somehow his visit was very important.

In his "Movie Journal" column in *The Village Voice* on September 19, 1963, Jonas wrote:

It doesn't have to be a great or complex work of art to be a witness of a passionate movement forward. And Warhol, for instance, is in the process of making the longest and simplest movie ever made: an eight-hour-long movie that shows nothing but a man sleeping. But this simple movie will push Andy Warhol—and has pushed me, and a few others who saw it, some of it—further than we were before. As simple as it is, it is a movement forward that carries others with it. Therefore it is beautiful like anything that is alive. Anything that is alive is beautiful—that is my statement for the week.

Jonas's piece gave *Sleep* credibility.

ON SEPTEMBER 9, 1963, John Cage organized a performance of Erik Satie's *Vexations* at the Pocket Theater on Third Avenue and Thirteenth Street. An epic repetitive work for piano, written in 1893, it had never been performed before in its entirety. The highly idiosyncratic work for solo piano was a 52-beat segment, accompanied by detailed instructions that it be played softly and slowly 840 times. Twelve relaying pianists performed the piece, each of whom played a twenty-minute segment, for fifteen repetitions. The performance lasted eighteen hours and forty minutes, and ended the next afternoon.

The Pocket Theater was a narrow storefront theater that seated about sixty people. Most of the twelve musicians were my friends. The performance started around six. I got there about an hour later and met up with Andy, and we sat together.

Andy loved Satie and was fascinated by how he understood intrinsically how boredom worked with an audience. "Oh, it's so boring, it's great," said Andy. It was repetitive, but it was also nineteenth-century music. "Oh, I don't know, it's old-fashioned art."

I stayed for about two hours, then went home, because I was

tired and wanted to sleep. Andy stayed until one o'clock, went home, and then returned to the Satie performance, staying I don't know how long. He was on speed and could handle it.

I took home from the performance a mimeographed and stapled six-page program. The front cover featured a nineteenth-century photo of Satie. Inside, in a dark, old-fashioned type, the program included an explanation of the performance and a description of Rosicrucian formulas used by Satie, along with several examples: ABCBCBCD, which were presumably the magical use of numerology. I kept the program in my apartment and occasionally found it open, by chance, to that page with the strange formulas. It would take years for me to understand their significance.

ON SEPTEMBER 24, Andy went to Los Angeles, for his show of the *Silver Elvis* paintings at the Ferris Gallery. While he was gone, my life became an endless string of dinner parties, a return to the social life I had had before Andy. When he came back to New York in early October, Andy was very nervous about *Sleep*. It was already a famous movie, yet it had not been completed.

Andy needed more shots, specifically to be used for the repetitions. "Just a couple more," he said to me. "Now I know what I want. We have some, but we'll do them again."

"Yes, of course, anything you want."

So one night in early October, I left my door unlocked. Andy came over around one in the morning, when I was asleep, and he filmed. I woke up briefly, and we hugged, but the point was to be asleep. The next morning, as before, I woke up with the lights on and dozens of yellow film boxes and scraps scattered on the floor. The film was in the can, as they say.

Andy hired a seventeen-year-old girl named Sarah Dalton to work on *Sleep*. She and her older brother David had arrived in New York the year before, both of them brilliant, blond, delicate, and beautiful. Andy really liked them, and so did I.

"What should I do?" said Sarah.

"If you see anything interesting, cut it out, like John turning over or yawning, cut it out," said Andy, "and nothing beautiful."

Sarah made storyboards. In the cluttered rear room in Andy's house and in her apartment, she methodically and meticulously went through the thousands of rolls of film. She tried to reconstruct the shooting sequence. In three-inch squares, she drew cartoons of the sleeping position, close-up, full body, crop, any movement, dark or light. She worked for months, and it was no help. Andy still didn't know how to make it work.

I stayed out of the editing process and did not offer any ideas, keeping my mouth shut. I knew better. But as time went by, I began to feel left out of the process, and a little rejected. Finally, out of desperation, Andy said, "We should just use anything." It appeared that he chose several shots, almost arbitrarily, duplicated them, and strung them together.

Finally, he had a twenty-minute reel of footage. And on a cold day in late November, in Wynn's fifth-floor loft at 222 Bowery, *Sleep* had its first "rough cut" screening. It was arranged by Naomi Levine, and Jonas Mekas and a few friends were invited. On an old, clattering 16mm projector that was difficult to get working, we first saw *Sleep*.

Once again, Jonas was thrilled. "It's so unique, and so incredible!" he said with his Lithuanian enthusiasm. "It is a work of genius." In the January 1964 issue of *Film Culture*, which came out in December 1963, Jonas put a still photo, a close-up of the sleeping face, on the front cover. He again raved about the film, giving it a huge launch and jump-starting Andy's film career.

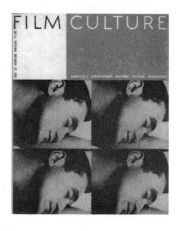

Cover of the January 1964
issue of *Film Culture*

SLEEP HAD BEEN announced in June, and over the months received enormous amounts of publicity. It was talked about in every art magazine, and by December 1963, the film was celebrated and notorious. Yet still there was really no movie. It seemed like a finished work of art, a successful conceptual work, and Andy would have loved to move on and forget about it. It had already accomplished its goal.

A week before the premiere, which was scheduled for January 17, Henry Geldzahler asked Andy, "What is the soundtrack for *Sleep*?"

Andy got a worried look on his face.

"If it doesn't have a soundtrack," said Henry, laughing, "it's a silent film."

Now Andy looked frightened. He had been tortured for eight months making the movie. Everyone was expecting a great film, but he was not a filmmaker. And the thought of a soundtrack had not even entered his mind. "Ohhh! I don't know."

"Satie," said Henry with a little chuckle. "What about Satie?"

Andy's expression changed. He had a look I knew well, when he heard a good idea, but didn't say anything, and just let it sink in.

A bit later, he said, "*Sleep* doesn't need a soundtrack. Satie is too arty!"

The next day, Henry gave Andy a cassette of *Vexations*, a bootleg copy made by someone in the audience. We played it on a small cassette tape recorder.

Andy liked it. "I'm going to use Satie on opening night," he said. "It's so boring, it's perfect."

"The sound quality isn't so good," I said. "And when it gets amplified, it'll sound really bad. Maybe John Cage has a better recording."

"Oh, it doesn't matter," said Andy.

The world premiere of *Sleep* was on January 17, 1964, at the

Gramercy Arts Theatre on East Twenty-Seventh Street near Lexington. The *Village Voice* advertisement read: "ANDY WARHOL'S EIGHT HOUR SLEEP MOVIE. Friday, Jan. 17; Sat., 18; Sun., 19; Mon., 20. Starting 8 PM (one show every evening). The only New York showing for some time. Contribution: $2. Benefit show for the Film-Makers' Cooperative."

The film ended up being six and a half hours long, not eight. "Satie was eighteen hours," I said to Andy. "Five and a half hours is not enough sleep for me. Please, make it longer!"

"I can't," said Andy, laughing. "I can't stretch it any more." He knew exactly the footage to repeat and loop, and it worked perfectly. Any more might have been too much.

For the premiere, the small cassette recorder was placed at the edge of the stage, and Satie's *Vexations* was played, and the bad sound quality was perfect. Opening night was the only time that Satie was played with *Sleep*.

I went into the theater a few times over the next nights, briefly, with Andy. It was fun, because I had no expectations. I was not an actor with a strategy for a film career, I was a poet with a dream of being a movie star.

Henry Geldzahler sat in the front row for the entire premiere. In his piece for *The Village Voice* introducing *Sleep*, he wrote:

Andy Warhol's films conceal their art exactly as his paintings do. The apparently sloppy and unedited is fascinating. What holds his work together in both media is the absolute control Andy Warhol has over his own sensibility—a sensibility as sweet and tough, as childish and commercial, as innocent and chic, as anything in our culture. Andy Warhol's eight hour [sic] *Sleep* movie must be infuriating to the impatient or the nervous or to those so busy they cannot allow the eye and the mind to adjust to a quieter, flowing sense of time. What appears boring is the elimination of incident, accident, story, sound and the moving camera. As in Erik Satie's *Vexations* when the same 20-second [*sic*] piece is repeated for eighteen hours, we find that the more that is eliminated the greater concentration is possible on the spare remaining essentials. The slightest variation becomes an event, something on which we can focus our attention. As less and less happens on the screen, we become satisfied with almost nothing and find the slightest shift of the body of the sleeper or the least movement of the camera interesting enough. The movie is not so much about sleep as it is about our capacity to see the possibilities of an aspect of film carried to its logical conclusion, *reductio ad absurdum* to some, indicating a new awareness to others.

Sleep was a great triumph. All of New York, uptown and downtown, came or had something to say about it. A cause célèbre!

"You're a star," said Andy. "You don't know what I've done for you."

"I do! And I appreciate it," I said, laughing. "I told you I want to be Marilyn Monroe."

"Oh, John!" said Andy, laughing, and we leaned into each other.

Implicit in my words were hopelessness, impermanence, and delusion; fame, glamour, and death were empty. "I want to be like Marilyn Monroe."

ON MAY 27, 2007, *Sleep* was shown in Turbine Hall at Tate Modern in London, with Satie's *Vexations* performed in accompaniment. Andy had been dead for twenty years. The film was projected on a gargantuan screen and twelve pianists played in rotation for over seventeen hours straight. The Tate film curator invited me to perform at 7:30 p.m. at the beginning of the concert, and after it ended, the next day at 3:00 p.m.

The performance took place over a long holiday weekend, but

it was unseasonably cold for late spring. A huge crowd was expected to camp out overnight, but only several hundred people did, bringing blankets and sleeping bags. I tried sticking it out, but shivering on the concrete floor in the freezing cold became too much. At 3:00 a.m., I went back to my hotel. I slept for three hours, and was back at seven in the morning, committed to seeing it through to the end. I went to the green room, where the pianists were resting between sets, the stress and strain apparent on each of their faces and bodies. Theirs was a heroic effort.

Watching the vast image of *Sleep* and listening to Satie was amazingly powerful. I got through the whole thing by treating it as a meditation, letting my mind rest without discursive thoughts, hearing the sound and seeing the abstract images, and watching my breath and mind.

At one point, Brandon Joseph, an art historian at Columbia University, came up to me. "I have seen *Sleep* a thousand times," he said, "and I have plotted the repetitions. They are repeated in a regular way. What appears to be a formula or pattern."

Suddenly, I remembered the program for John Cage's performance of *Vexations* back in 1963, how I had often found it on my desk open, by chance, to that final page with the strange formulas. Maybe Andy had the program on his desk opened to it by chance too.

"Brandon, do you know what that means?" I said. "Maybe Andy used Satie's Rosicrucian formula to edit the film."

I don't remember what magical use the Rosicrucian formula had. But it's curious that Andy, by a combination of accident, chance, and desperation, may have used a magic spell to make *Sleep*.

SUPERSTAR

In the months leading up to *Sleep*'s premiere, Andy and I were together all the time, and I was drawn even deeper into his life.

These were some of the most memorable experiences of our relationship.

In October 1963, I went over to his house, and found him working. He was drawing scratchy lines with a grease pencil; a bottle of Coke, a thermos, and a jar of Vaseline lay on the desk beside him.

A cover design had fallen through at the *New York Herald Tribune*, he explained, and the art director had asked him for something. "I'm just touching it up. I did it a couple of months ago for the *Times*, and it was rejected."

For gay men at the time, a jar of Vaseline meant one thing: anal sex. So I was thrilled at what I saw as secret homosexual subtext. "A Vaseline jar on the cover of the *Herald Tribune*! Andy, that's so brilliant!"

"I need the seventy-five dollars," said Andy. "I have bills to pay."

I was surprised at the implication that commercial art wasn't great art. It was a gay image in mass media.

"It was originally for a summer issue, and people have Coke bottles, thermoses, and Vaseline jars on the beach," he explained.

Now that it was October, the illustration could seem out of season and its gay connotations too obvious. But that day it was 90 degrees and humid, and the coming Sunday was supposed to be just as hot. "You lucked out with the weather," I said.

The image ran on October 20, a three-quarter-page drawing on the front of the Sunday Business and Financial section. The cover story that it illustrated was about corporate trademarks being used as generic images and lawsuits that such companies as Merriam-Webster, AT&T, General Motors, Dow Chemical, and Whirlpool were pursuing against people using their trademarks as ordinary words.

It was also an obscure, ironic joke by the editor of the *Tribune*, a friend. This was before Andy became really famous, changing the culture and art history with his use of the found Pop image. Andy would become the king of trademark infringement.

ON HALLOWEEN 1963, I went over to pick Andy up for a show, but as we got ready to leave, Andy said, "My mother wants to meet you."

"What! . . . Why! . . . Great!" I was shocked. Nobody had ever laid eyes on Andy's mother. He talked about her and was deeply attached to her, but she was a big secret. She lived on the ground floor, in an apartment behind the kitchen.

"She's heard about you."

"What!"

"She's heard you on the stairs coming in and out."

I was horrified. The night before, I had come back to his house, drunk, and when we said good night and walked down the stairs to the front door, we hugged and kissed, sloppy and affectionate. "She heard us last night!" I gasped. "Oh, no!"

"She just wants to meet you."

Andy took me down the back stairs in the darkness, where I had never been. It was off-limits. "Let me put on the light." Andy knocked. His mother, Mrs. Warhola, unlocked and opened the door. "Ma, this is John."

"Pleased to meet you!" I bowed slightly, warm and gracious as I could be.

Andy's mother was an old woman. She had a gentle face, gray hair, a wide waist, and strong arms, and she wore a cotton floral housedress and slippers. She smiled and we laughed as we gazed at each other.

"I am very happy to meet you."

"Good to meet you." She was filled with loving kindness.

Andy and his mother talked about something, in what I thought was Czech. (Later, I would learn they were not Czechoslovakian, but in fact Carpatho Rusyn, a small ethnic group from the Carpathian Mountains.)

Listening to them talk, I realized this was a very important moment. Andy introducing me to his mother was a statement, an affirmation that we were lovers. I was thrilled that it was really true. Then I said to myself, Stop thinking stupid thoughts and just be in the moment.

Her room looked and smelled like the home of a Central European refugee: boiled cabbage and beat-up furniture, a new Frigidaire refrigerator alongside a table with a big Motorola television.

"She wants to know how you feel."

"Really good!"

While Andy and his mother talked, I shifted from foot to foot, and stretched, and took in more details of the room. There was a new kitchen stove and an old enamel sink, a table covered with oilcloth, a chair facing the TV, and a broom resting in the corner. Against the far wall was a simple single bed and one pillow. On a chest of drawers at the head of the bed were small religious statues—the Virgin Mary, the Infant Jesus, a plastic St. Anthony—and a set of rosary beads. On one wall was a picture of Christ with outstretched arms, a bleeding heart radiating from his chest.

Andy said that she went to church every day, and on Sundays traveled down to East Fifteenth Street and Second Avenue, to St. Stephen's Church, which had a Czechoslovak congregation. Sometimes Andy, a secret Roman Catholic, went with her. Coming myself from a semilapsed Italian Catholic family, I found this a little perplexing. But I had no negative thoughts about it; it was their spiritual path, and that made it wonderful.

"You're a good boy," she said with an accent, smiling. Andy Warhol's mother approved. Set off the fireworks!

"She wants to know if you want something to eat . . . Oh. Ma, no! We're going out." She said it again in Czech. "Oh, Ma!"

"Very good to meet you." I touched my heart. "It was a joy."

Andy and I walked up the dark stairs. "She likes you!" He was happy, and so was I.

And how perfect that it was Halloween! I had met the witch. I had seen her broom in the corner and the wart on her nose. Brimming with mirth, I was about to blurt this out, but I kept my mouth shut, not wanting to hurt Andy. Mrs. Warhola was a white witch with great kindness.

We took a taxi to the Green Gallery. It was the seminal gallery of the early 1960s. Everything happened there first. Dick Bellamy, who owned it, was the most visionary art dealer, but not a good businessman.

The show was Robert Morris's cube boxes. There were only about twenty people, standing around drinking wine. Dick's children ran screaming around the room, bumping into the boxes, his girlfriend Sally chasing after them.

"I see Sally is giving a Halloween party," I said as we moved through the gallery, laughing and talking to whomever we ran into.

Andy kept looking at the art. Placed randomly on the floor, Bob Morris's boxes presided with pristine brilliance. Andy stood apart from everybody and obsessed over them, with what I noticed was an uncommonly strong intensity.

"Oh, Bob should just pile them up," he laughed.

This was Andy's second visit to the show. He had been to the crowded opening and had come back tonight to see the work again, and think more about the potential of its shape. Earlier that year, he had stenciled Campbell's Soups on a wood cube that he happened to have, but nothing came of it. I could tell, though, that Andy wasn't done with the idea. As it would turn out, this show of Bob Morris boxes was a landmark moment in art history.

A WEEK LATER, Andy and I were at a dinner party in Wynn's Bowery loft. We were in the kitchen, drinking and smoking cigarettes and joints while Wynn cooked. Andy said, "I have a problem. I have to do a piece for the World's Fair and I don't know what to do."

Andy had been asked to create work for the outside of the New York State Pavilion, which was being designed by Philip Johnson for the big upcoming 1964 exposition in Queens. The building was circular with places for ten pieces of art. David Whitney, Philip Johnson's lover—who was a friend of all of ours—suggested that Philip choose Henry Geldzahler to curate the artists. Henry chose Andy, Roy Lichtenstein, James Rosenquist, Bob Indiana, John Chamberlain, Bob Rauschenberg, Ellsworth Kelly, Peter Agostini, Robert Mallary, and Alexander Liberman.

"Oh, I don't know what to do!" said Andy. "They keep asking me, and the time is getting close."

"Bob Indiana," I said, "is doing a twenty-foot electric sign of EAT. That's great!"

Andy got more nervous. "I have to think of something! The building is round and has sort of ten sides."

"I have a great idea for you," said Wynn. "The ten most wanted men. You know, the mug shots the police issue of the most wanted criminals. They're so beautiful."

"Oh, what a great idea!" I said.

"My boyfriend is a cop," said Wynn. "He can get you all the mug shots you want. He brings home a briefcase of them every night."

"What a great idea!" Andy said. Everybody laughed in agreement.

The idea was quintessentially Warhol: silk-screened black-and-white photos, Pop, gay and straight, hero and outlaw. World's Fair president and New York City planning mastermind Robert Moses had to approve all the art, but Andy was unconcerned. "I don't care," he said. "I'm going to do it!"

"Ask Henry," I said, pleased to see Andy's determination, but also pragmatic. "You realize those 'most wanted men' posters are in every post office across America!"

The next day, Andy asked Henry Geldzahler, who liked the idea. David Whitney and Philip Johnson approved as well. I was happy to hear nobody thought it was a problem, giant photos of criminals at the World's Fair.

Andy took risks all the time. Amphetamines make a person

bold and tenacious. Like Jack Kerouac writing *On the Road* for thirty-six continuous hours, or Jimi Hendrix maximizing his virtuosity, speed allowed Andy to accomplish great things and change history. But speed can ruin or kill you. Andy's use would end in just a few years, after his being shot in 1968, and with it would end his risk taking, and his great breakthrough period of making art. But in 1964, the "most wanted men" was Andy at his most fearless.

Wynn's lover, the mug-shot procurer, was a third-generation New York City cop named Jimmy O'Neil. He was thirty-six, half Irish and half Italian, looked like a movie star, and was hip, beautiful, and smart. Some time after Andy's request, he came home and pulled from his black accordion case an envelope stuffed with photographs—crime photos, mug shots, and archival images. But what most caught Andy's eye was a printed pamphlet of collected mug shots from the New York City Police Department, entitled "The Thirteen Most Wanted." These would be Andy's men.

Five months later, on April 15, 1964, Andy's twenty-by-twenty-foot painting of the thirteen mug shots, silk-screened on square Masonite panels, was installed in the New York State Pavilion. Giving the painting a gay undertone, Andy had positioned the profile head shots to be "looking" at the other head shots (in one case, two guys looking right at each other), as if they were attracted to each other, homoerotic rough trade. It was an intensely political piece of art, I realized, and not just because Robert Moses was sanitizing the city for the World's Fair. For years, the New York police had systematically raided gay bars and closed theaters showing gay porn, while plainclothes policemen arrested guys cruising. Just before the fair, the police busted Jonas Mekas's Film Culture screening of *Flaming Creatures* and other films, many of which were confiscated and lost.

And there was a subtextual controversy, which Andy may not have known about: seven of the thirteen men were Italian American criminals, and Governor Nelson Rockefeller, then running for the Republican nomination for president of the United States, did not want to offend Italian American voters in Queens.

Backlash to the painting was swift. As soon as Robert Moses saw it, he freaked out and ordered it removed. Two days later, I drove out with Wynn and Naomi Levine to see *13 Most Wanted Men* before it was gone, but it had already been painted over in silver.

Surprisingly, the empty panel felt beautiful and perfect. The thirteen rough-trade men had been transformed into silver monochrome bliss. It was a great triumph for Andy, I felt, and he agreed. "It's more me now," he said.

As a replacement/alternative to the *13 Most Wanted Men*, Andy did a silk-screen portrait of a smiling Robert Moses on twenty-five Masonite panels. It was not a joke. Andy thought the portrait was a very good work, but the powers that be did not agree. He was hurt by the second rejection as much as he was the first time. So, in the summer of 1964, Andy made a silk-screen-on-canvas painting of twenty-five repetitions of the Robert Moses portrait. Andy was fearless. Then he had the idea for another replacement, panels of silk-screened paintings of flowers, but that never got anywhere either. The idea became the *Flower* paintings, which would be shown at the Leo Castelli Gallery that November.

Undeterred by rejection and still fixated on the mug shots, Andy went on that summer to make paintings on canvas with the silk screens from *13 Most Wanted Men*. He made a painting of each mug shot, front and profile, changed it from a square format to a portrait presentation of 40 x 48 inches, and put back the name and "numbers" of the criminals, which became the titles of the paintings. In 1967, they would be shown at the Ileana Sonnabend Gallery in Paris.

In the larger scope of Andy's work, the World's Fair *13 Most Wanted Men* painting represents a brief, transitional style: photos by different photographers, from different angles and different sizes, in one painting. Soon, Andy would give this up in favor of a more successful technique, repeating the same image at the same size several times.

But for me, *13 Most Wanted Men*—both versions—is among Andy's most profound work. All the other art at the New York State Pavilion felt like cartoon miniatures—Jim Rosenquist's advertising images, Roy Lichtenstein's laughing comic-book redhead woman, Ellsworth Kelly's red-and-blue paired monochromatic forms, and Bob Rauschenberg's postage-size images all were out of scale on the huge building. The silver painting alone was profound. It remained for the rest of the World's Fair, and after two years of sun, wind, rain, and snow, *13 Most Wanted Men* reappeared slightly through the fading silver paint, before it was put in the garbage.

13 Most Wanted Men at the 1964 World's Fair

I HEARD JFK was shot when I was downtown, and Andy heard when he was walking through Grand Central Station. I got to Andy's house on Lexington Avenue at about one-thirty, just after he did. In the back room with the *Liz Taylor* and other paintings stapled on the wall, we sat on the Tiffany couch among the clutter, watching live TV coverage from Dallas. We heard Walter Cronkite say, grave and sonorous, "President Kennedy died at one o'clock Central Standard Time, two o'clock Eastern Standard Time, some thirty-eight minutes ago."

Andy and I grabbed each other, hugged and hugged, pressing our bodies together, trembling. We both started crying, weeping big fat tears. We pressed our faces together and kissed. It was the first time we had ever properly kissed, sober and intentional. It had the sweet taste of kissing death. It was exhilarating, like when you get kicked in the head and see stars.

I did not particularly like Kennedy, and I had never voted, but his assassination changed all that. "They shot my man."

We spent the afternoon watching the live coverage. The telephone rang several times in the front room, and Andy answered it.

I said, "His death is the best thing he's ever done!"

Andy had a funny look on his face. Later, we watched Jacqueline Kennedy get off Air Force One, live, wearing the bloodstained pink Chanel suit. She had refused to change her clothes. Andy said, "Oh, it's the best thing she's ever done!" The image was indelible, like seeing a great work of art, or something perfect.

Andy went downstairs several times to see his mother in her room, where she was also watching TV. She was very upset, crying, which made Andy more upset. When he returned upstairs, his face was ashen white.

Andy said, frightened and confused, "I don't know what it means!"

"A bad omen," I said. JFK's murder rang like a death knell in my heart. It portended what was to come, the failure of our aspirations, the 1960s delusion of love and light, flower power and peace. It all ended five years later in bad politics.

About five o'clock, we tried to continue our lives. I went home to rest, and came back at eight, and we went to a party. The first person we met there was the editor Bea Feitler, who exclaimed in despair, "Andy!" It was a raw night in New York.

Two days later, en route to a party in New Jersey, I heard on my tiny transistor radio that Lee Harvey Oswald had been shot, but no one else in the car would listen. Finally, Andy responded, "Ohhh!"

We arrived at Billy Klüver's ranch house. Billy, a laser engineer at Bell Labs in New Jersey, first introduced the concept of artists working with engineers and technology, which would give rise to many great collaborations.

He greeted us at the front door, repeated the news, and welcomed us in.

The frigid air and bright sun outside, the dry, overheated house, and the adrenaline rush of the second shooting heightened everyone's sense of clarity. There were about thirty or forty people at the party, including almost all of the Pop artists before they became famous. Olga, Billy's wife, gave me a Bloody Mary, and went around with a pitcher, filling glasses. Andy drank a Coke.

I had an attack of paranoia. "I don't know why I'm here," I whispered, as we stood by ourselves in a hall. Nobody was talking to us.

"I don't know why I'm here," Andy repeated, laughing.

People were scattered about the house and everyone took turns in the living room watching TV. JFK's coffin was being taken through Washington, D.C., from the White House to the Capitol. It was deeply moving for everyone and nobody talked much. Andy and I watched TV, then went out of the room for a while, returned to the coverage, took another break, and then watched again.

Andy kept saying, "I don't know what it means!"

The next morning was JFK's funeral. I got to Andy's house at eleven. We sat on the couch in the back room for the whole day, watching TV. JFK's death was the first great live TV event, capturing for days the hearts and minds of the whole world. It was the first time a vast public was held captive to the television set as a sad event unfolded. Andy and I didn't know what to make of it. We were dumbfounded.

Most striking was Jacqueline Kennedy in a black suit and a long black veil, royal widow weeds. "She's so great. She's done it again," I said. "Two days ago, she refused to change her blood-stained dress; and today, she is Queen Mary at the royal funeral." In the freezing cold, Jackie led the cortege, followed by heads of state and dignitaries from across the world.

"She's so fabulous," said Andy.

Throughout the afternoon, in the deep sadness, the extraordinary presence of Jacqueline Kennedy was overwhelming. "Andy, you should make a painting of her with the black veil," I said.

"Oh, I don't know." Andy was skeptical, because the image was too new.

"That image," I said, "will be a Pop icon. It's happening live, now; but the image will be an icon. Trust me." Other people also suggested it to Andy several weeks later, and in early 1964, Andy did the series of paintings *Jackie*, from newspaper photos of JFK's assassination and funeral.

Andy answered the telephone in the front room several times. A few people visited briefly on the pretext of business, but really just wanting to be with Andy in the sacred moment. Everyone was very respectful of one another's personal spiritual reaction.

Andy went downstairs every once in a while to see how his mother was doing. "She's watching it on TV. She's very upset."

After they lit the eternal flame in Arlington Cemetery, I hugged Andy, said goodbye, and went home. Later that night, we went to a party. JFK's assassination and Andy were forever linked for me. Our good fortune was being there to help each other in crisis.

ON DECEMBER 4, 1963, Wynn threw me a birthday party in his loft. He gave lots of great parties and this time, I was the excuse. It was billed as a birthday party for John Giorno, a young poet and the star of Andy Warhol's movie *Sleep*. Nobody knew me or cared, it was just a good opportunity to get together.

There were about eighty people. Andy, Patty and Claes Oldenburg, Roy Lichtenstein, Jim Rosenquist, Jasper Johns and Bob Rauschenberg, who had broken up as lovers three years before (Jasper left just before Bob arrived with his boyfriend, Steve Paxton, whom they had broken up over), Yvonne Rainer and Robert Morris, Frank Stella and Barbara Rose, Merce Cunningham and John Cage, Larry Poons, George Segal, Al Held, Larry Rivers, John Ashbery, Kenneth Koch, Frank O'Hara (who arrived with a retinue), Alex Katz, Trisha Brown, Jill Johnston, and Carolee Schneemann, among others—in sum, everyone in the art world.

In this extended group of young painters, sculptors, dancers, musicians, and poets, nobody was really famous yet. John Cage was a little older and some were more established. They were artists who worked and lived in lofts in the Village and downtown, where they had gravitated through an intuition that there were people of similar mind. They were just beginning, having their first shows, and they went to one another's openings and birthday parties because they liked each other's work. I did not know they were the greatest artists of the last half of the twentieth century. I met and hung out with them by chance.

But since I hadn't yet accomplished anything, I didn't really exist for them. Still, they liked me well enough. It was a Pop birthday party for a young poet. On some subconscious level, they saw themselves as a family, a group that supported one another. I was very lucky to be used for the occasion, a great moment, riddled with intrigue and joy. By 1965 or 1968, everybody was very famous, so for a long time nobody went to anybody's party, unless it was thrown by someone who would help their careers. But that night was still pure.

The artists brought the vitality of their art with them from their studios to the party, invisible and secret. They all were at peak creativity, making their greatest works. Sally Stokes Cram (who would marry Wynn two years later) came with Prince Alexander Romanov and the Italian jewelry designer Mimi di Niscemi. Another budding young talent in jewelry was Kenneth Jay Lane, just launching his own business after working for Christian Dior.

Then there was the entertainment. The week before, Wynn had been to the Village Gate and seen an unknown singer named Tiny Tim. Wynn recognized genius, and asked him to perform at my birthday. On the day of the party, there was much haggling about the price. But Tiny Tim showed up and gave a brilliant performance. He sang in falsetto, with a plastic toy ukulele. He was scrawny with long greasy hair—a queer and a mess. It was a look that he nurtured, and he eventually would become a cultural icon.

Tiny Tim was doing his signature song, "Tiptoe Through the Tulips," when the filmmaker Ron Rice, drunk on whiskey and high on speed, decided it wasn't cool. Ron, a straight guy with a beautiful body, took off his clothes and pranced around naked behind Tiny Tim, who was annoyed but kept on singing. Ron tripped and fell backward into the paper backdrop, which came crashing down, ending the performance. Tiny Tim marched out in a rage. It was fabulously perfect.

Andy and I were sitting on a couch in the living room, opposite Ruth Yorck—Countess Yorck, as she liked to be called. She was old, with white wrinkled skin, dyed black hair, and a long nose, like a witch. As a girl, she had been Wassily Kandinsky's and Pavel Tchelitchew's lover, and had lived a famous bohemian life. Countess Yorck was a friend of Mme. Lyne, a French couture fashion designer and an old friend of my mother.

"How is your mother?" she said imperiously.

"Wonderful!" Countess Yorck was a troublemaker and I dreaded what might come next. "Great!"

"Why isn't she here tonight?"

"She's on Long Island . . . But I'm going out with Mme. Lyne this Saturday. You should come with us for the weekend." I trumped her.

Countess Yorck turned away, and said, "Why are we here tonight?"

"It's John's birthday," said Andy.

She ignored Andy, and said again, "Why are we here tonight?"

"Today is my birthday and Wynn has given this party."

"Has he now! Aren't you a lucky boy!" Countess Yorck was always unkind to me. At best, she thought she was being mischievous; in reality, she was a demon.

"It's so wonderful!" I was not going to allow her to spoil my night.

"John is the star of my new movie," said Andy.

"You are a lucky boy!" With disdain, she ended the conversation. She didn't like Andy Warhol either.

Wynn called me into the studio for a champagne toast. There was a big birthday cake from Ferrara's bakery on Grand Street, with lots of candles. Sally Cram and Patty Oldenburg lit the candles. Everybody sang "Happy Birthday."

"John, make a wish," said Patty.

"Make a wish." Wynn laughed.

It was one of those seemingly important opportunities, whether wishes work or not, and I had to do it, so why not be grandiose? I wished that I was a great artist, like everyone around me, but with greater compassion, and Marilyn Monroe on top of it; fame, glamour, and death, as a way out; one quick thought and mostly nonverbal. I blew out the candles, with the help of Sally, Patty, and Clarice Rivers, Larry's wife. We banged our heads together as we blew big breaths.

The author and Wynn Chamberlain on the
beach in Southampton, 1969

A WEEK LATER, I picked Andy up at the Lexington Avenue house
to go to an opening and a party. It was an extremely cold night
and I was feeling doomed by the temperature and my depression.
Andy opened the door and let me in, then stood in the hall, block-
ing me. "I have a surprise for you. Close your eyes."

"What?"

"Close your eyes."

I shut my eyes and Andy led me by the hand through the door
into the back room.

There on the wall hung what I thought was the painting of my
friend Marcia Stillman's suicide. It struck like a bolt of lightning.
A year earlier, on Thanksgiving, November 22, 1962, she had
taken LSD and committed suicide. She was at dinner with her
family in their apartment on Park Avenue at East Sixty-First.
She felt a little dizzy and hot, excused herself, and went to her
bedroom. The weather was 70 degrees on that late November afternoon. She opened the window, and sat on the wide stone ledge,
to have a breath of air. Marcia fell eight floors to her death, into
the courtyard of Christ Church next door. She was twenty-two
years old, beautiful, an actress, and had a brilliant mind.

Marcia's suicide had become an obsession of mine and I nagged
Andy for a year to make a *Disaster* painting of her death. I thought
it would give her death, which haunted me, some meaning. JFK's

assassination, three weeks earlier, occurred on the first anniversary of Marcia's death. It triggered my depression and constant thoughts of suicide. I had also asked Wynn to ask his boyfriend, Jimmy, to go the police precinct near where Marcia had died, and get the photo on file of the crime scene of her death. I nagged Wynn for five months and reminded Jimmy, who said he would do it, but never did. I had given up thinking it would happen.

But apparently, I thought, Andy had secretly gotten the photo, made the painting, and not told me. There it was in all its magnificent glory. The image was Marcia dead, lying facedown, crushed on the brick pavement in the courtyard, having fallen from the eighth-floor window, surrounded by three policemen and a male nurse leaning over her body. Perfect composition. The black silk screen was repeated thirteen times on the seven-foot-square white canvas. "It is so great, I can't believe it!" The painting and the room around it radiated a dazzling clarity.

"It's for you. A present."

I hugged Andy. "Thank you!" I was a bit overwhelmed. Andy really did love me! I walked up close. "It's fresh—the paint is still wet. It is perfect!"

"It came out right." Andy smiled warmly.

"It is one of the great paintings in the history of art. A masterpiece!" Another burst of joy when I realized that the futility of Marcia's suicide had been transformed into a great work of art, like the *Mona Lisa* or a Caravaggio. Then I had a moment of doubt. Everyone always thought their artist friends made great paintings. Was this truly great, or was it my obsession with and love for Andy?

"Oh, I know, it's so great!" said Andy, happy and confident.

When I looked closer, I realized it wasn't a photo of Marcia at all. I asked Andy where he'd gotten the image.

"I found it in the photos Jimmy gave me." The painting was from a photo of a girl who had committed suicide by jumping out of a window at Bellevue Hospital. It was later renamed *Bellevue II*, after Andy made another version for himself.

It didn't matter that it wasn't the actual photo of Marcia's death. The *Suicide* painting was a glorious surprise.

Andy showed it in the back room and everyone loved it. After about two months, I said, "Can I have my painting?"

"I made it for you," said Andy, smiling.

I had to keep reminding him, but it never came. "You said you wanted to give me something. I want Marcia's *Suicide*." I knew it wasn't really her, but I wanted to live with the painting, to be reminded that her death, or the idea of it, had been transformed into art.

Finally, one day Andy said, "How are we going to get it to your place?"

"You carried it here from the firehouse and I can carry it to Seventy-Fourth Street."

A week later, on a cold sunny afternoon, I carried the large rolled canvas very carefully on my shoulder. I went back another time for the stretchers. A week or so later, Andy came and stretched it. "You don't know what I've given you." He was testing me.

"I do! I do! I do!" I hugged Andy. The large skylight lit the painting radiantly. *Suicide* hung magnificently. "It is a totally, truly great painting and for me it is the fulfillment of something."

The painting remained at East Seventy-Fourth Street until March 1965, when I moved into the poet Ted Berrigan's old apartment on East Ninth Street. When I went to Morocco in February 1966, I rolled the canvas, stored it in the attic of my family's house in Roslyn Heights, and forgot about it for four years.

On Christmas Eve of 1963, it was my turn to give back. It was a numbingly cold afternoon as I stopped by Andy's house. "I have some Christmas presents for you."

"Ohhh, no."

"We are not exchanging gifts, but you've given me so much, I want to give you something. Winter solstice, new year offerings."

I had three presents for Andy, all wrapped in colored paper. The first was a pair of fine black leather gloves from Brooks Brothers. "When broken in, they'll go well with your black chinos."

"Ohhh, they're so . . . ," said Andy, caressing them with his delicate fingers.

The second was a paper collage that I made as a Christmas card using found images, pictures from magazines, some of them pornographic, and overlaid heavily with jewels from the Tiffany catalogue. "A Rauschenberg!" laughed Andy.

"Why not!"

The third present, wrapped in white tissue paper, was a gold wedding ring. There was a pawn shop next door to 222 Bowery, one of the last surviving ones on the street. In the window, on a blue velvet tray, were twenty or thirty old gold men's wedding rings. They always caught my eye as I went to visit Wynn. For a Christmas present, I bought one for Andy. A thick, rich, glowing yellow-gold wedding band.

"Ohhh!" Andy was shocked. "I don't know!"

"I'm not asking you to marry me. I think it's a really sexy gift." Andy looked frightened. "It's so large, he must have had a big dick."

I wondered if I hadn't made a mistake. A dead man's wedding ring or a failed marriage, but it was too late to take back. "It's so strong and sexy!"

"Did you get one for yourself?"

"Guys don't wear wedding bands!" We hugged and kissed.

With a dusting of snow outside, Andy and I spent the evening together, an intimate and almost corny Christmas Eve.

The author in front of 222 Bowery

IN EARLY JANUARY 1964, we went to the Louise Bourgeois opening at the Stable Gallery. Eleanor Ward greeted us grandly at the door. "Andy Candy!"

Andy cringed. He hated when she called him Andy Candy. "Oh, hello, Eleanor."

"Lairs!" she said, wide-eyed, as if she were Joan Crawford in a Hollywood movie.

"Did she say lies?" I whispered to Andy.

We walked around the show, "Louise Bourgeois: Recent Sculpture." The works were made from plaster and latex, hung and folded. There were cave tunnels, rough-walled labyrinths turning in upon themselves, flesh-colored undulations hanging nestlike from the ceiling.

"They're like pussies," I said. "What do you think?"

"It's so boring," said Andy. "It's so terrible! It's nothing!"

I was surprised he felt so strongly negative, and happy to hear it. She was the old order, sullied by surrealism.

"Why is everybody here, thinking it's so great?"

"I don't know."

"Politics. She's powerful."

"Oh, I don't know. Yes."

We talked with people we knew. "Louise's last show was eleven years ago," said the art critic David Bourdon. "And it is said to be a totally new body of work."

Suddenly, Andy was confronted with Louise Bourgeois. Eleanor appeared and introduced him. "Oh, Louise," said Andy. "It's so great."

"Thank you for coming." Everyone was effusive and gracious.

"And this is John Giorno, a poet."

"Very beautiful," I said, shaking her hand.

We were introduced to Louise Bourgeois's husband, Robert Goldwater, who was in his fifties, handsome, and a WASP. "He is the director of the Museum of Primitive Art," said David. And we chatted.

"He seems a bit gay," I whispered to Andy.

"I know."

WARHOL FIRST MET Salvador Dalí on January 10, 1964. It had snowed more than fourteen inches, which was plowed into glaciers, and became dirty blocks of ice with canyons cut through. The wind was piercing. I had a hangover and found it all so depressing.

We were taking a taxi downtown. "Where are we going?" I said.

"We're going to meet Salvador Dalí," said Andy.

Dalí and his wife, Gala, were staying in a suite at the St. Regis Hotel. They had been in New York for about two years on this visit, and were a presence in the art scene. In early 1962, before I met Andy, I was at parties where Dalí and Gala appeared, entering as royalty. I watched Dalí, with his unmistakable mustache, from a distance. And Andy had been at parties, before he and I met, watching Dalí and Gala, the glamorous stars. Ultra Violet, an old friend of Dalí, was arranging for Andy to formally meet Dalí.

Dalí was a great artist in the 1920s, '30s, and '40s, but in recent years he had made a lot of mindless bad art, including a painting of Christ on a crucifix currently being shown at the Metropolitan. We were meeting somebody who had fallen, and who was slightly less than the great artist he had been.

We got out of the taxi, walked through slushy snow and ice and up the red carpet of the hotel into the posh lobby, and turned left. "Ultra said be there at seven," said Andy.

The King Cole Bar had a huge mural behind the bar, painted by Maxfield Parrish in an art nouveau style of medieval revivalism, a jocular King Cole surrounded by his entourage, the Pied Piper, noble Knights Templar with white tunics and red crosses on their chests, gay camp but very discreet.

We sat on the banquet seats along the back wall to the left of the entrance. The waiter came and asked for our order. "No thanks," said Andy. "We're waiting for somebody."

Happily, we were behaving like lower-class boys, immigrant waifs, the hired help waiting for the rich people. "Andy, you know this place is also a gay bar," I said. "A very discreet gay bar between the hours of five and six only."

"Yes, I know!" said Andy, laughing.

"Of course, I've always preferred the Oak Bar at the Plaza. Less discreet and more hot."

"Oh, John!" Andy moaned sensuously.

"Nothing is happening here tonight." The bar was empty. "But of course, it is seven." We both laughed.

I had another history with the St. Regis, I told Andy. I had gone with my parents and their friends to Italian American black-tie dinner dances in the ballroom upstairs, benefiting some charity.

"You did?!" said Andy with an intrigued twinkle in his eye.

"Yes." I didn't say any more, because I wanted to avoid talking about the differences between my high-end Italian American family and his working-class Carpatho Rusyn one. Even though Andy might have thought it glamorous, I was slightly embarrassed by my family's bourgeois world.

Andy and I sat trying to entertain ourselves. "They say Dalí signs pieces of paper," said Andy, "and has other artists draw whatever they want, and he sells them." Andy had a look of fascination on his face. "And it doesn't matter what they draw. Oh, I don't know! What do you think?"

"It's great I guess, why not?" I said. "If it's a great work, but if it's just to make more money to feed an expensive lifestyle, I don't know."

"Oh, it doesn't matter," said Andy, wide-eyed and intrigued.

"Oh!" I said. "It's a great Andy idea!"

Ultra Violet arrived, we kissed, and she sat down. "They will be down soon," she said. Ultra was very glamorous, with long, shiny corkscrew curls. On *The Tonight Show*, when Johnny Carson asked her, she said she rinsed her hair in Coca-Cola. She was wearing an Afghan coat and layers of brocaded clothing.

"Can I take your order?" the waiter asked.

"No," said Ultra Violet. "We are waiting for our friends."

"Is Billy Rothlein up there?" I asked.

"No," said Ultra. "I didn't see him today."

Billy Rothlein, a friend of Wynn, was twenty years old, an actor, beautiful and bisexual. We were attracted to each other, had deep-tongue-kissed, would have liked to make it, but never got around to it. In November 1963, Billy met Dalí and Gala at a party. Billy had an uncanny, striking resemblance to the young Dalí, when Gala first met him in 1929 in Cadaqués, Spain.

Billy told me that when Gala saw him, she exclaimed, *"My Ilad!!* He is my Ilad." Dalí spelled backward. They became lovers that night. Gala had a reputation for liking young men—and for paying for them. She and Dalí, apparently, did not have sex, but he sometimes liked watching her making it with a guy.

We settled in for a long wait, when suddenly they appeared. I saw them first, two pathetic old people standing there who I thought would move on to another table. Ultra Violet exclaimed, "Hello!" and once Dalí and Gala were recognized, they became themselves, inflated, filled with energy.

Ultra introduced Andy, and the couple shook hands with him. "Hello."

"Oh, a young poet, John Giorno," said Andy. They shook my hand.

When I had seen Dalí at parties before, he was suntanned and looked like a playboy. Now in January, Dalí was old-man white, his pallor accentuating his dyed black hair and mustache. Dalí and Gala were charming and gracious with the seeming self-confidence of superstars, the modest prince and princess.

I looked at the loathsome mustache, and looked away, and looked again and looked away, and looked again. It was ugly, but I suppose a great idea, since it captured your attention in both photographs and real life.

They appreciated meeting Andy, as they knew his work. You

could see on Dalí's face that he recognized something. It was early in the history of Andy; he had just had his first exhibition one year before.

The waiter returned again to take our order. "What would you like?" said Gala, taking charge of the situation, becoming the center of attention, and making everything flow smoothly. "Andy, what would you like?"

Everybody looked at Andy. "I don't know!" Andy was trembling. It was an unanswerable question, like a nightmare. "Ultra, what would you like?"

"Gala, what would you like?" said Ultra Violet.

"Perrier," said Gala.

"Yes, I'll have Perrier too," said Ultra. "Dalí, what would you like?"

"Wine," said Dalí. "Red wine." He had said something.

"Andy?" said Gala.

"Oh, I'll have a Coke," said Andy. "Coca-Cola."

"John?"

Because Dalí had ordered wine, I could order alcohol too. "I'll have a vodka and tonic," I said. What an ordeal just to order drinks.

It was clear that it was impossible to talk to Dalí. He had nothing to say and was not interested in what anybody else said. He was the kind of passive-aggressive heterosexual man who used his wife as cover. The wife took care—with cunning, cleverness, and laughter—of the social world outside, and the husband surfed on the energy. Dalí was one of those heterosexual men who were only interested in women, and the rich and famous. A young gay man, poet or not, was off his radar.

"Andy is making a movie," said Ultra. "It is called *Sleep*. A man sleeping for eight hours."

"*Merveilleux,*" said Gala, laughing.

"It's John who's sleeping," said Andy. Dalí and Gala fixed their eyes on me for the first time. "But it's only about six hours. It's hard to do."

"It opens soon," said Ultra. "When is the premiere?"

"In two weeks," said Andy, "on January twenty-fourth."

"Where?" said Gala.

"A small theater downtown, near City Hall."

"We will be there," said Gala. She and Dalí nodded to each other.

"I want to see it," said Dalí.

"John, did you have difficulty sleeping?" said Gala, leaning toward me seductively.

"No, I love sleeping," I said.

Gala and Ultra Violet, with cheerful, chirping voices, managed to keep a banal conversation going, and Andy and Dalí occasionally responded with short phrases. Finally, Gala said, "We must go. We have a dinner at eight-thirty."

Andy and I had a rush of good feeling; we had gotten through, it was over. We said goodbye, laughing happily. I kissed Gala and Ultra Violet, and shook Dalí's limp hand.

In the 1970s, Andy and Dalí became good friends, co-conspirators of sorts, making huge amounts of money through their art to support extravagant lifestyles. Andy made endless celebrity and society portraits to finance the Factory and his compulsive collecting. And encouraged by Gala, Dalí made endless bad art to pay for their luxurious life.

Andy and I took a taxi uptown. He dropped me off at my apartment on East Seventy-Fourth Street, and went home to Lexington Avenue to work. "That was amazing!" I said. "Nothing happened, but it happened."

Gala and Salvador Dalí

ONE DAY IN MID-JANUARY, I had a terrible hangover. I had been out drinking the night before until five in the morning. I spent the day in bed with an aching head and a scorched mouth and stomach, in a brain-dead depression. I got up every so often to sip from a club soda bottle in the refrigerator and piss. This had happened many times before and I just had to wait it out, until my energy and vitality came back.

Andy called around noon. "What are you doing? Oh, don't tell me, I know, sleeping . . . I'm having my hair cut by Mr. Kenneth." Andy sounded very pleased. "And there's an opening at Sidney Janis and a party downtown."

"I feel so horrible, I can't go. I'm a disaster. I'm not getting out of bed."

"Oh, I'll come over."

I didn't answer. "Who's opening tonight?"

"Maybe I should come visit after Sidney's. The party isn't until late."

"Yes, wonderful." But it wasn't wonderful. I didn't want to see anybody, my nerves were wrecked, but I couldn't say no. I hoped he was just saying it and wouldn't come. Nor was I in the mood for the inevitable blow job.

Andy called about seven. "I haven't seen you in so long. I haven't seen you in three days. Are you sure you don't want to come, or I'll come over."

About nine-thirty, my doorbell rang. It was Andy. I went back to bed and Andy sat on the floor, leaning on the low bed. We gossiped about the day.

"I had my hair cut by Mr. Kenneth. He's so chic! He's so *fabulous!*" Mr. Kenneth was Jackie Kennedy's hairdresser.

Andy slowly slid his hand over the blanket, and timidly felt my cock through the covers. I loved Andy, but I was not sexually attracted to him. Since he had a reputation as being asexual, I never thought about having sex with him, except in times like this, when he decided he wanted to suck my dick.

"What did he do?"

"You're in a room all by yourself." Andy was very happy with his hair experience. "They put a gown on you and you lie there." Andy slipped his hand under the bedsheet and touched my cock.

"You took your clothes off?" I resisted a little, and let it happen.

"Oh, no! Kenny is so *fabulous*!"

I got hard and Andy sucked it. He really liked doing it, his fingers trembled with excitement. I reached out and grabbed and squeezed Andy's crotch and ass. His dick was hard in his white Jockey shorts. Andy had a very nice cock. He pushed my hand away, just like always. It was a distraction and not what he wanted.

Propped up on pillows, I watched the silver hair go up and down on my dick. I knew the silver hair was a wig, but we never talked about it and I never touched it. I sensed it was difficult for Andy. There was some gossip that he had had a fever and lost all his body hair.

While his head was bobbing up and down, I noticed the hair on the back of his neck, below where the silver hairpiece ended. I saw five bands of dyed color, each one-quarter inch wide, precision cut, a thin line of blond, a thin line of brown, a thin line of white, and closest to the skin a thin line of black, on top of which sat the silver wig.

"Will you please explain your hair?" I said as he sucked my dick. "There are five or more colors in your real hair. Look at that! Blond, what is blond doing there, and brown, and white, and black, and even gray. And the colors are in a funny order. Which one is your real color?"

"Only my hairdresser knows!"

"Would you please explain your hair, young man! . . . Why did Kenny do that! It is a hard-edge painting. Your hair is a Frank Stella. Your hair is a work of art. Or is it a Méret Oppenheim?" We were laughing.

"Oh, John!" Andy knelt on the floor with his elbows on the bed. Andy ran his tongue around the head of my dick. It was always a pleasure making someone happy.

"Do you want some poppers?" I asked.

"No."

"I'll have some." I reached in a box and got the amyl nitrite.

I shot a huge load of cum in Andy's mouth and on his face, big white globs of it dripping down his cheeks and chin. I was careful with the hair. Andy kept licking and swallowing, and said, "Ohhh! Ohhh! Ohhh!"

"I love your hair!" After, Andy went home.

A 1962 advertisement featuring Mr. Kenneth

"WE SHOULD MAKE another movie," I started saying to Andy after *Sleep*.

"Yes," said Andy, laughing.

Time passed, and I said, "When are we going to make another movie?"

Finally, in early 1964, he said, "Let's do another *Screen Test*."

I half thought he said it to shut me up. We had shot the first *Screen Test* in June 1963 and would shoot the second in March 1964. But it wasn't enough. "Another movie idea! I want to be a movie star."

"You are a movie star!"

"I am a movie star, but I want more." I did not give up. "Andy, when are we going to make a movie?"

"There are so many ideas . . . What should we do? . . . How about *Hand Job*?"

"*Hand Job*. Yes! Brilliant! Totally great! It's my part."

"I thought so," said Andy.

"You know what it looks like."

"A tight head shot of your face, while you jerk off and cum."

"It's Elizabeth Taylor in *Cleopatra*." I was thrilled. It was my role.

Time passed, and nothing happened. Andy was busy, and kept putting it off, and I kept saying encouragingly, "When are we going to shoot the movie?"

"How about Saturday? On Forty-Seventh Street."

Andy had just rented a loft on East Forty-Seventh Street, the first Factory. It was still raw, industrial space, a couple of months before his friend Billy Name put silver aluminum foil and silver Mylar up everywhere. There was no heat in the building on Saturdays and Sundays, which was when Andy liked to shoot, because it was quiet.

I met Andy at three o'clock on a bleak, freezing-cold Saturday afternoon in early February. The Factory was dismal. "Where are we going to do it?"

"In the back."

We walked to the rear of the loft. There was a toilet, old and dirty, paint peeling off the walls, and graffiti. "A sleazy toilet! Andy, this looks gorgeous! It looks like a subway toilet."

"Oh, I know!" said Andy, very pleased.

He set up the camera and lights. I smoked a joint and a cigarette and we talked. It was cold. Andy was ready. I took out my dick. "Suck it and get it hard."

He crouched down on his knees on the dirty concrete floor and sucked. He was nervous. I relaxed affectionately, to make it easy for him, and I put my hand behind his head and fucked his face, but his throat wouldn't open up. He sucked my dick like a nipple—not a good blow job. Andy trembled with excitement.

"When are we going to make the movie?" I said, laughing, pulling his head off my dick, and stepping back. "That must be a classic line!"

Andy focused the camera on my face and I masturbated. To stay hard, I thought of pornographic images and scenes from my fabulously promiscuous life. After three minutes, Andy had to change the film roll.

It was frigid and I could see my breath in the air. "This is hot! I can see my breath! Will you be able to see it on film, steam coming out of my mouth? . . . Come and suck my dick to keep it hard."

Andy's hands were really shaking, partly from the cold. The moment felt very important. He was trembling and fragile, and seemed deeply moved. That was reason enough to do the film, although it was also a great idea for a movie.

I took another deep sniff of amyl nitrite (Andy declined) and drifted off into a low-grade bliss. Andy changed the film again. It took a very long time for me to cum. Eventually, I shot gobs of white cum in a high arc that splattered on the concrete floor.

"I have bad news," said Andy.

"What?"

"I only had two rolls of film in my bag and I thought I had more here."

"You shot two three-minute rolls, and the rest of the time you were shooting blanks."

"I'm sorry. You looked so great. I couldn't stop."

"I had a good time. I like jerking off, as you know, and with you."

"We'll do it again next Saturday."

"Yes, of course." But I suspected we never would. We said goodbye around five o'clock on a dark, cold, depressing winter afternoon. It augured bad things.

ON MARCH 14, 1964, Andy and I went to the opening of Cy Twombly's show at the Leo Castelli Gallery. The work was lyric Abstract Expressionist paintings on primed canvases where the imprint of the artist's fingers and hand marked the void.

"What do you think?" I asked. The paintings were wonderful, but I had a knee-jerk response to feel neutral, because they were not like the works of Andy and the Pop artists, Bob and Jasper and the others I liked.

"Oh, they're so creative," said Andy, his ultimate put-down.

It was a cheerful night, and of course I had no idea that this was a cataclysmic moment in Cy Twombly's life—that he would receive bad reviews for the exhibition, and be rejected by the art world for not being in tune with the times.

Andy and I left the gallery and stood outside on the sidewalk with about twenty people. It had been an unseasonably hot day and the evening was warm.

"It's what they call a false spring," I said.

We were talking with the Pop Art collectors Bob and Ethel Scull, as well as Roy Lichtenstein. "Let's have dinner together," said Ethel.

"Oh, yes!" said Andy.

"Where?" said Bob Scull. "La Côte Basque, but they probably won't have a reservation. I'll try." He went back inside the gallery, telephoned, and returned. "No reservation, completely full." I also thought perhaps, understandably, he did not want to pay for everybody.

There were lots of suggestions of restaurants and nobody made up their mind. About ten of us walked to Madison Avenue and Seventy-Seventh and stood on the corner, trying to decide. The indecision went on interminably, and everyone left, except Ethel and Bob, Andy, and me.

"I know a place," said Andy. "On Lexington and Eighty-Sixth."

"Let's go there," said Bob.

We were relieved a decision had been made, took a taxi, and got out on the corner of Lexington and Eighty-Sixth, in front of Sabrett's Hot Dogs, in all its red and yellow and white glory. It was near Andy's house and he and I had eaten there on occasion, when we were hungry and in a hurry.

Ethel and Bob were very surprised. We laughed and laughed, Bob with tears in his eyes.

"Very Pop!" I said obnoxiously. And it was very appropriate, since the Sculls were nouveau riche and quite vulgar. She was overbearing, and he was probably a crook, having made a small fortune from a fleet of taxicabs. Years later, it was revealed that he was addicted to prescription drugs and connected to the mafia. But their shortcomings were overlooked because they were buying the right art.

We ordered hot dogs and orange sodas. Andy asked me, "How many do you want?"

"Just two," I said. We had come two nights before, and I had ordered three hot dogs, as I hadn't eaten all day and was starving.

That night Andy had sighed sexually, "Ohhh, will they fit in there?!"

Now, the Sculls were thrilled that Andy had taken them to a hot dog stand. "Andy always surprises ya," said Bob. "Fabulous!"

We joyously ate the hot dogs. The Sculls and I were a little drunk from the opening at Castelli. Andy was very pleased with himself. As we said good night, Andy told the Sculls, "Come to my studio on Saturday, I want to show you my new work."

Andy, we saw that Saturday, had officially entered his "box" period. In a pile on the floor were about twenty white cubes, each advertising in red and blue lettering: "Brillo soap pads . . . 24 Giant Size Pkgs." He had silk-screened them days before, so they were fresh. They radiated greatness. Elsewhere were several other similar works: supermarket packaging for *Heinz Tomato*

Ketchup and *Campbell's Tomato Juice*; not the bottles and cans themselves, but the boxes that would contain them. A small crowd of friends and critics just stood around looking.

"You've done it again," I said. The work was inconceivably wonderful.

Andy had been playing with the idea of boxes for some time— the cans stenciled on a cube the year before, another ketchup box just this past January. It was a little bit a parody of Bob Morris, whose seminal show of cube sculptures Andy and I had seen the previous Halloween. By chance, the art dealer John Weber happened to see Andy's first *Heinz* box and asked to borrow it for a show of boxes he was putting on at the Dwan Gallery in February in Los Angeles. Instead, Andy started on a series of different boxes, sending one of the *Heinz* boxes and three *Brillo* boxes to Dwan, then expanding his work to what we were seeing that day.

The Sculls arrived. Ethel was thin and chic, wearing a blue pantsuit and gold jewelry, and sporting a Miami Beach suntan. Bob wore a polyester leisure suit. They were too good to be believed. Ethel walked right up to the *Brillo* boxes and said, "They're fabulous! I want some." Everyone laughed. "Bob, how many should we get?"

"As many as you want!"

"And some of those." She pointed to the *Heinz Tomato Ketchup* boxes.

The Sculls were lucky. They were in the right place at the right time, and even though they weren't particularly sophisticated, they were smart enough to seize the opportunity. They weren't enormously wealthy but had just enough money to indulge their passion.

Ethel and Bob had come from their Saturday rounds visiting the art galleries. "We bought this at Knoedler's," said Bob, pulling a small bronze statue of a male god from ancient Greece from Ethel's handbag. "I just liked it!"

"Oh, it's so beautiful," said Andy. Everyone was astonished and laughed. We all looked at it.

I whispered to Andy, "Only a gay man buys a statue of a Greek god."

"I know," said Andy. Bob Scull was a hunky, refined truck-driver type. "I can see him cruising the baths."

When the *Brillo* boxes opened at the Stable Gallery in April, they were a great success. The Sculls offered to pay for a party at the Factory. I went, made several walks through the crowd, chatting, but the loud noise made it difficult to hear anything. Everybody was trying to get his or her picture taken, trying to be famous. Many were high on speed, and the level of adrenaline aggression was overwhelming. It was a nightmare and I left abruptly.

Bob Scull complained that nobody was taking Ethel's picture. And the next day in the newspapers, there was a photograph of the southern-belle scenester Marguerite Lamkin at the party, but no Ethel. The Sculls were furious and refused to pay for the party after all, and it was wonderful gossip. Weeks later, Andy whined, "They still haven't paid for the party. I think that's terrible."

I encouraged him to delight in their outsized crassness, but he wouldn't.

A few years later, when the really rich collectors bought Pop Art, the Sculls were completely eclipsed and forgotten, and their world collapsed.

Ethel and Bob Scull

ON MAY 25, 1964, Andy and I went to a black-tie preview gala at the Museum of Modern Art, celebrating its reopening after months of expansion and remodeling (it still hadn't quite eaten the Whitney building). As we waited outside in the crowd to get in, Edie Sedgwick arrived in a limo and made a grand entrance. She was wearing lilac pajamas. Andy had met Edie a week before for the first time, when someone had brought her to the Factory.

"Look at her! Ohhh! Look at her! Ohhh!" Andy was captivated.

Andy and I met up with Bea Feitler and her *Harper's Bazaar* colleague Ruth Ansel and entered the museum. We went up in the elevator to the curator's offices, where Bea was supposed to meet someone, but they weren't there, so we came back down.

In the elevator, looking me up and down, Andy said, "What are you doing? Look at you! What are you doing?!" Everyone laughed. "Where did you get that?"

I was wearing black tie: a Brooks Brothers tuxedo, patent leather shoes, and late-nineteenth-century Tiffany oriental pearl studs. I blushed. "From my family."

Bea reassured me. "John, you look great."

Andy was wearing a seedy black jacket, black chinos, a black necktie, and scuffed shoes.

IN APRIL, Andy made *Blow Job* starring somebody else. I was deeply offended. That was supposed to be my movie, I thought, the perfect sequel to *Sleep* and far better than the aborted *Hand Job*. How could he have done that? It was going to be my starring role, and he gave it to somebody else. I was devastated and furious but did not let it show. I couldn't help but see it as a sign, an early death knell signaling the end of our relationship. Andy was moving on, as I always feared he would.

THAT FALL, Andy and I were supposed to meet at Castelli's for a Roy Lichtenstein landscape show. When I got there, Andy had already left. My heart sank. This happened often these days. He would tell me a time to arrive, but when I got there, I would have just missed him.

Andy was tired of me. And the new Factory was full of new people pushing their way in front of the camera. Edie Sedgwick was center stage and I was last year's news.

A YOUNG POET

In October 1964, something happened to seal the growing distance between me and Andy. One late afternoon, we were walking down St. Mark's Place to Jonas Mekas's Film-Makers' Cooperative, when we ran into the art critic Gene Swenson, who had a very serious look on his face.

"Fred Herko is dead. He committed suicide. He jumped out a window at Johnny Dodd's."

It was incomprehensible. Fred Herko, young and beautiful and gay—completely crazy, a brilliant dancer and choreographer, and the star of Andy's movies *Rollerskate/Dance Movie* and *Haircut (No. 1)* and many others—was dead. We were dumbstruck.

"It just happened," said Gene. "At five o'clock, Fred was at Johnny's, dancing, and he jumped out the window. I spoke to Johnny. He is devastated."

"Oh, no!" I said. "It's five-forty. It's so fresh!"

Andy said, deeply moved, "Oh! . . . Oh! . . . Oh!"

"Dancing naked and jumped!" I said. He was such a great virtuoso.

Gene's eyes were shining with water. "Johnny says he found Fred at Joe's diner, dancing on the counter, and took him back to his place and suggested he take a shower. He was high on LSD and speed. After he showered, he started dancing, rehearsing a new piece. All the windows were open, because it is so hot. Mozart's *Coronation Mass* was playing on the phonograph full volume. Freddie danced naked, leaping and spinning in circles. Johnny sat on the couch watching."

"Ahhhhh!" I said. There was a very long heartbroken moment. "I saw Freddie the night before last."

Andy was trembling and his body shaking.

"He was talking strangely. I knew something was up," I said, recalling the run-in.

I had been leaving a building on East Sixth Street and saw Freddie in the hallway. We were happy to see each other and walked, talking, to the corner of Avenue A. Freddie looked as he always did. He wore a long black cape and carried a lute in a black case as well as a cloth bag of flutes. He was gaunt from shooting speed—the black circles around his eyes were darker than makeup. He had pushed his limits of endurance and it had taken its toll. He was ravaged. I was told he felt that he had ruined his dancer's body. He had become more and more out of control, and the line between reality and delusion was blurred. Everyone saw it, but nobody could do anything to help, afraid of being brought down too. We were paralyzed watching.

Freddie and I kissed and hugged, said goodbye, and went in different directions.

Andy repeated, "Oh! . . . Oh! . . . Oh!"

"I saw Diane di Prima yesterday," I went on. "She said Freddie didn't have a place to stay and was sleeping on the street."

In the sky above St. Mark's Place, black thunderstorm clouds rolled in and turned the early evening into night, the world turned upside down. A deity destroyed, his dance and music unfinished, the Pipes of Pan ended. It was an overwhelming sense of finality, a tragedy. I thought of the *Suicide* painting Andy had made. Could death be made into something beautiful?

After the horribly sad, long moment, I tried to change it into joy. "Fred has attained through dance the absolute state of Nijinsky. The madness of Nijinsky is a great accomplishment."

Andy was terrified. I had never seen him like that. His eyes wide open, he was frozen, not breathing, in a state of shock.

"*Le Sacre du printemps*! Fred is a god, and transcendent in dance. It's okay," I said in denial, knowing it was not okay. "Suicide is a song of aspiration."

Gene Swenson was wearing tight, washed-out Levi's and his dick hung down the crotch. In the golden age of promiscuity, we could have made it with each other right there. I didn't think there was any contradiction in sexual desire arising at such a mournful moment.

Andy said, a little angry, with tears in his eyes, "Why didn't he tell me! . . . Oh, I'll never forgive him . . . I would have made a movie . . . I can't believe he did it and didn't tell me . . . He knew I wanted to make another movie."

"*Suicide*. What a great idea!" There was an ache in my heart, and I suppressed the tears, not to spoil Freddie's glorious moment. *Suicide*, that was *my* movie, the proper sequel to *Sleep*.

"If you ever do it," said Andy, "you better tell me."

There was a brightness and clarity in the air. Fred's consciousness filled the space around us. When a person dies, in the hours after the breathing stops, the consciousness is in an intermediate state between two worlds and can travel quickly anywhere to people thinking of him. Fred was with us in the street, glorious.

Black storm clouds swirled in the sky, lightning and thunder raged, warm rain poured down in torrents. We said goodbye. Andy and I ran down the street, gusts of raindrops splashing on our faces and in our tears. We ran as fast as we could and cried as hard as we could, because it was raining and nobody could see us crying.

We turned right on Second Avenue and stopped in a doorway. The rain lightened, and we continued running down Second Avenue. Naomi Levine came running toward us, weeping hysterically, screaming, "Fred is dead."

"I know," said Andy.

"Fred is dead. I can't believe it. Everyone is going over to Diane's to say prayers and be together for Fred. I'm going." Tears streamed down Naomi's cheeks. "I want to light a stick of incense for him."

I left Andy at the Film Coop and took a taxi up to East Seventy-Fourth. I couldn't wait to get home and cry some more.

Fred Herko's death symbolized the absolute failure of all our lives. He was not spared. All of us, completely pure, with pure intentions like Fred, were lost. It was worse than we thought. There was no alternative, no way out, but to follow the heart. Marcia Stillman's suicide, and my own attempt before that, came rushing to the surface, and feelings of utter hopelessness erupted inside me like a volcanic explosion. We were broken children. I sank to the floor, paralyzed by the depression that had crippled me since childhood. Freddie was lucky he got out.

Spiritually, we were taught nothing about death by the religions from which we came, Catholicism, Protestantism, and Judaism. They taught us nothing about the reality of death—what it was, or how to work with it. We were exposed to nothing more than a priest saying a few prayers as the body was put in the ground. That was it.

Each of us had to find out by ourselves what death was, had to discover it through reading and from our own personal experiences. Because we were looking for answers, innate wisdom arose in our minds. I appreciated the intuitive spirituality hidden in people's hearts, some more highly evolved than others.

At the apartment of Fred's best friend, the poet Diane di Prima, and her husband, Alan Marlowe (who was also Fred's lover), people gathered every night to mourn. Nobody knew how to deal with death. We were young and it was a time of ignorance. Diane was a practicing Zen Buddhist, and I and a few others felt drawn to Buddhism, but most people were not religious. The day before Fred's death, Diane, by chance and in a stroke of genius, went to Samuel Weiser's bookstore on Broadway and bought *The Tibetan Book of the Dead*. Every night between seven and eight o'clock, for forty-nine days, people got together in her house and read it. We knew it was the right thing to do. People gathered in Diane's kitchen with a candle burning on the table and read and said the prayers, as well as we could, not really knowing what we were doing.

Nobody knew how to meditate. Tibetan Buddhism had not yet arrived in America and Japanese Zen practice was mostly in California. After the awkward reading, to everyone's relief, it turned into a party. People stood around or sat on the cushions and rugs, drank tea or wine, smoked joints, talked, and gossiped. More people arrived and the tall gay poet Alan Marlowe was very much the gracious host. It was a group of young, far-out theater and performance artists and dancers, and it was a time of great innovation. I did not go every night, but I liked being with them, because they were filled with love. A couple of nights, I was high on speed, Dexedrine, in honor of Freddie.

Standing around talking, Diane di Prima told us more about the week before Freddie's death. He had called for a big party to be held on the roof of his friend the poet Kirby Doyle's old Ridge Street house. "He was going to dance a new dance for us—a 'flying dance,' he called it—and he wanted me to read some 'flying poetry' while he danced. I stayed away that night, as did almost everyone."

"He invited me and I didn't go," I said, hugging Diane.

"Two or three people came, but there was no party: Freddie had gone on from Ridge Street to other adventures. Not sleeping, apparently, from that night until his death."

Andy came to join the mourners briefly. He was afraid of death. "Good to see you!" I said cheerfully.

"I have been here before," he said defensively. "I was here the other night." And he left quickly.

Frank O'Hara came a couple of times. He stood leaning against the kitchen doorjamb, eyes looking down, listening to Diane read from *The Tibetan Book of the Dead*. Frank died one and a half years later, hit by a car on the beach on Fire Island.

Many bits of information pointed to a long-planned suicide, which made it extremely sad. It wasn't just a moment of madness. We had all witnessed a tragedy unfolding, had seen it happening day by day, and were unable to stop it.

I remembered in the first rush of spring 1963, Freddie Herko had walked down the middle of Third Avenue near Cooper Union, on the white line, newly painted and very bright, playing his flute like the Pipes of Pan, an afternoon of the faun, while cars and buses and trucks swerved around him. "He's so brilliant," I said to Andy as we stood on the sidewalk with about twelve others, appreciating him and riding a wave of enthusiasm. It was a time when we innocently and heroically believed we were satyrs and nymphs. We looked at the bright, white, pure light, and got hit by the oncoming cars.

There was a memorial at Judson Church. Frank O'Hara, LeRoi Jones, and Diane di Prima read poems. The dancer Deborah Lee performed her solo in *The Palace of the Dragon Prince*, a ballet that Freddie had choreographed and danced in a few months earlier, a mad, heroic epic that frightened people and tested the limits of reality. I made a found poem, from Fred Herko's obituary in *The Village Voice*, using a technique I had begun to practice the year before. I picked something from the paper, a neutral-seeming article, and latched on to a sentence or phrase that I connected to emotionally, the pieces of the whole that radiated, and those pieces became the poem.

Fred's death had a profound effect on everyone. For me, it reawakened a long-festering frustration about my life and career. In some ways, I had it easy as a stockbroker at Fahnestock & Co. After all those nights with Andy and others, I worked only five hours a day, from ten in the morning to three in the afternoon, when the stock exchange closed. But I wasn't good at it, and it filled my mind with bullshit information, affecting my energy and creativity. Plus, it embarrassed me among my artist friends. I was a poet, and I needed to get out.

Fred Herko

ON NOVEMBER 21, Andy Warhol's show of *Flower* paintings opened at the Leo Castelli Gallery. It was his first show at Castelli, where he had moved after his show of *Brillo* boxes at the Stable Gallery in April. It was a well-calculated, political decision suggested and advised by Henry Geldzahler, a big move up.

The *Flower* paintings were Pop Art at its most pure. Brilliantly conceived, it was a popular image, which could be reproduced endlessly. Andy said he wanted to be a machine, all identity dropped, the individual gotten rid of, made anonymous. More revolutionary than Roy Lichtenstein, who still made paintings, Andy's work could be mass-produced on canvas. He had made the complete gesture. The *Flower* paintings were perfectly beautiful.

As much as I admired them, inside I ached. That night, I had arrived at Castelli alone. Andy and I no longer went out together. He had gotten rid of me, had moved on. He didn't answer my phone calls, because he was busy, and didn't call back. I wasn't told about parties. And when I saw him, he acted like nothing had happened. It was heartache. I loved Andy. I was his first superstar and I was the first one he got rid of.

Over the years, later superstars complained endlessly about Andy exploiting and getting rid of them. They spoke of his cruelty, his sadism. This was possibly true, as Andy was only human. It also might have been the result of the amphetamines. But at the time, being the first, I had no context. I couldn't understand why it was happening, and I felt only suffering and pain.

IN JUNE AND JULY 1965, when Andy was shooting *Chelsea Girls*, I received several phone calls from the Factory, requesting that I help them get my new friend William Burroughs to be in the movie. They had tried to get to William, through various people, and had received no response. I knew all about it.

While Andy was shooting *Chelsea Girls*, William's friend Brion Gysin and I were lovers, living in room 703 of the Chelsea Hotel. William had been staying there, too, before he went to London. Andy's and our paths never crossed in the elevator or lobby of the Chelsea, two worlds simply coexisting.

"We'd love him for a cameo," said Pat Hackett, Andy's frequent collaborator. "Can you help us?"

"I'll see. I'll ask him," I said obligingly and cheerfully. Andy had gotten rid of me, hadn't asked me to be in the movie, and yet wanted me to deliver William Burroughs. Andy can go to hell, I thought. I made sure William did not do *Chelsea Girls*.

My big, grasping ego and small-mindedness changed history in a bad way. William Burroughs would have given a great performance.

ON SEPTEMBER 25, 1965, Andy gave a party for John Ashbery at the Forty-Seventh Street Factory. The literary and art worlds anticipated it for a week, but I wasn't invited and I was devastated.

Apparently, it was a great event. Everyone was there, and talked about it endlessly afterward. Because I was a poet, it was a double insult.

Two weeks later, I ran into Andy at a party and he had the nerve to say, "Oh, you didn't come to John Ashbery's party."

"I wasn't invited."

"I told Gerard to invite you."

That was it! I never called Andy again, not for years. I allowed my anger to blossom into big changes. Andy was dead for me. I almost never ran into him, and if I did, I avoided him or, of course, greeted him cheerfully and moved on. But before that, I heard from him one more time.

On November 25, 1965, Andy telephoned. He hadn't called me in a year. "Come to the Sidney Janis Gallery tonight. I have a surprise for you."

"What? Oh, please tell me!" I was happy to hear from him. I couldn't help it.

"You'll see. I've done a Plexiglas of you. You're in the show. I thought you knew."

The Sidney Janis show was sculpture by nine Pop artists, all of whom were painters. Andy had done the *Brillo* boxes, but almost no other sculpture. I walked into the gallery and there was a huge, freestanding, thick piece of Plexiglas mounted on a heavy stainless-steel base. A still photo from *Sleep* was silk-screened in black on the clear plastic—a tight head shot of me sleeping with my arm thrown back over my head. It was in an edition of eight. It was a great work.

I was happy and surprised that Andy had done the Plexiglas of me. The legend of *Sleep* continued and grew. "Oh, Andy, thank you," I said. "It's so beautiful."

EVEN AS OUR RELATIONSHIP was dissolving, I came to realize how much more Andy had given me than a starring role in his art. Back in 1963, soon after we had met, we were sitting at the back of a packed, sweaty poetry reading. Up front, Frank O'Hara and John Ashbery sat at a table and read from a book with no amplification. Andy and I could not hear anything.

"Why is it so boring?" Andy asked.

"I don't know. I can't hear one word and I can't see them. There is nothing there."

"I know," he laughed.

It was one of those seemingly meaningless moments that change your life. "Why is it so boring? What's wrong?" echoed in my mind.

I went to many great performances all the time: rock concerts, new music, the Judson Dance Theater, Happenings, performances by artists. But poetry was dead. Poetry performance had not yet happened. There were exceptions: Dylan Thomas, Allen Ginsberg, sound poetry. But in the early 1960s, hanging out with my artist friends, it was clear that poetry was seventy-five years behind painting, sculpture, music, and dance. The golden age of poetry was just about to begin.

My inspiration was the young artists I happened to meet, seeing how they lived and worked and made their art. If an idea arose in their mind, they made it happen. If they could do it for painting and dance, I could do it for poetry. I was fearless. I learned that from Andy, mostly. If he had an idea, he followed through. If it didn't work out, so what?

In February 1965, I had a meeting with my mother and father—drinks in front of the marble fireplace and the burning logs on Old Brick Road—to tell them that I had quit my job on Wall Street. I was a poet, and I wanted to spend my life writing and working on poems and poetry. I asked for their help again, another chance, and the support of an allowance. They believed in me with wonderful purity, and they happily agreed.

"We trust you," said my mother, "and wish you all the best."

Thus began the rest of my life.

I wanted to do more than write poems. I wanted to broaden the ways that poets could connect with audiences. The poet should use modern technology and invent new methods for making and communicating their work. There were boundless ways for poets to make art. Anything and everything was possible.

To receive and raise money for my poetry projects and events, I needed to create a not-for-profit organization, and that organization needed a name. So I took something commercial and industrial and gave it a wry metaphoric spin: Giorno Poetry Systems.

When I began, no other poet was doing anything like it. I was inventing it as I went along, without reference or help; and it was like walking blindfolded in traffic. I did not know what I was doing but did not allow doubt to arise in my mind, and hoped for the best.

PART TWO

WILLIAM AND BRION AND PAUL AND JANE

In January 1965, I wandered through a party at the heiress Panna Grady's apartment in the Dakota. This wasn't just any party. It was a party in honor of the world-famous cult-hero poets William Burroughs and Brion Gysin. They had arrived in New York two months earlier on a mission: to make book deals, for Brion to sell his Dream Machine (a hallucination-inducing strobe light), and to work on a collaboration called *The Third Mind*. Panna gave lots of parties for the duo and, in doing so, she created an amazing scene around her. I had been to a few of these events. I was an eager young poet, after all.

At fifty, William was mythic, more famous than anyone. By 1965, lots of people I was friendly with in the art world had become really famous. But William was more: junkie, aristocrat, great writer, he went beyond. Thin, gentlemanly, and courtly, he dressed in imitation Brooks Brothers suits. He had the power, a strong magnetizing quality, to attract people to him. He looked humble and shy, like fame was the last thing he wanted, which made him even more attractive. At a time when no paths to spiritual liberation seemed available, other than drugs, William was a saint.

When I first met William alone, he left me speechless and in awe. With Brion standing by his side, however, I instantly had great rapport, ease, and attraction.

Neither had been to New York for about ten years. They conceived it, with naïve joy, as a historic visit, an assault on the bastion of America. Their sword of wisdom was to cut through ignorance. They viewed New York as the media capital of the world, which controlled and manipulated people's minds, the capital of corrupt world politics and wealth; it was the home of evil. And Brion believed that the New York art and literary worlds were controlled by women and Jews, who were in a conspiracy against him. Being anti-Semitic and misogynist in New York was not a good beginning.

But I ignored this as best I could. Despite their ignorance, the point was the true brilliance of their minds.

They were staying at the Chelsea Hotel, they told me. Brion complained bitterly about the place, but William liked it. It suited his tastes; drugs, in one form or another, permeated every room. Stanley, the owner, accepted art in lieu of payment, so William thought him very sympathetic. Those were the Chelsea's golden years of sleaze.

Not long after our first meeting, William received the news that his father, Mortimer Burroughs, had died of a heart attack in Palm Beach, Florida. I saw him at another party soon after he came back from the funeral. "What happened?" I asked respectfully.

"My father's famous last words, before he died, were 'How did I get into this mess?'" he replied, tight-lipped, making an elegant hand gesture.

I looked at William and sort of smelled the freshness of his loss: A father dying was very important in a person's life. Something connected to the DNA was cut, and there was a karmic scream, powerful and unexplainable.

"Did you have a feeling about your father's consciousness? What was the state of his mind?" Since I had read *The Tibetan Book of the Dead* for Fred Herko, just a few months earlier, death was constantly on my mind. The journey of the consciousness, having left the physical body, resting in the bardo. But as hard as I tried to get something out of William, he wouldn't give an inch.

"I went down and saw his body in the coffin. Some kind of priest said something."

"Was he buried?"

"He was cremated," said William neutrally, puffing a cigarette.

It wasn't yet the time for William and me to have this conversation. Our exploration of death together was still in the future.

ON A COLD, bleak, lonely Valentine's Day, William gave a reading at the East End Theatre on East Fourth Street. The weather was a reflection of my bad state of mind.

Just weeks before, Diane di Prima and Alan Marlowe had moved their long-roving New York Poets Theatre into the space, an old Ukrainian dance hall. There was a stage at one end and Alan had bought old theater seats and was in the process of making it into an extraordinary small house. "It's a jewel box," said Frank O'Hara when it was finished. "Like the best of the art theaters of Europe."

The theater seated about a hundred and was packed that evening. Everyone from the downtown scene was there: the filmmakers Jack Smith and Conrad Rooks; the artists Larry Poons, Roy Lichtenstein, and George Segal; Jill Johnston and her lover, the dancer Lucinda Childs; the poet/musician Ed Sanders, who had just formed the band the Fugs.

Wynn Chamberlain and I smoked a joint while we waited in our seats. A big piece of red velvet cloth had been tacked to an overhead beam, hung crookedly. "Alan said he bought the red velvet today," Wynn told me.

"It's tacky." We laughed.

This was the first time most people were laying eyes on William Burroughs. Expectations were high. *Naked Lunch*, which had been published six years before, was already a myth and William was the most revered icon of the underground literary and art worlds.

William and Brion walked down the center aisle and everyone got silent. Head bent and looking down, William went up the right side and backstage, and then reappeared through the red velvet curtain. He was a pale white, pencil-thin junkie. Everyone applauded thunderously, cheered, and stood screaming. He was our Beatles.

William took off his gray fedora and overcoat, revealing a suit, vest, and necktie, shabby and cheap, but elegant. He sat in a big leather chair and placed a black leather attaché case carefully on a table before him. He opened it, took out his papers, and arranged them neatly, along with a cassette tape recorder. With his dry, drawling raspy midwestern voice, he read pieces featuring one of his recurring characters, bloody Doctor Benway, sending the audience into crazy laughter. It was the union of Beat wisdom, upper-class elegance, and drugs. Everyone was spellbound.

We didn't know, but this was one of William's first readings.

"He's better than Will Rogers." I was electrified. "Will Rogers with absolute wisdom."

"And W. C. Fields on drugs," said Wynn.

Next, William played a cut-up experiment on the cassette recorder. He and Brion were known for their cut-ups and I was familiar with the technique and concept. This one was made from sound tapes of a Piper Cub airplane crash on Jones Beach, official dispatches from the American armed forces in Vietnam, a book he was writing called *The Last Words of Dutch Schultz*, and a cops-and-robbers caper. The tape was rough, barely audible, boring, and went on forever. But it was astonishing and beyond concepts. It was a heroic new way of seeing the nature of reality.

William got up humbly and bowed, and a thunderous ovation roared from the audience. He gathered his things, walked behind the red curtain and down the left side, and stood at the front row. It was a magical display. He was a great writer and a great magician.

William stood in front with Brion, talking to people and shaking hands. As they were about to leave, I went up and we shook hands, and said a few words. William said, "Oh, hello, John." I was thrilled that he remembered my name. And a little anxious, as we were not yet friends.

I felt a strong affinity toward William and Brion, a sacred attraction to their minds; and being with them was what I wanted. My heart beat faster in their presence.

William Burroughs and Brion Gysin

THAT SPRING, Wynn hosted another poetry reading by William in his loft on the Bowery. It snowed the day before, a late storm and a reminder that suffering never ends, slushy and gray. There was a select group of seventy invited guests, including Andy Warhol. By this time, he and I were well out of touch but still adept at pretending in public that nothing had changed. "Everyone is here!" he gushed.

I had a hangover and was not having a good time. I was a poet, and young, and I knew my poems were not yet great or even that good and I had a big ego and low self-esteem. I felt like a fly on the wall. "Everyone is here, but I don't know how to use it."

Andy laughed. "Oh, I don't know how to use it!"

Andy, Marisol, and I huddled together, as we had often done at those early 1960s parties, because they were usually boring and nobody had anything to say, and we protected one another. Despite my estrangement from Andy, we kept to this routine.

"Oh, I don't know why everyone is here!" said Andy. There was the essence of the uptown and downtown art worlds.

"William is a sacred demon," I said. "Every culture has a sacred demon. And he is it!" I leaned into Andy, and whispered, "As are you."

I really wanted to get to know William and had a deep yearning to form a relationship. Perhaps there was a karmic connection in past lives, and we were meeting again, or I was just a shameless hustler. I didn't care. I wanted him.

Brion and William were one, a union acting together. And Brion and I had a visceral attraction. Our eyes hooked in deep, fathomless love and there was a hot, physical vibration between our bodies. And Brion was the route to William.

Mack Thomas opened the reading. He was a novelist and an acquaintance of William from the Beat Hotel in Paris. At first sight I knew he would be nice, but no good. Mack read from his rather childish—some called it sweet—memoir, *Gumbo*, and then launched into some weird Southern Baptist hymns. It was nuts.

Writers in the audience, such as Frank O'Hara, Kenward Elmslie, and Joe Brainard, were appalled. Frank said to Sally Stokes Cram, by now Wynn's girlfriend, "What kind of shit have you invited us for?"

Then William read and everything changed. He again read some Doctor Benway passages, from *Naked Lunch* and *Nova Express*. He was a gifted performer, captivating everyone with the sound of his voice and the wisdom of his words. Everyone sighed with relief and delight.

Frank O'Hara whispered to Sally, "Isn't he the greatest?" Frank could be a bitch, but William had passed the test.

Finally, with a quiet aggression, William turned around and ripped down the white-bedsheet backdrop behind him, exposing a giant rubber tarantula, wiggling menacingly. There was a collective gasp, and a burst of applause. William took New York.

After the reading was a lively party. I talked with Brion and remained standing next to him while everyone else came up to talk to him, and we all had a great time together. Brion and I made a date to get together for drinks: "Next Tuesday at five."

BRION AND I became lovers. Andy and I had loved each other, but with Brion, it was about incredible sex. I slept with him every night in the Chelsea Hotel. Every morning about ten, after fucking, a cup of coffee, and a joint, we both went to work. Brion went down to William's loft at 210 Centre Street. William liked to start work at nine or nine-thirty. He went to bed drunk and early, and was an early riser. They worked all day on their book collaboration *The Third Mind*. I went to my apartment on East Ninth Street and worked on poems, as well as on the beginning of my new poetry endeavor, Giorno Poetry Systems.

Brion and I rendezvoused back in room 703 for drinks at 6:00 p.m. Once or twice a week, we met in William's loft on Centre Street for drinks and then went to dinner at a Chinese restaurant on Mott Street. Located downstairs, in the cellar, it was greasy and dark and had the feel of a restaurant in Hong Kong or Shanghai. It was William's favorite place. He always said, "Good, cheap food." I thought he liked it because it looked like the outer room of an opium den.

Every night we got completely drunk on bourbon and water (vodka and tonic for William), smoked endless joints and cigarettes, and took whatever drugs appeared as gifts. There was always brilliant conversation.

And then Brion and I went to bed. In the sweltering heat of his un-air-conditioned room, we fucked endlessly. Love and bliss and wisdom (in between his negativity and complaints about professional rejection), all the time, morning, afternoon when free, evening, every day and every night, insatiable sex and drugs. Too much was not enough. We were gods fucking in a god world, demons fucking in hell, hungry ghosts fucking in the spirit worlds, and blissfully suffering men, until we collapsed in each other's arms in sleep.

Brion introduced me to LSD. My first thirty-four LSD trips were with Brion in room 703. We took acid every three or four days for five months. He led me into his powerful, magical world and was a great teacher and guide. He first introduced me to the nature of mind, the absolute empty true nature of mind. And I realized a glimpse of emptiness and compassion through bliss. He transformed a dumb kid into someone who actually began a spiritual path.

I really fell in love with Brion. I was at my sexual peak, and the LSD blew me open. He was the first one I loved with such vastness and abandon. I was still young and not yet formed, and Brion had my body and soul. He was a powerful psychic influence, blissfully and brutally. He imprinted me, politically and spiritually radicalized me, and showed me a world of magic. He introduced me to so many possibilities, like empowerments, opening and enabling me.

One was the use of electronics and technology in poetry. Brion opened me up to sound poetry, or *poésie sonore*, and we collaborated making sound pieces of several of my poems. One was based on a poem called "Subway," which I had taken from ads posted inside trains. Brion loved it and we went underground to record him reading the poem, as well as the echoes and rumbles of the underground. *Subway Sound* was sent to Paris and presented by the French sound poet Bernard Heidsieck at the Paris Biennial of the Musée d'Art Moderne in October 1965. I was thrilled that my first piece had such a success.

William and Brion liked my book of poems called *The American Book of the Dead* (which hadn't been officially published). They agreed quite seriously that I was something else. Years later, Brion said, "John Giorno had the brightest eyes, the most sparkling eyes of anyone. That's why we let him in."

William and Brion became the center of my world, twenty-four hours a day. They were great magicians, and I assumed they had a secret pact—black magic or something—between them. Brion was a great demon king and William was a great demon king. They had enormous power and cared only about themselves.

That spring and summer, many people came to visit the Chelsea, magnetized by Brion. In July, Paul and Jane Bowles, who rarely came to America, stayed at the hotel for a few days. I was a great fan of Jane's fiction and was in awe of her. They were on their way back to Tangier after visiting Jane's mother in Miami. One evening, William, Brion, and I had drinks with Jane and Paul in their room. Being with the four of them, I was speechless.

Jane was irresistible, having the quality to inexplicably attract. She was dysfunctional, but so were we all. In part, we were dysfunctional from all the drugs and alcohol. Jane was just more so. She was scattered and lived in torturous indecision. Trying to decide on which bar or restaurant, she would change her mind for two hours. We eventually went, where we always went, to El Quijote downstairs off the lobby. In the evening, we rarely ventured out of our rooms, and when we did, it was there, or the local bar down the street, which was always empty.

After dinner, returning to Brion's room, William Burroughs said, "She is clearly brain-damaged. A mere blurred and impoverished travesty of her true self!"

The Chelsea Hotel

AT THE END OF AUGUST 1965, William flew to London and Brion flew to Tangier. I joined Brion in February—in part because of my infatuation with Brion, and in part because of my curiosity about Paul and Jane Bowles, who were his neighbors.

As presented in the pages of *Vogue*, the public image of Jane and Paul Bowles and their life in Tangier was infinitely refined, oozing with good taste—intellectual chic, the elegant and civilized international writers and socialites. Most insiders knew that they created this image to hustle money. When I arrived in Tangier, I saw that their life was far less glamorous: sordid, dismal, and boring.

Brion, Jane, and Paul lived in the Immeubla Itesa, a concrete apartment house built by the Italian government in the early 1940s, a peculiar run-down building with small, uncomfortable modern rooms. There was none of the power of the ancient, sleazy Tangier casbah. Each apartment had a small balcony overlooking a strip of land that was a rustic pastoral field where goatherds passed, grazing their flocks. It was crisscrossed with paths used by Moroccans on their way to work, and on the far side was the back of the American consulate compound. While it evoked the period of Humphrey Bogart and Ingrid Bergman, in reality, it was just plain depressing.

One afternoon in June 1966, just after lunch, Jane Bowles paid a visit to Brion. She lived right next door, while Paul lived one flight up. Brion, his cook Targuisti, and I were sitting around smoking kif and were very stoned. Cherifa, Jane's old girlfriend, knocked on the door to say that Jane wanted a few words with Brion. Jane's apartment, on the other side of our kitchen wall, only a few feet away, was a lesbian harem of sorts: Cherifa, Fatima who cooked, and an assortment of young Arab girls who stayed over. I had been in her apartment only once, briefly, and occasionally ran into Jane in the hall. Paul visited Brion almost every day, but Brion's and Jane's paths never crossed. Jane knew very well that Brion was a misogynist and hated all women, particularly her. So when Jane appeared in Brion's doorway, it was a shock.

She was wearing a short-sleeve white blouse, a khaki skirt, and brown shoes. She had an uncertain limp, slightly dragging her foot, which made me feel uneasy. Her hair was dark henna (a specialty of Arab women) and her complexion was very white.

Brion welcomed Jane with effusive graciousness, and they started gossiping. She had come to inquire about a mutual friend who was sick, to find out if Brion had any news. Targuisti served sweet tea with fresh mint to Jane and refilled our glasses.

Jane was very kind and very charming, and I loved her immediately. I had a big ego and thought that she might also have come to see me. Jane's speech was a bit slurred from the stroke she had suffered nine years before, and she compensated by trying to be more amusing.

"I saw Martha about two weeks ago," said Brion cheerily. Princess Martha Ruspoli, Jane's current lover, lived in a villa on the mountain outside Tangier.

"How nice," said Jane, who had been out of town.

"It was delightful. John and I had dinner with her." It had been an intimate dinner for three. Brion had accepted Martha's invitation, I assumed, as a political intrigue, because Jane was away. For me, it was very exciting.

Jane said to me, warmly sympathetic, "Where are you from?"

"New York!" My throat was very tight. I was in awe of her. I loved *Two Serious Ladies*, which was one of the great novels of the twentieth century. "We met last year," I said breathlessly. "When you were at the Chelsea Hotel." I was sure she didn't remember me, as I had said almost nothing.

"John is a poet," said Brion grandly. "A very special one!"

"How nice!" Jane smiled at me happily. I was exhilarated.

Jane sat on a Moroccan couch, which was alongside Brion's double bed. She was leaning back on the bed with her legs stretched toward the mirror on the opposite wall. I first sat cross-legged on the bed behind Jane, and then I moved next to her, leaning back on the couch, occasionally looking at her in the mirror.

Jane's knees were akimbo and her skirt had crept up a bit, and I noticed that she had thick legs. Occasionally, I caught her sneaking a look at her reflection. Vanity, I thought, naïvely. But who was I to judge, as Brion and I had positioned the mirror so we could watch ourselves having sex. She started laughing and I started laughing, rolling around with our heads together in the mirror. I had no idea what we were laughing about, just spontaneous joy.

"Pretty place you have here!" Jane said to Brion. I thought for a second, with pleasure, that she meant the two of us in the mirror. *"Pretty place you have here!"* she said again, giggling and fluttering her eyes. Jane spread her legs toward the mirror. She was looking at herself, looking up her skirt, laughing, pulling her knees up, moving her thighs back and forth, squeezing her knees together like a little girl, then opening her legs in some kind of bliss posture. During all this, Brion and Jane made witty small talk.

After about twenty minutes, we cheerfully said goodbye and Jane went back next door. "Did you see what happened?" said Brion, outraged. "She was looking at her cunt in the mirror. Did you see?"

"At her pussy?" I said with surprise. "I thought she was looking at her piano legs."

"She looked at her cunt in my mirror!" Brion was getting steamed up. "I saw what she was doing!" Targuisti smiled, nodded his head seriously, and said in Arabic that he too had seen her doing it.

"You saw her cunt?"

Brion choked, wide-eyed with his head shaking. "Yes!"

"Her thighs are so fat, how could you see up?"

"It is unthinkable!" Brion was really angry.

"And when she said, 'Pretty place you have here!,' she meant her pussy in the mirror, and was oblivious of me. Jane is so brilliant . . . On your bed!"

"On my bed! . . . That Jewish cunt!" Brion's voice had a deep resonant disgust.

"Did she have panties on?" I said, laughing uncontrollably.

"And no panties!" Brion was getting more angry; blood had rushed into his face.

"I saw everything," he continued, apoplectic.

"That's enough to turn you to stone, isn't it?" I said ecstatically. In a situation like this, there is only one possibility: make it worse. "She defiled your mirror!"

"How dare she! That brazen bitch!" Brion was high on his own anger.

"She has stained your mirror," I said. "Is that the same as a curse?" The mirror is a very powerful symbol, very powerful magic, and a metaphor for the illusory nature of all phenomena, and the empty nature of mind. "Do you think the stain is indelible?"

"The witch!"

"Perhaps Targuisti should wash the mirror immediately." I was still laughing hysterically. Sweat poured from my face, mixing with the tears of laughter.

"I shouldn't have let her in the door." Brion seethed resentment.

It was a pleasure rubbing Brion's nose in it. He was on the verge of tears from loathing and despair.

"I can still smell it," he said, lighting a stick of incense and waving it around.

"Jane is so brilliant." I couldn't resist.

"She did it on purpose!" Brion was so upset, his speech was slurring. "And you lay there with her. Both of you laughing at me." Brion trembled with rage and paranoia, and then he started crying. I put my arms around him, hugging his body, kissing his face, pressing him to my heart, and offering him love, kindness, and strength.

"All of you are loathsome," Brion said.

I thought back to what had happened: I lay next to Jane on the couch, looking at her in the mirror. Looking into her eyes in the mirror, and her eyes were enraptured. I remembered her legs akimbo, and her spastically opening and closing her legs, and the fat on the inside of her thighs. Then, a moment of shock recognition, and I yelled joyously, "I saw Jane Bowles's pussy and I didn't know I was looking at it!"

We went onto the little balcony and looked out over the dry field, deserted of goats and sheep and shepherd boys and people passing, and the white walls of the consulate, quivering like a mirage in the very hot afternoon. Then Brion and I took our afternoon nap and forgot about it.

Jane and Paul Bowles

THE VERY NEXT AFTERNOON, just after lunch, Brion, Targuisti, and I were once again sitting around drinking mint tea and smoking kif in the ovenlike heat, when there was a loud knock at the door. Paul Bowles appeared, very agitated.

"Something terrible has happened!" said Paul. "I am distraught." He was impeccably uptight, wearing seersucker pants and an off-white sport shirt. "The parrot ate Jane's food, and keeled over dead."

"What?"

"The parrot is dead. Inexplicably dead and it ate some of Jane's food."

"When?" said Brion, very interested. This was the parrot on Paul's shoulder in the famous photographs of him that appeared on the book covers of *The Sheltering Sky* and *A Hundred Camels in the Courtyard.*

"Just now! Fifteen minutes ago! Jane and I had finished lunch and we were talking. Fatima hadn't cleared the plates yet. I noticed the parrot picking at some leftovers in Jane's dish. The next thing I knew it had gone to its perch and fell to the floor with a thump, dead!"

"Oh, no!" This time there was a happy resonance in Brion's voice.

Paul, who prided himself on never showing any emotion, said, "This is very serious!"

"Poison!" said Brion.

"Exactly, poison!" said Paul, pacing the room and puffing a cigarette. "I am beside myself with worry. What are we going to do?"

"Don't ask me," said Brion joyously. "Cherifa is poisoning Jane."

This was a little game that Paul and Brion played with each other, and played with their friends, but kept hidden from the outside. The game was: Jane was being slowly poisoned by Cherifa, her jealous old Moroccan lover who was accomplished in magic and potions. This time it was because Jane was having a love affair with Princess Martha Ruspoli. Jane was being poisoned but yet she wasn't. It was all a game, a child's fantasy that Paul and Brion created to amuse themselves, and was not true at all. They believed it and they didn't believe it, so they were free of blame and responsibility.

"Who knows how long this has been going on!" Brion giggled. "She does it slowly, over long, long periods, and the poison is undetectable."

"What am I to do?" Paul puffed on a cigarette in an ivory holder.

"I must tell you. Jane paid me a most curious visit yesterday." Brion feigned outrage. "Do you know what she did? She looked at her cunt in my mirror." He told the story in gorgeous detail, and we all laughed and laughed.

"The poison might explain her behavior yesterday." Brion seemed a little consoled.

Paul was astounded that Jane had come into Brion's apartment, and more so that she had done such a thing. "I am so worried about Jane. She's so pale."

"White as chalk," said Brion. "Ah!!!"

"Arsenic makes the skin so beautiful!" I joined in.

"What is worse, Jane scarcely ate anything at lunch today, less than I did," said Paul, resigned to the inevitable.

"Cherifa has concocted a potent brew," said Brion, laughing.

"Revenge of the demon kings!" I said, tickling Brion.

We went on like this: Brion goading, Paul anguished, me laughing along but also a bit worried that Jane was actually being poisoned. I got the feeling I was interfering with their little game, so I tried to keep my mouth shut.

We all knew that Jane drank a lot and took tranquilizers, a very dangerous combination. In 1958, the year after her stroke, Paul had authorized five electroshock therapy treatments in a London hospital for Jane, which is the worst thing for a person with brain damage from a stroke.

It occurred to me that the day before she might have been high on poison. Being stoned on poison was the reason she had come, as she knew Brion hated her. Imagine her crazed suffering.

Poison can also be a psychedelic and can distort the illusion called reality. This can be both painful and enlightening. I wondered what Jane Bowles saw yesterday as she lay on Brion's couch, a little dazed, looking at her pussy in the mirror. I wondered what she hallucinated. Did she see the semiwrathful aging fertility goddess? So powerful to have penetrated Brion's protective envelope, and violate his mirror?

A week later, Paul stopped in to see Brion. The electricity had gone out and we had lit a couple of candles. Paul said, "Nobody is ever going to find out about all this."

"Don't be silly," said Brion, smiling. "Everyone will know. We all write letters to each other."

"And you all gossip," Paul said.

There was an odd silence. Then I looked clearly at both of

them, and said to myself, I will be the one who writes your story.

They continued talking.

You underestimate me, I thought. I will write about you, and the horror of it all.

The unhappiness we caused each other in Tangier. It wasn't long before my relationship with Brion disintegrated, clouded by negativity, and we stopped sleeping together. We became each other's demons. Of course, each of us was the cause of our own suffering, and there was no blame, but we were the instruments of each other's misery.

Jane suffered even more than us, because she was a little deranged. Nobody could help her. She seemed amazing and lovely, but underneath was bottomless pain. Her mind and her body were poisoned. It was all like Italian opera, and we laughed insanely at the unbelievable magical display. Even though she was right next door, our paths rarely crossed and there was nothing I could do. I was frozen in hell like everyone else.

One morning, as we were having breakfast, I told Brion of a dream I had just before I woke. I was in India, with my friend Peter Zimels, and it was a Buddhist dream, intense and complicated.

"You've come to the wrong place," said Brion, point-blank.

I felt a bright light flash inside my head, the truth unexpectedly revealed. I should not have followed Brion to Tangier. A mistake and a dead end. I managed to say, "What is the right place?"

"Where the others of you go?"

"India!"

"Yes, I guess so," said Brion, laughing.

I felt deeply shocked that I had come to the wrong place. It was true that my attachment to Brion had led me down the wrong path. I had chosen Brion as a lover, come to Tangier, and offered him the blind faith and devotion of a disciple, and it had all been a mistake. His mind was brilliant, but he did not have a spiritual path.

I always felt a deep connection with Buddhism, considered

myself a Buddhist, and even before I studied Buddhist philosophy, literature, and art at Columbia, I felt attached to India. But my karma hadn't ripened. That door hadn't opened for me yet.

Brion Gysin in Tangier

ART AND TECHNOLOGY

I arrived back in New York in early September 1966, on a Yugoslav Line freighter from Casablanca to the company's pier in Brooklyn. I telephoned my father and said cheerfully, even though I was horribly depressed, returning home after still another failure, "Hi, Dad, I'm back!"

My mother and father were very happy to see me and have me back, like all loving parents. I was failing at a noble aspiration, a heroic love affair, and being a poet, a big defeat. Back to square one, back to where I began with my family. But I knew the game and acted positive, and everything was okay. I regaled them with stories about Morocco. My parents were wonderful and, as usual, kind, generous, and supportive, giving me enough space. "Rest and recover your strength," said my mother.

At the end of summer, our house was especially beautiful and luxurious, and the gardens and grounds—flowering bushes and shrubs under the old oaks—were in a state of lush green. The gardeners kept the lawns perfectly cut and the flower beds turned. My parents had recently put in an underground automatic sprinkler system that watered the lawns; it went on in the early morning and in the late afternoon, keeping everything fresh. After the torture of Tangier, being there was a welcome relief. I lay in bed a lot, hiding my depression, reading, working on poems, taking naps, and looking out the windows. When I was asleep, and just after I woke up, all my problems were forgotten, and I felt peaceful and happy. I rested for as long as I could in this state, awake and dreamy, with no thoughts, or eyes closed watching a donut of light, floating slightly in bliss.

By mid-September, I had to go on with my life, like it or not. I was a poet and had chosen this hopelessly difficult job. Knowing that fact intuitively fed my depression, but I had to figure out what to do next. I called my friends in New York and told them I was back, and I went into the city and visited them. It was urgent that I get an apartment, and not have to take the Long Island Rail Road back and forth to my parents'. I mentioned it to Wynn, who said, "I've just rented a loft on the third floor to store my paintings. There's a lot of space. You can stay there."

"Yes, thank you!" I said, surprised by the opportunity. "I'll pay the rent, and I'm happy to live with the paintings." It was cheap, fifty-five dollars a month, and a great loft.

Built in 1884 by the YMCA, and called the Young Men's Institute, 222 Bowery was the first of the modern-day YMCAs. Previously, the Ys on the Bowery were soup kitchens and shelters for the homeless. The Young Men's Institute was conceived to help men seventeen years or older who were from immigrant families get a better start in life. By offering gymnastics, classes in music and poetry, language, carriage building, etc., the Young Men's Institute "intended to promote the physical, intellectual, and spiritual health of young working men in the densely crowded Bowery." At the turn of the twentieth century, the Bowery was the main honky-tonk thoroughfare, surrounded by a sea of squalor and deplorable conditions, and the suffering of immigrants. The Young Men's Institute was a safe haven to countless young men until it closed in 1932.

Beginning with Fernand Léger in the early 1940s, 222 Bowery became an artists' loft building. Mark Rothko lived in the gymnasium between 1955 and 1961, and later Michael Goldberg and Lynda Benglis lived there, among others. The Romanesque revival building was designed by Bradford Gilbert, Cornelius Vanderbilt's railroad architect. In keeping with that style, my loft had twelve-foot-high ceilings, two big barrel-vault windows, Tiffany glass doors, and a giant baronial fireplace. There were a few bits of beat-up furniture: a big table, some chairs, and a couch of square, flat, foam-rubber cushions that was also the bed. What good fortune! It was a soft landing back into the New York art scene.

The first week, I settled in, started working on a new poem, and visited friends. The Irish-born artist Les Levine, his wife, and their newborn son lived in a loft above a store at 119 Bowery, a run-down, three-story nineteenth-century building. Below them lived my friends Jill Johnston and Lucinda Childs.

I invited Jill and Lucinda to tea at 222 Bowery. "Wow, John, what a great loft!" said Jill as she walked in.

"I know, I lucked out." We talked, and I caught up with art world gossip.

Bob Rauschenberg, they told me, was working on an amazing new project with the Bell Labs engineer Billy Klüver (whose New Jersey party I attended with Andy the weekend after JFK was killed). "Artists collaborating with engineers," said Jill. "The coming together of art and science."

"What they are doing is really interesting," said Lucinda.

But, Jill went on, "they're having a little trouble. I think they're in over their heads." Jill looked at Lucinda and they both laughed. "And it opens in two weeks!"

"He's brought together an extraordinary group of people," said Lucinda, rattling off a list of artists I had known and admired since 1962 or '63. "John Cage, David Tudor, Yvonne Rainer, Öyvind Fahlström, Robert Whitman, Steve Paxton, Alex and Deborah Hay, and of course, Bob."

Lucinda, who was also performing, insisted that even though the engineers were all "straight guys in suits," some exciting things were happening. But Jill was skeptical. "Is it the wave of the future," she wondered, "or Bob on another ego trip?"

The performances would take place over nine nights in the Armory on Twenty-Sixth Street, Lucinda went on, an homage to the 1913 Armory Show, which featured Duchamp's *Nude Descending a Staircase* and introduced modernism to America.

"Now, it's Rauschenberg descending the stairs," Jill poked again. "And he's introducing art and science to America."

"It sounds really interesting."

"You should get involved," said Jill. "They are looking for volunteers. Steve said they are desperately looking for help."

"I would like to." It seemed like a good idea, and it might fit with the sound compositions I was making. But what I did was so primitive—loops and overlays on tape recorders—that working with engineers and advanced electronics to make poems was incomprehensible. I had a bit of low self-esteem, feeling like the injured chick that had never quite flown, had never really gotten off, that I was incapable of flight. "But how could I help?"

"I'll have Steve Paxton call you," said Jill. "He'll fill you in." The next morning, the telephone rang, and it was Steve, asking if he could come visit that afternoon and explain what was happening.

Even though the project sounded exciting, I was a bit reluctant, because I had just moved into the loft a few days before. I wanted to begin working on poems and settle in, and not get distracted by I didn't know what. But my intuition and common sense said art and technology was also poetry and technology, and this might ratchet up what I was doing with sound poetry into the real world of brilliant engineers. It might be a chance to move on from the technical amateurness of Brion Gysin and William Burroughs. Although it was a scary challenge, I knew something important was being offered to me.

At 3:00 p.m., the door buzzer rang. Steve Paxton was a dancer and choreographer. We had met before, and I had seen him perform many times at the Judson Dance Theater and other dance venues. He was not only an innovative choreographer but a fabulous dancer, inventing huge leaps and twists and pirouettes that were mind-boggling. I was in awe when I saw him dance. Over the years at downtown parties, I got to know Steve slightly; we had talked but never become close friends.

Steve was also Bob Rauschenberg's lover of five years. Steve had danced with the Merce Cunningham Company, and Bob designed sets and costumes for Merce. In October 1961, after a Merce performance in Connecticut, Bob and Steve made it, had great sex, and fell in love—while Bob was still with Jasper Johns. Steve was the reason for Bob and Jasper's breakup, which, gossip had it, had been very painful for Jasper.

Jasper was from a gentlemanly South Carolina background, and Bob was from Port Arthur, Texas, and his parents were poor white Christian fundamentalists. That background was ingrained in Bob's personality and imprinted in his mind, often in the best sense—as it was for Janis Joplin, who was also from Port Arthur. It didn't matter good or bad, it was their magical display; they were great artists.

I had met Bob and Jasper several times, separately, at openings and parties in 1961 and '62. I was introduced as "a young poet, John Giorno." We just shook hands, and I was always awed, almost speechless, as I was such a fan of their work.

That afternoon, Steve came bounding up the stairs, bright-eyed and beautiful, full of positive energy. "Tell me about the show," I said.

"Everyone's pieces are all coming wonderfully. The problem is bringing it all together in the huge armory space."

He told funny stories of what was happening between the artists and engineers. We smoked a joint and talked some more.

Spontaneously and simultaneously, we both tilted forward, fell into each other's arms, and kissed. We kept kissing and hugged, and it felt totally wonderful. We threw off our clothes, I got the amyl nitrite and Vaseline, and we lunged at each other and fell on the bed, making love with great passion. Needless to say, after the loneliness and disaster of Tangier, I was starved for love and affection. We balled to our hearts' delight. Steve was twenty-seven years old, and I was twenty-nine. He was extraordinarily beautiful. His dancer's body was hairless, hot-blooded, white as marble, lithe and hard and sinewy; it was a perfect classical sculpture, with the head of a Greek god, brow, nose, lips, locks of hair. And he had a big dick. He was dazzling to look at, and our physical connection was intense. We came in great orgasms, collapsed into each other's arms tenderly, and went to sleep. We woke, and continued giving each other love and affection, and gossiped about our work and friends.

We kissed goodbye, and Steve said, "I'll call you tomorrow."

Steve Paxton performing *Antic Meet* in 1963

STEVE CALLED, and we got together the next late afternoon, talked, had tea, smoked a joint, and made love again. I was very happy at my good fortune of having a beautiful lover, as it was totally out of the blue!

"I'm busy all day tomorrow with rehearsals," said Steve. "I'll call you the day after tomorrow."

The next day, Steve called and said, "I can come over tomorrow morning at about ten-thirty." The next morning, he called at ten-fifteen and said, "I'm free for a couple of hours."

The door buzzer rang ten minutes later.

We fell into each other's arms. "Good to see you," I said. We pressed our bodies together as close as we could. "Would you like some tea?"

"I just had some." Steve was beautiful and morning fresh.

"A joint?"

"Yes!"

I rolled a joint as quickly as I could, and we smoked. "What time is the meeting this afternoon?"

"Three p.m., at the Armory."

We just wanted to make love. Again we fell into each other's arms. It felt so good, and I felt so lucky. We fucked, and both came gloriously, rested in each other's arms, went to sleep briefly, and woke up happily.

I made tea, and we sat naked and talked for about twenty minutes about our friends—Jill, the dancers/choreographers Yvonne Rainer and Deborah Hay—and how the show was coming along.

The door buzzer rang, and I ignored it. It rang again. "It must be a delivery, but I'm not expecting anyone." It rang again. "It's too early for the mail." It rang again and again. "That's strange!"

"It's Bob," said Steve, with a worried look on his face. His already white skin had turned a whiter shade of pale.

"What?"

"Bob must have heard me when I called. He must have listened on the downstairs phone."

"Oh!" I said in amazement. Steve got dressed quickly. The door buzzer stopped ringing. We relaxed, and I continued making cheerful conversation. I thought whatever it was, was over, when suddenly there was a loud knock on the door. We froze. Somebody knocked again and again. A man's voice said, "I know you're in there, open up."

"It's Bob?" I mouthed, and Steve nodded "Yes!"

He banged more on the door. "I'm not going away until you

open." Everything fell silent. Bob had slid down to the floor, was leaning against the door, crying softly.

It was astounding. What was unfolding was a nightmare, only you wake up from nightmares; this was really happening, and no doubt would have irrevocable consequences. But it was also like opera or the movies, very exciting.

A minute later, Steve got up, unlocked and pushed open the door, and leapt out into the hall and down the stairs. He executed his exit with the grace of a dancer.

A few minutes later, I looked out the door, peering into the hall, a little afraid of what I would see, wondering if I might be attacked by a jealous lover. Nobody was there. Bob had gone.

I sat down, bewildered and sad. It was very upsetting. Something innocent and pure, two guys making it, had turned into an earth-shattering mess. A bad turn of events, and things like this always led to more trouble. I lay on my bed, resting, a bit exhausted, and girding myself for a downward wave of depression.

Ten minutes later, the phone. "Hello!"

"John, it's Bob Rauschenberg. Can I come and visit you? Please! I'm around the corner in a phone booth, please!"

"Yes, of course!"

One minute later, the buzzer rang, Bob climbed the stairs and came into my loft. "Hi, John," Bob said sadly.

"I apologize. I don't know what's happening, and don't want to cause any trouble, or anyone suffering."

"You don't have to explain," said Bob. He looked at me desperately, and his face wrinkled up in pain. He moved forward and fell into my arms. His face was buried in the crook of my neck sobbing big, wet tears. I held him as tenderly as I could, trying to generate good feelings to make him feel better. He moved his head up from my shoulder and kissed me on the mouth. I was shocked. We kissed gently at first, with an almost delicate sadness, then more strongly, and with passion and abandon (completely forgetting what had gone on just before), kissing and hugging. We were both hard and were rubbing our crotches together. An extraordinary turn of events!

I pulled my head away and said, "Are you okay?"

"Yes, I am," said Bob happily.

"Would you like to smoke a joint?"

"Yes!"

"And have a cup of tea?"

"Yes, John, thanks!"

I made tea, rolled a joint, and made cheerful conversation. It was like after an earthquake: the air radiated the power of a seismic change. I was a poet who used found words as found images, and while Andy Warhol was my first main influence, Bob and Jasper Johns were also huge inspirations. I was flabbergasted that I was kissing and making love with someone I so revered.

"I just returned from Tangier," I said, chronicling my journey from Morocco to Long Island to the Bowery.

"I've been to Morocco," said Bob. "I was there with Cy."

"Yes, I know," I said. Bob was there with Cy Twombly, when they were lovers. "I think we have some friends in common, Paul Bowles and Jane Bowles, and some people living on the mountain."

"Paul Bowles, no! What a horrible person!"

"I know very well! You left a few legendary stories behind." We laughed, but I did not elaborate, so as not to embarrass him.

One of those stories had taken place in a hotel in the casbah. Paul had given Bob a hashish and marijuana cake (a potent psychedelic), and Bob, who had never experimented with drugs, had an extremely bad, paranoid reaction. Comatose for ten hours, Bob had been, as Paul recalled, "covered by a bedsheet with an enormous erection sticking up in the middle like a tentpole, an enormous erection for ten hours."

Bob and I were sitting next to each other on the couch, drinking tea. We smoked the joint and were a bit high. Bob leaned forward, our lips touched, and we kissed again. I was surprised by his forwardness, given what had happened, but it felt good, and why not! My tongue went into his mouth, and we kissed and kissed. Both of us were very needy, and exploded into each other from the beginning. Something magical, unexplainable, and very strong happened. We pressed together with an electrical surge, one of those rare moments in life when, inexplicably, bliss is experienced. I didn't know it, but at that moment Bob Rauschenberg and I became partners.

We took off our clothes and made love. Bob was forty years old, eleven years older than me. He had a beautiful body, soft skin, and firm muscles. He had a big dick, thick with a silky foreskin, nine inches hard, and it felt really good. It was like making love to Alexander the Great or Emperor Hadrian. His body radiated the worldly power of great accomplishments. At the same time, I was surprised that he seemed to have the same desperate need for affection and tenderness that I did.

We woke up lovers and friends, and sat around smoking cigarettes. Any thought like "He doesn't seem very sad about Steve," I dismissed instantly. Their relationship was more complicated than I thought, and it was not my problem.

"I volunteered to work on the show," I said. "I'll do whatever they want."

"I need help. Would you like to work on my piece?" said Bob, smiling.

"Well, yes, I would be delighted to."

"It's a video piece that gets projected on a huge screen. You can be the cameraman. Do you know about video?"

"Well, yes, sort of, I'm a poet." Bob must have seen the panic in my face, as I was not a filmmaker, and knew nothing about how to shoot films.

"It's very easy," said Bob. "You just point the camera at me."

We talked some more about Jill and Lucinda and Yvonne. "I've never smoked marijuana before," said Bob.

"What?"

"I've had reefer, but only years ago. Never marijuana."

"Marijuana and reefer are the same thing," I smiled. His vocabulary confusion was endearing, as was the fact that he called grass by its archaic name "reefer."

But more than that, I was pleased that he was stoned and had relaxed into it. This was the first time Bob Rauschenberg had gotten high and enjoyed it, wasn't paranoid, and maybe experienced the mind-expanding possibilities of drugs. I felt so lucky that Bob went through that change with me. It seemed important in our new relationship, like a landmark.

After a while, Bob left, saying, "I'll call you later." That evening at about six, the phone rang, and he asked, "How ya doing? Can I come visit you tomorrow around two?"

"Yes, I am very happy to be with you. See you tomorrow."

Neither of us mentioned Steve, and I ignored the shocking fact that Bob Rauschenberg had a big enough ego that he could just take his boyfriend's boyfriend away from him, if he wanted, and he did. I suppressed any thoughts that he might not be a very nice person, because negative thoughts poison a relationship. I might have known that I'd pay for it. I happily went along with it, because a good-looking guy who was also a famous artist got dumped in my lap.

The next afternoon at two, the door buzzer rang, and Bob came up the stairs. We kissed and hugged, I made tea, and we talked more about the show and all the artists that we shared as friends. We smoked a joint and made love.

"Tomorrow, I rehearse my piece," said Bob. "Can you be there?"

"Yes! What time?"

"Four at the Armory on Twenty-Sixth."

The next day, I was there at four, and Bob was a little late. The Armory was a vast oval space, built before World War I but still used by the military reserve, and also rented out for events. On one side of the arena were bleachers seating a thousand people. A huge video screen hung down the middle from the ceiling. Opening night was two days away, so there was an exciting charge in the air.

9 Evenings: Theatre and Engineering was the brainchild of

Billy Klüver, an electrical engineer trained in Stockholm, Paris, and Berkeley, with help from his friend Pontus Hultén, a high-flying, Swedish, postmodern curator. Mix those ambitions with the dirt-poor American boy from Port Arthur, Texas—now a famous artist—and you had a potent cocktail, like a martini. The result was a seminal moment in art history.

We began to rehearse Bob's piece, *Open Score*. Bob sat in a chair in front of a gray background, projected onto the huge video screen. He wanted a relatively tight shot. So I focused the camera on his head and throat, and zoomed a little into his hairline. My idea was that's what happens when you kiss someone; you get closer. It was the only move I had to do. What a relief, not so complicated!

The artist Ken Dewey worked on the video, and the musician Jim Tenney on the sound; both were friends, and I felt comfortable with them. On another camera, Bob Breer rehearsed filming the screen and audience.

"That's a wrap," said Bob. "John and I are going. Bye, everybody."

We took a taxi to 222 Bowery. I made tea. We talked, smoked a joint, and made love.

"I'll call you tomorrow morning," said Bob as he left.

THE NEXT DAY, Bob didn't call. At about six, the phone rang. It was Billy. "Hi, John. Can you come over? There is a problem. Bob is sick. It would be good if you could come over."

"What?"

"You'll see when you come."

From my loft to 475 Lafayette Street was a short walk. (Bob would later inform me that it was exactly twelve minutes, as he walked it often and had timed it.)

Billy was waiting for me at the top of the stairs on the second floor. "He has temporarily lost the ability to speak," he said. Bob had been to see the doctors, who thought it might be something called Guillain-Barré syndrome. "They say it can last for a few days. They don't know."

"You mean he can't talk?" It was serious.

"Yes. We communicate by writing notes. He's been asking for you. We think you can help him."

We went into the kitchen, and Bob was sitting sadly on a chair at the table. We kissed, and I sat next to him. He grasped my hand tightly, trembling, and we sat with our knees touching. I tried to direct love and affection to him, a beam of tenderness aimed directly at his body and mind. Occasionally, Bob scribbled a note on a pad, asking a question, and I answered with a happy flourish.

Also in the kitchen or standing just outside were Yvonne Rainer, Bob Morris, and Susan Hartnett, all artists involved in *9 Evenings*. Dorothea Rockburne, an artist who worked for Bob, cooked a soup for dinner. Everyone was kind and gentle, trying to help Bob, offering the best they could to deal with the catastrophe.

Every once in a while, Bob had to go downstairs for something, or to the bathroom, and I went with him, and we hugged and kissed. He scribbled a note, "Thanks for being here." He invented little secret signs to show he loved me.

Steve Paxton came in and out. I made an effort to be kind, asked about his piece and how he was. He was full of smiles and said everything was going well. We acted as though nothing had happened. Steve was still living in the house and still sleeping with Bob, and I did not want to fuck up this amazingly fortunate occurrence in my life. So I tried to abide in the continual flow, and not have any negative thoughts. It was before I became a Buddhist and a meditation practitioner, but in times of extreme need, wisdom is self-arising.

At the same time, I felt very sorry for Steve. I knew he was suffering enormously. Bob was the love of his life, and he had lost him. Yet I felt no guilt. I hadn't asked for any of this, and I was also a victim of whatever games they were playing. I got handed Bob on a silver platter, and all is fair in love and war.

The kissing and hugging became a drug, and it was the one thing that made Bob feel good. We kept doing it, every few minutes, in the hall, when the room was empty for a minute before the next person came in. We continually and discreetly held hands, and Bob's was shaking slightly. It was a great expression of love. I got through it by not questioning what was happening, and having no thoughts other than dealing with each moment as it arose, and allowing the natural feeling of compassion to come through. The cause of Bob's sickness was, obviously, the stress of everything that was unfolding. I went home at about eleven, and Bob went to bed.

The next night, Thursday, October 13, 1966, was opening night, and Bob still could not talk, but he didn't have to. We arrived at the Armory just before the beginning and walked backstage smiling. The performances—Steve Paxton, Alex Hay, Deborah Hay (only some of the artists' pieces were in each show)—went off seamlessly. Bob bowed on stage with everyone at the grand finale. Then Bob was whisked away, before anyone could talk to him, as was I along with him.

The second night, Friday, October 14, was Bob's first performance. He still could not talk. Backstage, we met Julie Martin, who coordinated the production. (She was secretly Billy Klüver's girlfriend, and they would later marry.) She forgot not to bring it up, and offered Bob some sympathy. He wrote on a piece of paper: "Can't talk, no pity." Everyone who knew was wringing their hearts with worry and concern.

The performance of Bob's piece *Open Score* went off perfectly. I did my job as cameraman. David Tudor's piece *Bandoneon! (A Combine)* was wonderful. Bob bowed, smiling to the audience at the end of the evening in the grand finale. Then Bob was hurried away home again. The night was a great success.

The next day, Bob's speech came back slowly, and he began to recover. In the afternoon, he came to 222 Bowery and talked softly and naturally, and we made love.

October 23 was the last night. Bob's *Open Score* began with a tennis game played by Frank Stella and Mimi Kanarek, with the rackets wired for sound. The sound of the game controlled the stage lights. Each time the tennis ball hit the racket, it made a sharp popping sound, and one of the house lights went out— darker and darker with each hit. At last, when all the house lights were out, and the house dark, a cast of five hundred volunteers came on stage in the blackness. Their instructions were to do ordinary things, move about, take off a sweater, touch or hug someone. The hall was flooded with invisible infrared light, which enabled infrared cameras to film the volunteer performers. I was one of three cameramen, along with Bob Breer and Les Levine. We filmed the five hundred people, and the images were projected on the huge screen. I panned the camera over the crowd, zoomed slowly in on somebody, panned and zoomed out, panned and zoomed in. Then, suddenly it was over. What a relief!

Bob said in the program, "Tennis is movement. Put in the context of theater it is a formal dance improvisation. The unlikely use of the game to control the lights and to perform as an orchestra interests me. The conflict of not being able to see an event that is taking place right in front of one except through a reproduction is the sort of double exposure through action. A screen of light and a screen of darkness."

In Öyvind Fahlström's *Kisses Sweeter Than Wine*, I was the cameraman for Bob, who was dressed as an eighteenth-century idiot savant, someone who could remember and multiply infinite numbers. I figured out that if I stayed focused and relaxed, it would work out. The video image was projected on the huge screen.

In Steve Paxton's *Physical Things*, I got credit in the program for "Technical Help," but he didn't ask me to do anything. I had only caused him trouble and suffering.

Each artist used their friends in their pieces, so there were many artists in the cast, and it had the feeling of a celebration of an extended family: besides Frank Stella, the cast included Carl

Andre, Meredith Monk, Donald Judd's wife Julie, Walter de Maria's wife Susanne, Marjorie Strider, David Whitney, and dozens more.

The work in *9 Evenings* was good, but no single piece was exceptional. The artists were incredible, and their collaborations with engineers were wonderful, but somehow it didn't quite achieve greatness. Each artist was working in another medium and made cautious, determined pieces. The real great work of art was the concept of the entire event, a collaboration of Bob and Billy, artists working with technology. At the time, however, the art world did not give them credit. The art world hates crossovers; leaving one medium for another is unforgivable—traitors! Bob's piece was largely ignored.

The wrap party for *9 Evenings* was also a surprise birthday party for Bob. He hadn't wanted a birthday party or anybody making a fuss. He thought he was simply going to see, for the last time, the devoted participants of the show following what had been a traumatic time. It was arranged that I would pick him up, and we would arrive at the Armory, and at the right moment everybody would sing "Happy Birthday." After the huge success of *9 Evenings*, everyone, including Bob, was happy, relaxed, and exhausted.

Everyone was gentle with one another, appreciating the ordeal they had all gone through. In the emptiness of accomplishment was a silent, invisible resonance of joy and satisfaction.

"You all have done something heroic," I said to Yvonne Rainer. "When you do something for the first time, the obstacles and difficulties are always enormous. You have succeeded, and you are all heroes."

"Thanks, John!" said Yvonne, smiling.

I was still in startled shock at my stroke of good fortune, being the lover of one of the greatest artists in the world. Suddenly, I was a royal consort and given special treatment. I had not forgotten the difficulties in my life, the sadness of being ditched by Andy Warhol, the bad fortune in my relationship with Brion Gysin, or the mistake of being stuck in Wall Street. This time, I made a big effort not to do anything wrong.

Bob and I stayed for a short time, talked to everyone, then took a taxi back to Lafayette Street. We hugged and kissed, feeling the wonder of being with the person you love, when your hearts ring with happiness. It was rare when it happened to anyone, and I deeply appreciated it.

Experiments in Art and Technology

BEFORE, DURING, AND AFTER *9 Evenings*, there were press conferences, and fund-raising receptions and parties. Bob had a sunny personality—wherever he went, he brought a bright energy that made people feel good, particularly rich people. He was a natural Southern hustler. I saw him radiate and his radiance filled the world and my heart.

One afternoon, when I was with him in the Armory, he said, "You see that man over there. He's very interesting. You should talk to him." We walked over, and Bob introduced us. "Bob Moog, I want you to meet John Giorno, a poet working with sound."

"Hello!" Bob Moog was short, fat, and balding, with uncut greasy hair at the edges, and looked like he might have slept in his clothes. He was thirty-two, only a few years older than me, but looked like an old man.

A few days later, we saw him again, and Bob said, "Have you talked to him yet? He is doing something very important."

A few days after that: "Have you talked to Bob yet?"

Two days later, Bob said, rather annoyed, "John, you go and talk with him!"

"I will, I will!" I said, then went over and reintroduced myself, and we talked.

Over the preceding two years, Bob Moog had been creating and refining the Moog synthesizer, which was about to revolutionize the music industry. In 1966, only a handful of rock bands had one, and it had not yet appeared on an LP. But two years later, Wendy Carlos would release her album *Switched-on Bach*, in which she used the Moog to synthesize works of the classical composer; it went on to win three Grammy Awards. Soon after I started talking with Moog, the Doors, the Grateful Dead, the Rolling Stones, the Beatles, Frank Zappa, Devo, and Brian Eno—every rock band—would use Moog synthesizers, and it would be featured on almost every LP. It would profoundly change not just rock 'n' roll, but all music.

In January 1967, three months after Bob's encouragement, I visited Bob Moog in upstate New York to collaborate with him on making sound compositions of my poems. I took a Greyhound bus from Port Authority up to Ithaca in the windy, freezing cold after a big snowstorm that had turned everything into a two-foot-thick block of ice.

Bob picked me up at the bus station, and we drove to Trumansburg, a small town about fifteen minutes away. On Main Street, the only street, Bob had joined three redbrick nineteenth-century buildings together and renovated them to pristine condition inside and out. This was the factory where Bill Hemsath, Bob's chief engineer, and a small crew made Moog synthesizers. It was like being backstage in *The Wizard of Oz*. Bob Moog was a genius, and even though his invention hadn't quite taken off yet, I knew he was onto something great, and I was happy I had been pushed to meet him. I told Bob about my frustrations. "I'm trying to make sound poems, sound compositions of my poems using the sound of the words," I said. "But I'm not trained musically, and I don't know what I'm doing."

"Interesting you should say that," said Bob. "I didn't know what the hell I was doing! I still don't know what I'm doing."

"Good to be working with you," I said, and we laughed.

"I was doing this thing to have a good time," Bob explained. "Then all of a sudden someone's saying to me, 'I'll take one of those and two of that.' That's how I got started."

I brought prerecorded readings of my poems, and we made them into sound compositions on the synthesizer, with Bob acting as the engineer. I told him what I wanted: multitracks on a 16-track tape recorder of the same reading, each track slightly off sync, modified and modulated, different oscillations producing pitches and patterns, and subtle variations and vibrations; and one track in the mix was a clear voice. We composed pieces for each poem.

The Moog synthesizer was analog, not digital. Bob plugged in patch cords, turned knobs, and experimented, sending the voice through oscillators, filters, and amplifiers. The musical qualities inherent in the words, the onomatopoeia, was enhanced naturally and magnified musically with buzzes, swoops, whooshes, scrapes, gurgles, screeches, burps, and cackles. We chose what worked best.

Bob plugged patch cords by the dozens in an endlessly changing warren of colors, and played back different configurations. The interactions of waveforms generated by oscillators, and modulated by waveforms from other oscillators, or a noise generator, layered on top of the timbre of the clear voice; the tracks came together in miraculous symphonies of song. "How do you like that?" asked Bob.

"It's totally great! Thanks!"

Bob Moog had many amazing ideas and suggestions as he introduced me to a new world of technology. Although he was brilliant, he was simple and humble. He saw himself as a toolmaker, and he believed the musicians were the artists. He liked that I was a poet attempting to make poems into electronic music, and he was happy to help me do so for free. We became friends, and I would return to Trumansburg two more times in the next year.

"You know, John," he said one day. "I heard the U.S. Army is working on experiments with certain oscillations that release or relax the sphincter muscle, and make people shit. The idea is to use it in crowd control, and riot control."

Amused, I thought it through aloud: "So they play the sound over a public loudspeaker, and everyone shits in their pants, and becomes disabled."

"They're working on it. I don't think they've quite figured it out yet."

"What is the oscillation that does it?"

"Thirteen or thirteen point five," said Bob. "I think they're still doing research with combinations of modulations."

"Bob, please, we have to put it in our poem. What a great idea! Someone listens to the poem, and starts shitting," I said, laughing. "That's a healthy, real, physical reaction, that might feel good."

So we actually tried it. But it didn't work on us, nor on other people I played it for when I got it back to New York.

Many years later, a friend pointed out that at Cornell University in nearby Ithaca, the U.S. military had lots of top-secret programs doing research into the uses of technology in warfare. We wondered whether it was Bob Moog doing the research for the shitting project.

Bob Moog

BOB AND JOHN

In the middle of my new romance with Bob Rauschenberg and the madness of *9 Evenings*, I had a date I couldn't miss, a vestige of my old life. One day, Bob and I were talking on the phone; that evening, I told him, I had to go to a black-tie dinner at the Waldorf-Astoria with my parents.

"What?" said Bob.

"There is this black-tie ball at the Waldorf, a benefit, a dinner dance. My mother and father go every year. I haven't gone for the last couple of years, but I went every year since I was sixteen years old."

I was beginning to get dressed, and told Bob that I was having trouble with the bow tie.

"You're wearing black tie! You must come over and show me."

"No, it's too embarrassing."

But Bob was determined.

I finished dressing: Brooks Brothers tuxedo and patent leather shoes, a pleated white shirt with the oriental pearl studs that my mother had bought in an antique shop. I also sported black mother-of-pearl cuff links (circa 1920, from my father) and a silk handkerchief. It was the same outfit I'd worn with Andy at MoMA's Spring Gala a few years earlier. I put my coat collar up, got a taxi on the Bowery, and circled around to Bob's house at six o'clock.

Bob met me at the top of the stairs on the third floor. "Look at you!" We kissed and laughed.

"My boyfriend's wearing black tie," said Bob, very impressed. It was so unlike Andy's ridicule in the MoMA elevator. We went into the kitchen. Billy Klüver, Dorothea, and Susan were there. I had a bourbon and soda, we talked, and then I wanted to leave. Bob walked me to the top of the stairs, laughing. We were artists, and it was a joyous joke to be dressed up as a conservative.

"I love doing this! Thumbing your nose!" I said, going down the stairs, and as usual, trying to make a political statement sexual.

"Doing it both ways. AC/DC!" I also had the feeling that I was being obnoxious. But life forced me into both situations, and I had to see both of them through.

I took another taxi to the Waldorf-Astoria. My parents had driven in from Roslyn Heights, and I met them in the lobby. My father was in black tie, and my mother in a fabulous ball gown of her own creation. Every year for these dinner dances, she made for herself, or had her sample hands sew for her, a great gown. This year it was a long, pale blue silk satin gown in the Empire style with graceful folds and a short train, with rhinestone jewel flowers embroidered around the shoulders. The Jacqueline Kennedy look created by Oleg Cassini lingered on after JFK's death. "Very good!" I said. Happy to see one another, we took the elevator up to the Grand Ballroom.

This annual event was organized by Judge Paul P. Rao, who was at the peak of his career as chief judge of the U.S. Customs Court. He had been assistant attorney general in the Truman administration in 1946, one of the most successful Italian Americans in government. Everyone of any importance in New York Democratic politics was present. The dinner dance cost five hundred dollars a ticket, and it was supported by the rich Italian American community, those who had made great fortunes, lawyers and judges, and the political machine.

Every year, I couldn't help but think my mother, father, and I were the three most glamorous guests. My mother was charismatic, and beyond question the best dressed. Even though some Italian Americans were extremely rich, none of them dressed on that level of haute couture. I was young, handsome, and stylish, direct from central casting, and my father the reserved, perfectly elegant gentleman. We sailed through the general cocktail party into the private cocktail party, which was packed.

"There were supposed to be one hundred people here, and there must be two hundred," said Judge John Cannella, smiling at my mother. "Nancy, good to see you. You are exquisitely beautiful, as always."

At the other end of the crowded cocktail room, there was a swell in the density of the people, and the noise became a loud rabble. The bump in the crowd kept moving closer and closer. The crowd opened, the sea parted, and there was Senator Robert F. Kennedy moving forward like an armored vehicle, shaking hands as he went. He shook hands and said hello to Judge Cannella, whom he knew. Then Bobby Kennedy, with his hand permanently stuck out, pointed it to me, and I shook it. It was like a cold fish. He had a smile fixed on his face, like Madame Tussaud's waxworks. He said in the Kennedy Irish Boston accent, "Hello."

My heart was pounding, and I was amazed. He was tanned, locker-room-jock handsome, a movie star radiating light. But he was also a cliché of himself, a cartoon character, the dumb, ambitious, Irish politician working the crowd. In 1966, he was already looking ahead to the 1968 presidential election. I had a feeling that night was of historic proportions, in the context of the still lingering nineteenth-century ethnic animosity: Bobby was an Irish politician from Boston hustling the Italians in New York.

Trailing behind was Ethel Kennedy, looking like a tanned, dried-out tennis mom. It was like being sucked through the TV tube into the make-believe world of the news screen, but magically here in flesh and sweat.

"Let's go in to dinner," said my mother. "It's too crowded."

I followed my mother, who, with an ever engaging smile, talked to whoever was in her path: old Mrs. Buitoni and the two Ronzoni boys, from the spaghetti companies, Mrs. May of May's Department Store. There were lots of judges—federal, state, city—and New York City commissioners and state senators. For me, it was like playing a game of noblesse oblige, and I snobbily looked down on all of them.

Once happily drunk, I glided through the rest of the evening. I danced with a judge's mistress, withstood the boring speeches, and tried not to ask, "What am I doing here?"

Finally, I headed home to the Bowery, my new home. That was my last black-tie dinner at the Waldorf.

From left: Amadeo Giorno, Catherine Morolla, the author,
and Nancy Giorno at the Waldorf-Astoria

ONE DAY later that fall, Bob called at about one in the afternoon.
He was having a meeting with Leo Castelli at his gallery. It was
Thursday, and we hadn't been together since Monday, because we
both had busy schedules. Even though we talked several times a
day, we missed each other. We were addicted to sex, and this felt
like a very long absence. We yearned to be together.

"I'm at Leo's, I'm in the toilet, and I'm thinking of you," said
Bob. "I love you."

"Yes!" I felt really good hearing him say that. "There's a telephone in the toilet?"

"I took it in from Leo's desk." There was a small bathroom in
Leo's private office at the back of the gallery.

"John, something else. I have a hard-on thinking of you."

"Good!"

"And I'm jerking off."

I was a bit surprised, but phone sex was hot. I had done this
before with guys and I liked it. I talked porn to Bob, and he jerked
his dick. I jerked my dick, lying on the bed. We said sexy, lewd
things to each other, and it felt wonderful, making love over the
phone. We felt each other's breath and heat, and nerves trem-

bling, and his throaty voice was voluptuously wet. I felt Bob leaning back with his shirt pulled up, and cumming in a thundering
orgasm. I knew what it looked like, and felt his big cock shooting
a load of cum up into the air and onto his belly. I was close, and
brought myself up to an explosion of cum, and our minds in bliss
were inseparable, for a moment. Then we rested over the phone,
as if we had our heads together in bed.

"The bathroom smells of cum,"
said Bob, laughing. "I better
smoke a cigarette before I go out."

I was amazed! What a totally
wonderful, extraordinary expression of love between two people. I
was overjoyed that we were free
enough to do it.

The author and Robert Rauschenberg
kissing in a SoHo stairwell, early 1970s

ON TUESDAY, NOVEMBER 22, Steve Paxton left New York for two
weeks, for Thanksgiving and work. Finally, he was gone. The
night he left was the first time Bob and I slept all night in Bob's
bed in his apartment on Lafayette Street. What a joy! Sleeping
and waking with someone you love! We were together on Tuesday
and Wednesday; on Thursday I went to my family in Roslyn
Heights for Thanksgiving. Bob had a quiet Thanksgiving with a
few friends. By Friday night I was back in his bed.

The next day, he flew to L.A. to work on prints for the first time
at a new press called Gemini Gel. When he left, I suddenly had
time to tend to myself. We had been lovers for almost two months,
and to say that it had been stressful balancing a triangulation
was an understatement. My nerves were a wreck.

I took a breather, saw friends, and worked on "Capsule," one of two long poems I wrote in 1966. The other was "Freaked," and both were collages of found images. I had been doing the collage poems for two years, but being with Bob on a daily basis—and seeing how his mind worked, how he chose images and what he left out—greatly influenced my own work. Although my poems and Bob's work were completely different, I allowed my mind to work as Bob's did, trusting my intuition, letting clarity emerge, waiting for the display of illusory images to arise in empty space. His mind inspired mine. And when you sleep with someone, you sleep with your heads touching, and your chests and hearts touching each other all night, a blissful union of the minds.

I assessed what had happened. I was overjoyed at my good fortune of being with Bob, and deeply saddened by Steve. His grasping poisoned my joy, my grasping poisoned my mind more. I could not help but think that the nature of my union with Bob was tainted by the karmic injury to Steve, and was a bad omen. Generally, in situations like this, all three people end up suffering.

When Bob returned to New York the following Saturday, he called from JFK at about 6:00 p.m. "How ya doing?" Having been apart for a week, we longed to see each other. In an incredibly sensual voice, he said, "John, please, can you come over?"

A half hour later, I walked over to Lafayette Street. A taxi took about forty minutes to come in from the airport. I unlocked the door, walked up the five steps to the hall. The house was dark and empty. I was about to go toward the stairs and look for the light switch, when out of the blackness of the studio came a figure walking toward me. I froze.

"Hi, John!" said Brice Marden, appearing from the darkness. I saw his face in the slight window light from the street.

"Hi, Brice!"

"I stopped by to pick something up I've been working on here while Bob was away."

Brice Marden was an unknown twenty-eight-year-old artist who had recently started working as Bob's studio assistant. His first job had been to fold Steve Paxton's plastic tunnel, a prop for *9 Evenings*, but since Bob wasn't working much in the studio, Brice mostly swept and washed the floors and did errands.

At that very moment, still in the blackness, we heard a key in the front door, and Bob entered. "Hi!" We kissed and hugged, happy to see each other. "Hi, Brice! Let's turn on some lights."

We were about to go upstairs when Brice said in a determined voice, "Bob, I have been working here for a week. I have had a breakthrough. Can I show you a painting?"

"Yes," said Bob, smiling, as he loved painting.

Brice's being here was a setup. He had lain in wait for Bob. A bit pushy, I thought with annoyance.

Brice disappeared for a second around the corner in the studio darkness, then returned with a painting. It was a twenty-inch canvas painted gray. It was the first monochrome gray painting he did. "Encaustic," Brice said, referring to the mixture of wax and oil paint that he had used to give the surface a sheen.

"Wow!" said Bob. "That's beautiful!"

"You see why I think I had a breakthrough," said Brice. He had done oil paintings in 1962 and '63 that were two colors, light gray and dark gray, in various shapes and configurations. The breakthrough was one gray color in encaustic on one canvas.

"My white paintings, I did a long time ago," said Bob.

"I thought of them," said Brice. Bob really appreciated what Brice had done, and there was a brief moment of bliss between two artists. They talked a little more, and my mind wandered.

"Brice, it's great," I said, but I saw nothing, a gray painting—it could have been an art student's failed effort. I was still taken with bright Pop style. I had no idea that it was the seminal moment that would propel Brice Marden to the superstardom of a great painter.

We went upstairs to the kitchen. "Let's have a drink," said Bob. I got the glasses and ice, and made us a Jack Daniel's. Brice had a beer. Bob was happy to be back home in his kitchen, with its big black cast-iron stove; this place was the center of his life.

"Helen has been quite sick," said Brice, worried. "It has been going on for some time, but got worse while you were away. She was bleeding. She's at St. Vincent's."

"Sorry to hear it," said Bob.

Helen Harrington, Brice's beautiful girlfriend, had uterine cysts. "I had another big breakthrough while you were away. The painting was one," said Brice, "and the other is that I love Helen. How much I love Helen! She is more than the center of my life. It was shocking when I realized how much I love her."

"I'm so glad!" said Bob.

"I have asked her to marry me," said Brice.

"Congratulations!" said Bob. We appreciated his new level of commitment. We were all in love. I took it as a good omen.

Brice had accomplished what he wanted, got the cue, and said good night.

Bob and I flung together like magnets, kissed, and hugged. Letting our bodies and minds rest together, without thoughts.

We went downstairs to Bob's bedroom, took our clothes off quickly, and jumped into each other's warm arms, hot bodies, delicious smells, and luxurious kissing tongues. I got the Vaseline and poppers.

We sixty-nined, and rimmed each other, and then fucked. I loved fucking Bob, endlessly and tirelessly, sucking on poppers. I introduced Bob to fucking. With Steve, he didn't get fucked. With Jasper, I don't know what they did—Bob never talked about Jasper. With Cy, I imagine Bob fucked him. Bob still had a fundamental redneck imprint and was a little uptight. I loved fucking, and Bob became addicted to it, opened his soft, silken, voluptuous asshole, appreciating the extreme pleasure that occurred with carefully manipulated friction on the tissues at the moment of orgasm.

Bob was always great sex. When two people have the deep illusion of loving each other and opening their hearts profoundly, and they have great sex—a rare coincidence—they experience brief moments of profound bliss.

The next morning, over a breakfast of coffee, croissants, pain au chocolat left by Dorothea Rockburne, and cigarettes, I said to Bob, "Tell me about Los Angeles. What happened?"

"I worked with a great guy, Sidney Felsen, a master printer, and we did good!" Bob was very happy. "I made a breakthrough." He laughed. "They have these big stones, and they had just gotten them from Iowa. There was one very big stone, and I made the biggest print ever in the world."

"Wow! Congratulations!" I said. "Bigger than whenever, the eighteenth century?"

"The biggest in the world," said Bob. "It was the stone. It's very rare to get a stone that size. Sid had just gotten them from a nineteenth-century city hall that was being taken down. According to Sid, these kinds of stones are the very best for printing, and the most perfect he had ever seen, and the largest stones he ever worked with, and we used them for the first time."

"An amazingly fortunate circumstance!"

"I made an X-ray of my whole body," said Bob, "and put the X-ray on the stone, life-sized. Do you want to see it?"

We went downstairs to the second-floor front print room. Bob opened the tube he had brought back and took out a magnificent lithograph. "I call it *Booster*."

On the thick paper was the image of Bob's skeleton, even a little of the thick muscle of his dick appeared faintly—the classic, perfect, Rauschenberg image.

"Wow, Bob, it is so beautiful!" I had a physical feeling of joy in the presence of the work, Bob himself, and his unstoppable creative flow. Everything his mind touched, everything he took in with his eyes, entered a stream of consciousness and turned miraculously into great art, gold. A fecund cornucopia spewing great work, formally exacting and tender.

"John, I did this for you. I was thinking of you when I did it. I did it because of you."

"Bob, thanks!"

"It's a trial proof. I'll give you one when it's done."

"Bob, thanks!" It was very exciting. Bob was making the biggest print, breaking boundaries at this very moment, and the work itself displayed all his great qualities, all the subtleties of shape and shadow. And he was giving me one!

When the *Booster* print was finished six months later, Bob gave it to me, but I left it in the house to be sent to the framer, which was never done. A year later, when Bob and I were breaking up, I did not demean myself to ask for it. False pride and a mistake! I would have loved to have it, but I didn't want any implication that I was in it for material gain. I was the whore with the golden heart, no money, and I gave double. I was there only because I loved Bob's body and mind.

We went upstairs and had another coffee, this time with bread and jam and orange juice, and smoked more cigarettes. "I stayed with Stan and Elyse Grinstein. Stan is rich, and is Sid's partner at Gemini Gel. They live in a house in Brentwood, a big bourgeois house made out of fieldstone, like staying with a rich dentist, only bigger."

Stan owned a company that manufactured forklift equipment. He and Elyse were art collectors and patrons, founders of the Los Angeles County Museum.

"The best part," Bob continued, "was that down the street was Shirley Temple's house from the nineteen thirties. Wow!"

Sunday was my thirtieth birthday, and I had woken up with Bob. Sleeping with him all night for three nights was the best birthday gift in the world. Steve was coming back the next day, so it would stop; but I was still at the stage in my relationship with Bob where I did not allow one negative thought to arise in my mind, because negative thoughts were poison, and I was so in love with Bob, so overjoyed.

ON A SATURDAY NIGHT a few weeks later, Jill and Lucinda gave a Christmas party at 119 Bowery. Lucinda had just put in a gorgeous, perfect floor to dance on—a symbol of their love affair, a jewel in an otherwise shabby loft building—and obviously didn't want dirty shoes on it. So Jill asked their upstairs neighbor, Les Levine, if they could have a Christmas party in his loft instead.

Jill invited Bob, and surprisingly, Bob accepted. Bob went to parties only when he absolutely had to, and when he would be treated as royalty, all attention focused on him. He picked me up at eight. I gritted my teeth for the ordeal, as I would have much preferred staying home in bed with him.

We got there early, and Jill gave us some mulled wine and we talked with Les Levine. And then Jasper Johns arrived. Bob and Jasper had broken up five years before, when Bob and Steve became lovers, and Jasper never forgave Bob. It was an electrifying moment, since they rarely saw each other. Bob went up to Jasper. They shook hands, laughed awkwardly, exchanged a few words. Jasper graciously turned back to the choreographer Simone Forti, with whom he was talking. Bob and I talked with Les in a huddle, which made us feel safe.

Then Steve appeared, said hello to everyone, making a circle around. He nodded to Jasper, who barely nodded back. Steve looked cheerful and happy, but since things were difficult for him, I wondered what was below the surface. He was still living with Bob, and dependent on him, and he knew how involved Bob had become with me. I thought about the suffering and the confusion Steve must be feeling about his life. He moved among the people like a brilliant dancer making a guest appearance, and then departed from the stage.

I went to the toilet, then got myself another drink. I passed Jasper, who looked right at me. I stopped, and we talked. I had first met Jasper in 1962, when he was radiantly beautiful; over the years since, we had met a few times at parties. Jasper was very smart and challenging to talk to—he never allowed a sloppy thought, didn't let you get away with anything. He could often be quite cruel. Jasper had a great devotion to poetry and poets.

"Ted Berrigan showed me your collaboration with Frank O'Hara," I said. "Well done!"

Jasper laughed approvingly; I was okay. We talked, very much engrossed in each other. Then, from behind me, I heard Bob's loud voice with his mean Texan drawl: "Jap, what are you trying to do, steal my boyfriend?"

I turned red, froze, laughed, and backed away, and Bob joined me.

Two years later, Jasper Johns and I would become lovers.

CHRISTMAS EVE 1966 was wonderful. Bob and I spent the afternoon at 222, then crunched through two inches of dry snow to Lafayette Street to exchange presents that evening. He gave me two small brown paper bags.

In one were three small works of art, each two inches square, of his classic images. Bob had made these with his transfer technique, using alcohol to transfer magazine images onto paper. He had made about twenty of them, giving them to friends as Christmas presents. Mine were very beautiful. In the other brown paper bag was a sprig of fresh holly with red berries, and two Band-Aids attached to the two edges of the bag. I still have them in my archive.

I had several gifts for Bob. "This is the secret present," I said. "You mustn't show it to anyone."

Bob opened the blue paper and white tissue paper, and there was a gold wedding ring. I had bought it in the same pawn shop on the Bowery where I purchased the ring for Andy. Bob's was an old, thick, yellow-gold men's wedding band for a big finger like a big dick, and very sexy. Bob gasped. "I love it." He held it to his chest, squeezed tightly, and looked at me with tears in his eyes, so unlike Andy's half-frightened giggle. "Thank you," he said, and we kissed.

We went upstairs to the kitchen and had a drink, and over the hours many people came: Steve Paxton and Billy Klüver; Yvonne Rainer and Bob Morris; Bob's fifteen-year-old son, Christopher, who lived with his mother but often dropped by. I lost Bob in the dense cigarette smoke and loud talking.

ON DECEMBER 29, the phone rang, and it was Ted Berrigan. "John, I'm really happy you're giving a New Year's Eve party. What time should I come? Can I bring anything?"

"What?"

"When I heard you were giving a New Year's Eve party, I thought that it was the best news," said Ted. "And you have the biggest place."

"Ted, I'm not giving a New Year's party. I don't know anything about it."

"Now, who did I hear it from?" said Ted, who was famous for just that, inventing a party, asking if he could come over, then phoning twenty people and inviting them. He had done it to me before. Speed was Ted's drug of choice.

But why not! And so I gave a New Year's Eve party (the first in what would become an enduring tradition) for about fifty people, including Bill Berkson, Peter Schjeldahl, Ron and Patty Padgett, Joe Brainard, Aram Saroyan, the seventeen-year-old Jim Carroll, Anne Waldman, Bernadette Mayer—what was the second-generation New York school of poets. I bought lots of wine and we drank it all, and smoked joint after joint. These poets were my friends and peer group. It was good that Bob didn't come.

BOB BECAME the love of my life. I had never loved anyone more, in such an intense way, fulfilling both physically and mentally.

The union of the body and mind made our connection spiritual. We were artist and poet, he used found images in art, and I wrote poems using found words, shaping the images and collage. It seemed like our minds were in sync and flowed compatibly—the right person at the right time.

Looking back, our love affair had less to do with Bob, and more to do with me. Bob was just attracted to my sexual energy, and any suffering I caused myself was my own fault. Bob was enormously self-centered, egomaniacal, generating great magnetizing power; like all superstars, he fed off and exploited everybody around him. Loving Bob was loving a beautiful monster, and when the monster loves you back, obsessively, obviously, it is okay. I was useful to Bob at that moment in his life, but he was ruthless, and I knew it.

I was at the peak of my sexuality. The many LSD trips I had taken the year before with Brion Gysin had enabled me to begin the process of training my mind, offering glimpses into the mind's powerful nature. I was writing some of my best poems. I was completely mature, performing perfectly at my best. I had met Bob, a fabulous lover, one of the greatest artists in the world, whose work dovetailed with my own. He was rich, famous, and beautiful. These were all good reasons to abandon myself to love and attachment.

It became less about Bob, and more about my feelings and emotions, which set me up to be Bob's victim. There was no blame. Somehow, like everything in my life so far, I knew deep down it would not last. I was heading for a car crash.

On January 20, Steve left to teach a ten-day dance workshop in North Carolina. Wonderfully, Bob and I were spending all night together again. Bob was in his sexual prime as a mature man, newly experimenting with me. I don't think he ever had so many orgasms, or felt such excruciating pleasure. He learned to relax and appreciate it. My heart was completely open, Bob's heart was completely open, and it seemed a great blessing.

I loved Bob's ass, and loved to fuck it endlessly, tirelessly, and

Bob loved to be fucked insatiably. When I was inside him, some indescribable energy, some sort of bliss passed between us. We collapsed in each other's arms and went to sleep. We had sex two or three times a day, every day when we could.

Two months later in March, we got up one morning, and Bob was in the bathroom, looking at his tits in the mirror. "Look what you've done to me!" I loved playing with Bob's nipples, squeezing them harder and harder, which he really liked.

"They are gorgeous," I said. "They are hog tits. You should be proud of them." When Bob and I met, he had tiny nipples, but over the months his nipples had grown quite large.

"I have to keep my shirt on," said Bob. "What am I going to do this summer?"

I USED GAY IMAGES in my poems, which amused Bob, but he didn't use them in his work. I was annoyed by all the gay artists— Bob, Andy Warhol, Jasper Johns, and others—who never allowed themselves to use gay images in their art, because they did not want to ruin their careers or compromise their ability to make money in a homophobic world. But I also understood. They mostly came from poor families, and I was from the upper middle class, which gave me the privilege to do what I wanted. And poets have nothing to lose, anyway. William Burroughs's and Allen Ginsberg's liberating use of gay images had inspired me in the 1950s. It became my determination and heroic aspiration to take homoeroticism to another level in my work. Perhaps I did it a little too much. In my love affair with Bob, sex was very important, and sexual energy was interwoven in the daily process of making art and poems. It was my life, and I wrote about it.

Bob had an unspoken rule that no one was allowed to write about his being gay, under the threat of excommunication and wrath of hell, and nobody did. I understand why. Bob and his generation grew up in the 1950s with the extreme homophobia of the Abstract painters. Gay was the kiss of death. His use of heterosexual images was self-serving. Of course, he was a great artist and artists are allowed to do whatever they want. Just as he was allowed not to talk about being gay, I am allowed to describe it in detail.

In September 1965, I had written "Pornographic Poem," using excerpts from a mimeographed erotic story that I don't know how I had gotten my hands on:

Seven Cuban
army officers
in exile
were at me
all night.
Tall,
sleek,
slender
Spanish types
with smooth dark
muscular bodies
and hair
like wet coal
on their heads
and between their legs.
I lost count
of the times
I was fucked
by them
in every conceivable
position.
At one point
they stood
around me
in a circle
and I had
to crawl

from one crotch
to another
sucking
on each cock
until it was hard.
When I got all
seven up
I shivered
looking up
at those erect pricks
all different
lengths
and widths
and knowing
that each one
was going up
my ass hole.
Everyone
of them
came
at least twice
and some three times.
Once they put me
on the bed
kneeling,
one fucked me
in the behind,
another
in the mouth,
while I jacked off
one
with each hand
and two
of the others
rubbed

their peckers
on my bare feet
waiting
their turns
to get
into my can.
Just when I thought
they were all spent
two of them
got together
and fucked me
at once.
The positions
we were in
were crazy
but with two
big fat
Cuban cocks
up my ass
at one time
I was
in paradise.

It was a groundbreaking poem, using a pornographic image as a readymade, as an ordinary metaphor, as a found poem. Nobody had done that before. Ted Berrigan published it in *C*, a mimeographed Lower East Side magazine, which he handed out to everybody for free. "Pornographic Poem" became a cause célèbre in the fall of 1965. The U.S. Supreme Court had ruled Henry Miller's *Tropic of Cancer* to be non-obscene a year earlier, but *Naked Lunch*, another banned book, was still in the midst of an appeal to the Massachussets Supreme Court. "Pornographic Poem" was admired by all the poets on the Lower East Side, Andy and the Pop artists, and the art world.

In 1970, Ron Padgett included "Pornographic Poem" in *An*

Anthology of the New York School of Poets, published by Random House. Good fortune made it a seminal poem, but I also thought of "Pornographic Poem" as a guerrilla tactic. Being included alongside old-guard poets like Frank O'Hara and John Ashbery, I felt I had infiltrated the enemy world, where I could radically change it, expand consciousness, and liberate the mind.

Since late 1965, I had been recording poet and artist friends reading the two-minute poem. They would come to 222 Bowery; I would serve tea, and then I would record them. There was a remarkable freshness in reading a found image, and in this case, each recording reflected clearly and purely the sexuality of the person reading it. Peter Schjeldahl's reading was full of gawky, sexual energy. Henry Geldzahler's reading was smooth as silk. Patty Oldenburg, a totally liberated woman, gave a nervous reading. Nena von Schlebrugge, a fashion model and the former wife of Timothy Leary, gave a very sensual, elegant reading. Yvonne Rainer gave a strong and balanced reading, like a dance. Brice Marden's and Helen Harrington's readings were tight and straight. Lee Crabtree, a musician who later committed suicide, gave a breathless, trembling reading. Anne Ware from the Ann Arbor Theater Company gave an actor's reading. The artist Alan Saret's reading was as thin and hard as a line drawing.

I made sound compositions from each reading, laying down two tracks, one on each track of the stereo tape recorder, slightly off sync. The repetition created a rhythm and a beat, and brought out the musical qualities inherent in the words and the person's voice. The emotional vulnerability of each reader, the hidden sexual nuances, each person's sexual hang-ups and their openness were magnified into musical phrases. The piece was twelve voices in succession. It really worked, which made me very happy.

I also asked Bob to read the poem, and he agreed. As November 1966 passed to January 1967, I asked him several times, but it was never the right time. At the end of January, he and I had been drinking heavily for days—dinners in the house, going out to parties, drinking to five in the morning every night. One day we woke up about one-thirty in the afternoon with enormous hangovers. We went up to the kitchen, had coffee, and both said, "Let's go back to bed!" We spent the afternoon submerged in a semiunconscious, underwater world of sex and sleep, with the weight of the hangovers and bliss of our bodies.

About five o'clock, we got up, went to the kitchen, and had coffee and snacks. He had to go out for a fund-raising dinner, so we went back to bed for one final half hour.

We got up again and were wide-awake. We walked into the front print room. I saw the Wollenberg tape recorder and said, "Bob, one of these days you have to record 'Pornographic Poem.'"

He smiled, nodded his head, and said softly, "Now."

"What?" I said. "You mean, now?"

"Yes," said Bob happily.

I felt a rush of adrenaline. Although I had been asking him for weeks, I couldn't quite believe it was going to happen.

Bob read the poem brilliantly. It took two minutes. It was a gay pornographic poem, and we had been fucking all day. Bob's voice was incredibly sensuous, oozing with sexuality and pleasure, deep, thick, wet, throaty resonances from the residue of bliss.

"Bob, what a great performance—thank you!"

We hugged and kissed; and now he was a little late.

IN APRIL 1967, I released *Raspberry & Pornographic Poem* in a tape edition; it was a reel-to-reel quarter-inch tape in a square box. Les Levine designed the cover, a collage of close-up photos of my face in different sizes, printed in bright red, as well as the liner notes on the back cover. My first rock 'n' roll album cover! I assembled it at 222 Bowery, duplicated the tapes on two reel-to-reel tape recorders, and pasted the printed covers on the boxes. It was a Giorno Poetry Systems project, a limited edition. I sold twelve, gave twelve to friends, and kept ten for the archive. It was a pleasure seeing it float around Bob's house from floor to floor and room to room that spring. It had an audience of a few hundred people in the poetry and art worlds, and they all liked it.

In December 1967, it was released as an LP, with "Pornographic Poem" on side 1 and "Raspberry" on side 2, funded by the artist Dorothy Ioanonne's wealthy husband. We pressed one thousand albums. Les did a poster, we did PR, and we sold a few hundred LPs, giving away about three hundred.

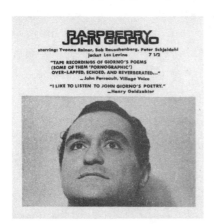

Yvonne Rainer really liked "Pornographic Poem" and chose three of the readings—Bob Rauschenberg's, Peter Schjeldahl's, and her own—for the soundtrack of a dance she did at the Brooklyn Academy of Music in 1968.

Raspberry

BEFORE THE RECORDING of "Pornographic Poem," I stumbled into another dilemma with Bob over gay content in art. This time, the tension started with my work and ended with his.

Almost a year before, in his apartment on East Eleventh Street, Peter Schjeldahl—friend, poet, and editor of the Lower East Side's seminal *Mother Magazine* and Mother Press—had offered to publish my first book of poems. I was taken by surprise and overjoyed. I was a poet who thought a poem could take many forms—that poetry was the expression of ultimate wisdom. I did not belong directly to the literary lineages of the New York school of poets or the Beats, lyrical poetry or modernism; as a result, I was an underdog. They all tolerated me, were amused, but didn't take me seriously, and were jealous because I was becoming somewhat famous. "Peter, I can't believe it!"

"I love your work. You are the greatest!" Peter, tall and thin, from Minnesota, of Scandinavian descent, had a delightful awkwardness that always reminded me of Ichabod Crane.

Over the next months, I put together the book, *Poems by John Giorno*, half from *The American Book of the Dead*, an unpublished book of poems from 1962 to 1964, and the other half poems from 1966 to 1967, including "Leather," "Outlaw," "Paratrooper," "Janitor," "Alone on a Beam," "She Tasted Death," "Easy to Grow," "Pornographic Poem," "Problems," and "Head." I could really see how my work had developed over the past five years.

In early October, Peter asked, "John, who do you want to do your book cover? You know, artists do poets' covers."

"I don't know." I hadn't thought about it.

"What about Andy Warhol?" said Peter. "Why don't you ask Andy?"

I was horrified. It was the curse of my life: people wanting me because they wanted something from Andy. I was finished with Andy, I didn't want to ask him to do anything, and I was Bob Rauschenberg's lover. How embarrassing!

"I don't know," I replied.

"Think about it," said Peter. Over the weeks, I saw Peter at readings, parties, and meetings about the book. He said again and again, "Have you asked Andy?"

It was like a toothache. There was no way out. I reluctantly bit the bullet and telephoned Andy.

"Yes! I'll do it," said Andy, laughing happily. "Let me think about it."

A while later, Peter asked again, "Have you spoken to Andy about the cover?" I called Andy, and he was still thinking about it.

In early November, Andy called, and said, "I have an idea for your cover. A condom laminated between two sheets of plastic, and you write the name on it."

"Andy, what a great idea!" I completely trusted Andy; all of his ideas were great. "It's brilliant."

"Yes, I know."

I told Peter, and he said, "Wow! That's amazing! Let me check out the costs."

Another time on the phone with Andy, I asked, "New condoms, or used ones? We'll need a lot, maybe from the street, isn't that hot?"

"Oh!" said Andy in a low drawl.

"Yes, scumbags from the street." I was stoned on speed and pot, and the idea seemed pure and sexual.

But the cost of laminating a one-thousand-plus print run was too much.

As an alternative, Andy proposed on the phone, "Let me take some photos of you with a condom."

We made a date, and I knew from the beginning it was an excuse for Andy to suck my dick, and the photos probably wouldn't be usable. It was a long shot, but I wasn't sexually exclusive with Bob, and I was a pragmatist: anything for a great book cover. I went to the Factory at nine at night when everybody was gone, and we did the shoot.

Andy was happy being with me and I was happy to see him again, and for something real, a shoot. In a corner, we started by doing relaxed, sexy poses with a condom, holding the packet up like in a straight magazine ad, every pose possible. Then came the inevitable: I took out my dick, and said, "Andy, suck it, and get it hard."

"Oh, John!" That was just what he wanted to hear. He was down on his knees sucking. He got my dick hard, I put on a condom, and he took photos. He sucked it again with the condom on, and took more photos. I sniffed poppers to try to enhance it. I jerked off in the condom as he took pictures.

I don't think Andy had sex often, and maybe not at all during this time, and sex was always traumatic for him. His head was shaking, his forehead was sweating (I remembered to be careful of the wig), his body and his hands trembled. The Nikon shook in his hands as he tried to focus, eyeglasses disheveled, stumbling around in the dim light, almost having a nervous breakdown, taking photos of a condom on a hard, half-hard, soft dick.

The passion between us was gone, the sex was not great, but it was still a pleasure. There was a sweetness in seeing Andy overcome. We still loved each other, despite how completely our lives had changed. It was a funny, wonderful moment together.

A week later, I called Andy. "How are the photos?"

"I don't know," said Andy.

"You mean not right for the book cover."

"Yes."

"That's okay. I'll do something else. Andy, thank you!" What a relief! My dick would not be memorialized on the cover of my book.

Forty-six years later, the Andy Warhol Museum in Pittsburgh dug up two of the condom photos from their archive and published them in a show catalogue. In one photo, I'm holding up a condom

like in a magazine ad; in the second, I'm unrolling a condom at my crotch with my pants on. I am wearing a new white button-down shirt with thin blue stripes that Bob had just bought me.

The author holding a condom, photographed by Andy Warhol

IN MID-DECEMBER 1966, Peter Schjeldahl said, "John, I have a great idea for the cover. Bob Rauschenberg."

"What?" I was more horrified.

"Could Bob do your book cover? I'm sure he would really like to."

"I don't know! Let me think about it." I worried that it would seem I was exploiting my relationship with him to further my career. In the end, I hadn't really minded asking Andy. We were in the past. But Bob was different. I did not want that negativity to sully our love, and my poems did not need it. At the same time, I was thinking, Yes, what a totally amazing cover it would be.

In January, Peter reminded me several times to ask Bob, but I didn't do it. I didn't want to hustle him. One day Peter said, "I'll come over and ask him for you."

"I'll do it. I promise." I waited for the right time. Bob and I were alone in the kitchen, drinking bourbon, smoking joints, and feeling good, and I blurted it out, like jumping into cold water. I explained how Peter was doing a book of my poems, and the Andy story. "Would you do the front cover of my poems? It's Peter's idea." My throat was constricted, I could barely say the words, and I was sweating and shaking.

"Yes," said Bob lovingly, with a big smile on his face. "I would love to do your book cover."

"Thank you!" I said with a rush of pleasure at his happy, instantaneous response, an expression of love. I was awed by the thought of a work of art by Robert Rauschenberg being on the cover of my book of poems.

In early February I gave Peter the final manuscript. It was typeset, we proofread it, and the layout and pasteup were done. Peter kept nudging me over the weeks to ask Bob for the art. On occasion, I gently reminded him. Les Levine did the frontispiece collage of close-up photos, and we were ready to print.

One day Bob said, "I have something for you." He had done it. The cover was red and orange-red. It featured the big breasts of a woman, a white astronaut with parachute from above, the profile torso of a swimmer with a soft dick, and a transfer photo of a frontal dick with crayon scribbles and patches of pale orange paint. It was dazzlingly beautiful.

The images in Bob's work were often secret signs and magical messages. Here's how I interpreted the cover: the woman's breasts were my playing hard with Bob's tits, and his nipples having gotten so big. The dick in the profile was about the size of Bob's dick soft, a generous offering from him. The luscious red iris flower was Bob's asshole. The parachute and astronaut, a recurring image in his work, were us in transcendent bliss. Using male nudity and sexuality was a breakthrough for Bob, someone who still had the residue of Texas fundamentalists. The red cover was our secret gay love.

My book came out in April 1967. The downtown poets, the second-generation New York school of poets, very much appreciated the poetry, arranged just the way I wanted. And the painters, sculptors, and art world were in awe of the cover.

The cover of *Poems*,
designed by Robert Rauschenberg

ON OCCASION, Bob and I talked about LSD. I had had profound experiences on my first trips with Brion Gysin. In the mid-1960s, before it became a sex and party drug, LSD was very pure, and people took it with respect for the sacred. For me, it offered my first glimpse of the true nature of mind, experiencing, for an instant, what I had only read about in books. LSD was important to the culture, and so Bob was thinking about trying it.

At about eleven on a Tuesday morning in January, we were having coffee, Steve was out of town for the ten-day dance workshop, and I was getting ready to go back to 222 Bowery and work on poems. Bob said, out of the blue, "I would like to take some LSD. What about you?"

"What?" I said stunned, realizing my good fortune. "Yes! What a great idea! . . . You know I have some . . . When?"

Bob had seemed afraid of LSD when we first talked about it, so I hadn't pressed. LSD was very powerful and could be difficult for the mind, and I did not want it to jeopardize our relationship. That he was smoking joints had been a breakthrough; now, that he wanted to take LSD was heroic.

"Tonight," said Bob. "Now that Steve's away, we have an opportunity."

"Yes!" I was very pleased to hear Bob say that, to bring up our complicated relationship. During all of it, nobody talked about how we were feeling, that I might be suffering, that Steve was suffering. It was all centered on how Bob felt.

I came back to Lafayette Street at seven that evening. We each took a tiny, barrel-shaped, bright orange pill. We began by breaking them in two, and only taking a half, to be cautious. But as we started getting high, Bob said, "Let's take the whole thing."

The acid took about twenty minutes to begin working. I felt a very pleasant tingling in my blood and mind. After forty minutes we were pretty high, and in one hour, completely. The next two hours of an LSD trip were the most important, the peak. I was always careful of how I used the time, what I did with my mind, the circumstance and where I was. The drug, among other things, numbed nerve ends, allowing the natural clarity of the mind to flow free.

Bob and I hugged and kissed, just sitting in the kitchen, reveling in the miraculous display of each other, the expanding joyousness.

At one hour and fifteen minutes, the doorbell rang. It was Billy Klüver coming to visit. Bob made him a drink, and they talked and talked, about a fund-raising event for Experiments in Art and Technology, an organization they were starting, inspired by *9 Evenings* and devoted to artist-engineer collaboration. Then Dorothea Rockburne arrived and went over details of running the kitchen. Soon after, Alex Hay came, got that Bob and I were on something, and smiled. For everybody but us, it was just a normal night.

But for me, the worst had happened. My head was reeling; the warp and woof of reality was pulling apart, and I had to act normal. It was before I became a Tibetan Buddhist meditation practitioner, but things arise out of necessity, and out of desperation, I practiced what I would later call meditation, abiding in patience, watching the breath flow in and out, letting the mind rest for brief moments, not following thoughts. I did not want to be with these people, I just wanted to be with Bob. It was my fault, and my obscured mind could not relax and accept the guests as a beautiful accompaniment. Instead, I heard their talk as nails on a blackboard.

Finally, they all left. "Wow! What happened?"

"Give me a hug," said Bob. We were exhausted and fell into each other's arms, hugged, and kissed.

"Let's go downstairs."

I do not know what happened to Bob on his first, and maybe only, LSD trip. For me, some trips were full of color display and fabulous hallucinations—but not this one, maybe because of the strain of having to socialize in the kitchen.

We went down to bed and made love, vast and open. We fell asleep. Half the LSD trip happened in our dreams, and I didn't remember them.

IN EARLY FEBRUARY, Bob began a new sculpture called *Revolver*, working again with an engineer.

The sculpture consisted of five clear plastic disks, each six feet in diameter and one inch thick, silk-screened with images, sitting vertical in a cradle made of aluminum on rubber belts, which were moved on wheels, like tank tires. There was a handheld control panel, and each plastic disk could be rotated at different speeds. The viewer looked at and through the disks, and manipulated them, moving them forward and backward, stopping to look at new configurations as the images changed in relationship to one another. Illusions moving through space, seen through other illusions, in the vast universe of the mind.

In the beginning, *Revolver* was filled with positive energy, and was an aspiring work of art. Bob silk-screened the plastic disks in the rear loft at Lafayette Street. They were gorgeous. After the design was worked out with engineers, it was then fabricated.

In early March, as the pieces arrived and were put together, the trouble began. The sound of the motors turning the disks was like the sound of a dentist's saw grinding teeth. The handheld control panel was an ugly clunker, with one-inch-thick cables going to the motor drive. The motors broke down all the time; one or two didn't work at all or would move in only one direction. Another problem was the enormously heavy weight of the plastic disks on the rubber belts and small wheels. It was 1967, but they used 1950s technology, post–World War II hardware, which was all that was available. This was just before transistorized, lightweight materials were invented.

Bob had big problems getting it to work, but one of his best qualities was perseverance. Seeing him work with the difficulties that arose, the obstacles that came daily—with patience and diligence, and a commitment to allow the process of art to arise naturally—was an important teaching for me.

He worked on the piece with Billy Klüver and an engineer named Fred Waldhauer, who was helped by Julie Martin. By late spring, *Revolver* was more or less finished, or as good as it would ever get. The critics said, "Is it art, or a new hunk of junk?"

I loved the piece. We never talked about it, but it has always seemed to me like a result of his LSD trip. His classic images seen in another dimension, as the mind sees the unreal nature of phenomena. Veils of illusion revolving in space.

I was happy it was a collaboration of art, drugs, and technology, and that he had risked it.

But I was also worried. *Revolver* was a noble failure, something that was born of a great, pure aspiration, took a lot of work, and fell short in the execution. I feared that somehow it might have an effect on our relationship or, just as bad, was a reflection of it.

ONE AFTERNOON, I was on the third floor of Bob's place on Lafayette Street, talking to Susan Hartnett. In the kitchen, Deborah Hay and Bob were having a meeting about performances she was organizing. "Why don't we ask John to do a piece?" I overheard Debbie say.

"Yes, why not!" said Bob.

What did that mean? My adrenaline started running. A few minutes later, in the kitchen, Debbie asked, "John, we're organizing performances at the School of Visual Arts, and we would like to invite you to do a piece."

"Yes, I would be delighted to," I said, disguising my panic attack.

I had only performed my work live once before—in 1962, at a reading on Fourteenth Street for *C* magazine, which had published two of my poems. At the event, Ted Berrigan had announced, "And the next poet is John Giorno." He had not told me I was going to read, he assumed I knew. I was taken by surprise; I had not rehearsed. I got up and began to read, my hands and legs shaking, my body turning to jelly, trembling and pouring sweat. But my voice was surprisingly loud, as I said each word clearly and precisely. The poems were two explosions of energy, and when I was done, I sat down. I had shocked myself. What happened?

Since then, I hadn't been asked to do any more readings. I had concentrated my efforts on writing poems as well as on developing and evolving a new style using found images. And after my success with *Subway Sound* at the 1965 Biennial at the Musée d'Art Moderne in Paris, I had continued to experiment with and develop the sound poems. The School of Visual Arts was to be my first performance/installation, engaging a live audience with the sound poems—it was a big challenge.

Les Levine designed a dark brown poster with a photo of the enlarged head of his cat. Bob, Steve Reich, Trisha Brown, Debbie, and others performed. And Debbie asked me to be in her piece as a non-dancer dancer. She was revolutionary in introducing pedestrian movement in dance, a democracy of ideas and bodies, and a mix of sense and non-sense.

And then there was my piece. I chose an early version of "Pornographic Poem," featuring only three readers: Yvonne Rainer, Peter Schjeldahl, and Bob. I also included sound poems I had made with tape loops, as well as overlaying tracks recorded using two tape recorders at 222 Bowery. These were many-layered sound compositions of my poems "Chromosome," "She Tasted Death," "Outlaw," and "Leather."

I had a second set of speakers placed halfway down each side of the auditorium, in an effort to make the sound completely fill the space. On the right and left sides of the stage, I had two spotlights, which I had instructed volunteer operators to move slowly over the audience, pausing to highlight people in the passing beam. The idea was to spotlight people in the audience, rather than the performer. I had hoped that the audience would hear the words with clarity, the way the performer feels when performing in the blinding light of the spotlight, eliminating everything but the sound of the words and the light. And every single person in the audience was the star.

The actual effect was the opposite. People felt uncomfortable

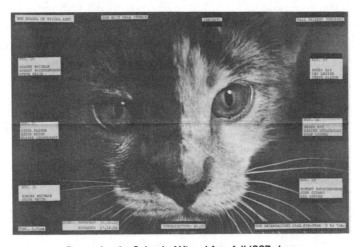

Poster for the School of Visual Arts fall 1967 show

JOHN GIORNO

when the spotlight was on them, and it made them hear less, as they were thinking about their discomfort. It was a noble failure, like Bob's *Revolver*. But just as Bob persevered through challenges, so would I. In the effort to present poetry in a new way, I was just beginning.

LOOKING FOR MOMENTUM after the SVA show, Les spoke with Irving Sandler, the director of art education at New York University, about showing his videos at the Loeb Student Center. Irving suggested that Les do it with me, with a performance of my sound poems.

I was taken by surprise, and said to Les, "Why not!"

"Oh, John, that's wonderful," replied Les, and we talked some more. Then he said, "Oh, something else, Irving asked if Bob Rauschenberg would do something with us, too."

I had a flash of anger. Obviously, it was Les's idea to exploit my relationship with Bob. I had known Irving since 1962, and he liked me, but as a devotee of the New York school of poets, he didn't like, or get, my work. "No!" I shot back. "Bob doesn't perform anymore." Les kept pushing, and I kept saying no.

This was shaping up to be a lifelong syndrome: an invitation to perform, followed by the not-so-subtle attempt to rope in my famous lovers or friends, too. But I was pragmatic about poetry: my poems, on their own, were presented to the audience, and anything that got them there was okay.

I told Les I'd think about it, and he kept saying, "Why don't you ask him?" I said yes, just to end the conversation. A few days later, he asked if I had asked Bob, and again a few days after that.

It lingered in my mind, and I dreaded doing it. One night, I popped the question, fully prepared for Bob to say no, and for me to say, It was Les's idea, I don't care.

"Yes!" Bob said instantly and happily. "I'll think of something."

Unexpectedly, we were on! *Three Events* was scheduled for Tuesday, March 7, 1967. I was happy, but I had also already learned that nothing was a big break. At best, things were just successful and worked, and that was all.

There was a poster—a photo of Les, me, and Bob, from the waist up looking into the camera. I noticed how similar Bob and I looked, the same skin and body tones, slightly puffy from too much drinking, but so young. We stood straight, but there was an invisible body connection, a flow between us. Lovers get to look like each other, I thought. Another joy!

The poster for *Three Events*

TWO DAYS BEFORE the performance, I called Bob and said, "Hi! Whatcha doin'?"

"I'm working on my piece," said Bob, rattling off a list of performers from the Armory event in October.

"What? You're going to show the movie of *9 Evenings*?"

"No. I'm doing a new piece."

"But you don't do that anymore!"

"I'm going to surprise you. And I want you to be in it," said Bob. "You wanna be in my piece?"

"Yes." I had a moment of total panic. At that time, I was just a poet, and had only gotten as far as making sound compositions of the poems. I wasn't much of a performer. Then I had another burst of joy; Bob had asked me to be in his piece, in his art, no greater good fortune. So I did what I always do in difficult situations: don't think about it, trust it'll be okay.

Loeb Student Center, on the south side of Washington Square Park, was an ugly 1950s building, plastic and aluminum, dead institutional modern. The auditorium, which doubled as a basketball court when the hoops were lowered from the ceiling, had a U-shaped balcony and a small stage at one end. We had the folding chairs removed, so the audience would stand. On March 7, about five hundred people showed up.

Bob went on first. His piece was called *Outskirts*, and had three parts. Since the stage was unworkable, he had to use the space under it. In five four-by-four-by-twelve-foot compartments under the stage, five dancers (Trisha Brown, Lucinda Childs, Yvonne Rainer, Elaine Sturtevant, and Deborah Hay) performed dances specially choreographed for their boxed-in spaces.

For the next part, the audience was invited to the second-floor terrace or out on the street to watch a projection on the wall of the church next door: color movie footage of a jet fighter taking off from an aircraft carrier. The film on the brick wall was like a moving silk screen and the wall was like a Combine, a brilliant union of Bob's painting and sculpture. But in the freezing, uncomfortable cold, the audience did not seem to get it.

The third part of *Outskirts* was the procession, and it was the best. Earlier in the day, Bob had said, "You're in my piece with me. I asked Max Neuhaus to play a bass drum and walk on us."

"What?" I said.

"Max is going to play a big drum, and walk on our chests, one foot on yours and one on mine."

"I can handle that," I gasped.

"He's going to walk all over us," said Bob, laughing.

He wasn't lying. In the middle of the crowd, Bob and I lay down on our backs on the floor. Max banged on a thirty-six-inch bass drum, put one foot on my chest and one foot on Bob's, then lifted his foot off me to walk. I shimmied forward, and he put his foot back on my chest, and lifted his foot off Bob's chest, then Bob slid forward. We slid forward with each step, over and over again. It wasn't easy, as the dirty floor was wet with black snow from peoples' shoes, and my shirt and jeans stuck to the mess. And it was hard for Max, six feet two and skinny, to keep his balance. The thunderous beat of the bass drum banged six inches over our heads.

Following us in the procession was the blue light. Billy Klüver and the engineers at Bell Labs had developed long, flexible plastic tubes of blue light. Two performers, wearing only their underwear, carried the tubes, gently moving the three-foot magical ropes, like snakes of light. A chorus of other performers followed.

The crowd roared like in a coliseum, screaming and cheering, pushed and pressed in, and we were completely in the dark. It was as painful as torture, and I went into a quasi-state of shock, but I did it until it was over.

Then Bob and I pulled ourselves up and ran backstage.

We hugged and kissed and I felt the pain in my chest subside. "I'm not brokenhearted," I said, laughing.

After Les's portion of *Three Events*, a video of art critics talking, I went on last. My piece, *Raspberry & Pornographic Poem*, was the sound compositions of my poems, and included the three sound poems I had made with Bob Moog on the Moog synthesizer. They were played on a multispeaker system surrounding the audience. I had rented ten ultraviolet neon tube fixtures, which were attached to the edge of the balcony and ringed the audience, and created a giant black-light purple soup. The sound was overwhelming.

The concept was that in turning the mind upside down, in disorientation, senses sharpen, become alert, and consequently listeners *hear* better. And to dissolve the barrier of the proscenium stage, the poems were played from multispeakers and heard all over the space equally. The poems, sound compositions, were music, filling the air completely. The installation was a support, creating for the audience a space more conducive to hearing poems. It was a great improvement on what I'd done at SVA.

Decades later, *9 Evenings* is commonly thought of as Bob Rauschenberg's last performance piece, and this event at the Loeb Student Center has been almost forgotten, even by me. But in 2009, when I visited the William Burroughs Collection at the New York Public Library, I unearthed a letter from me to William describing *Three Events* in detail, and it all came back, the procession most of all . . .

Lying on the floor in the crowded dark and the pain; and Bob, my lover, next to me, which made it okay.

TWO MONTHS LATER, my pursuit of synergy between sound and light reached a breakthrough, once again thanks to a random encounter at Bob's. I was hanging around waiting for him at Lafayette, as was Fred Waldhauer, another Bell Labs engineer. In the context of a chat about artists, poets, and technology, Fred told me about a new sound device he was working on.

I was intrigued. "Can I use it with my sound poems?"

Thus, we began a collaboration, working together for much of the summer. Fred built for me an organ that analyzed the light content of sound—high-pitched voices or notes were in red and yellow, and lower-pitched voices or notes in green and blue—with volume registered in brightness. It was a groundbreaking invention that Bob would soon use, too, and in the next decade, it would usher in disco lights.

Fred specially adapted this device, a "light organ," to my sound poems, and in late 1967 I began to use it in performances and installations. In February 1968, I performed *Purple Heart* at the Architectural League of New York as part of a series of installations called ESPE, Electronic Sensory Poetry Environments. I used the compositions I had made with Bob Moog, the light organ analyzing their sound and displaying it in banks of four colored lights. And as part of my ongoing effort to involve all the senses, soap machines dispensed bubbles from the ceiling. It was a great success.

The next month, I brought the light organ to Toronto for a complicated new piece called *Johnny Guitar* at the Ryerson Institute's SightSoundSystems Festival. Three poems made into sound compositions fed through Fred's organ to banks of colored stage lights, which flared out onto the audience.

Earlier at the same event, Marcel Duchamp and John Cage played a game of chess on stage, electronically hooked up to a computer and to a large screen displaying their moves, which generated music by three composers. It was an amazing historic moment—which, much to my disappointment, I missed by just a day.

But to see my name on the festival poster with those of Marcel Duchamp and John Cage was astounding! With all my insecurities, it made me feel like I was an artist and a poet.

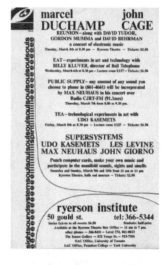

The poster for the
SightSoundSystems Festival

NOT LONG AFTER performing with Bob in *Three Events* came an even more exhilarating possibility: performing with Bob *and* using my sound compositions, *in the very same piece.*

For her latest spontaneous dance festival, I hooked Deborah Hay up with the perfect space: Mike Goldberg's studio at 222 Bowery, the old YMCA gymnasium, a spacious loft with a thirty-foot-high ceiling.

Then, maybe because she'd seen how well Bob and I slid around the floor together at Loeb back in March, Debbie asked Bob and me to be in her piece for the festival. Why not!

Bob and I stood on two tall platforms with our backs touching the wall. Our simple instructions were to rub our backs against the wall, back and forth, back and forth. "It's about friction," Debbie laughed during rehearsal.

I wore a dark blue Izod Lacoste sport shirt, and by the time of the performance, the rubbing had worn an oval spot in back that eventually became transparent. Bob wore a tan short-sleeve shirt. It was a hot, humid night, and the air was stifling in the loft, packed with a hundred sweaty members of the cutting-edge downtown art scene. We were supposed to be in complete darkness, but there was one twenty-five-foot-high opaque glass window letting in some indirect light, making us shadows. In the silence of the packed house, there was only the sound of our shirts rubbing the wall for fifteen minutes.

Bob and I took it very seriously. It was a way for us to secretly and magically love each other. This was very much the way Bob's mind worked: in the darkness, everyone was looking at us, but nobody could see us.

We let our minds rest together. Meditation is inherent in everyone, the union of two minds, becoming one mind. And the movement of back rubbing proved to be a great metaphor for this. Friction is a very sexual movement; it generally culminates in orgasm. But Bob and I only got dull, irritating discomfort. And since it was not blissful, we were beyond bliss.

Then it all fell apart.

Debbie had intended for my synthesizer sound poem "Rose" to be played in the final five minutes, but Steve Paxton was running the tape recorder and forgot to turn it on. In those last minutes, waiting for my poem to come on, I rubbed my back against the wall in a crescendo of anxiety, ending in fury. Just as people began to applaud, Steve remembered and the sound came on.

The lights came up, Bob and I bowed, and we got a huge round of applause. Everyone said it was a beautiful piece, and Debbie was thrilled.

But I was furious at Steve for his passive-aggressive negligence, and held on to that anger. Nine months into my relationship with Bob, Steve was still the cause of unceasing obstacles. He had not intentionally forgotten to turn on the tape, but it was just the latest in unconscious, all-pervasive, negative phenomena that enveloped our relationship. Steve took over Bob's bed every night, which was agony for me. But when anger arose, I had to completely suppress it because of Bob.

As the applause petered out, I didn't say anything, but I was ashen white, and a few people noticed something was wrong. Suddenly, standing there, I fell into a deep depression, as if a trapdoor had dropped out from under me. Afterward, I stood around talking to people and continued to act cheerful for a while, then I ran upstairs to my own loft and locked the door.

In some ways, this wasn't unusual. Every day, I worked intensely on poems and poetry projects, and I took a small chip of a Dexedrine pill once a week to intensify and clarify my work, so I was always crashing a little. I was stressed by all the activity. But this time, it felt different. Again, it felt like a bad omen.

I let Bob in to say good night, and I went to sleep in a black hole.

ABOUT A MONTH LATER, Bob went to Los Angeles to sign *Booster* and other new prints at Gemini. As he was leaving, we kissed in the downstairs hall, and he said, "I already miss you."

The next day began like any other but became one of the worst days of my life. I did errands, went to the post office and supermarket, talked on the phone, and tended to the details of poetry projects. Around four in the afternoon, I settled in to work on a new poem. I took half a Dexedrine and, while waiting for it to hit, smoked joints and cigarettes, and drank vodka and soda, which was a chemical combination that went extremely well with my work. I worked on the poem with absolute concentration, choosing images that joined one another in a magical display, made line breaks, wove the threads of the nonlinear narrative, created repetitions by doubling and tripling the lines for depth of meaning and musical force, trying as hard as I could to make it perfect. I worked for as long as I could, about six hours, until my mind got very tired, and then I stopped. I lay down on the bed, rested, and girded myself for the painful process of crashing from speed and alcohol. I was pragmatic; anything was worth a great poem.

About two in the morning, I went for a walk, from the Bowery over to the West Village and the crowds of gay men cruising the trucks. I was very depressed, and was not trying to pick up anybody, just trying to pass time until I detoxed. I walked up to Madison Square Park at Fifth Avenue and Twenty-Third Street. It was the morning of July Fourth, and the city had a powerful, vacant feeling with many people away for the holiday, save tourists, and the poor dregs and misfits like me. It was already 90 degrees at 4:00 a.m., and the air was wet. The full moon lit the lush trees, which moved like underwater plants.

I sat down on a park bench. Something in my mind snapped, broke, as if hit by lightning, and I started crying, weeping, and I screamed in pain. Nobody was in the park, so I could let it go, torrents of water pouring down my face, a weird sound of despair squeezed from my lungs, writhing and shaking on the bench. I had no idea what was happening, but I had to let it happen.

It was at that moment that Bob Rauschenberg and I broke. For no reason, nothing had happened, nothing had changed in our relationship. I believed it was a precognitive recognition, seeing the future, clairvoyance. We would split up. I had lost him.

I lay on the bench, having occasional spasms of tears, the sun rising low and hot, when I realized somebody was sitting there.

"It will be okay, it's okay," said a middle-aged man with short gray hair. "You are so beautiful!"

I bolted up and sat erect, wiped the tears off my face, and backed away from him. "What?"

"Let me help you," he said.

"Thank you. I don't need any help, Thank you." I got up, hurried away, and took a taxi home.

My mind was weighed down with depression. It was as when tectonic plates make a big sharp move and bring ruin to the earth, causing great sadness, unthinkable loss. A giant bell over my head rang a deafening gong, and sent me into a state of shock. After that, I got the message, and it was not good.

Two weeks later, Bob came back from L.A. and was very happy to see me, and for a while everything went on as before. But Bob had returned from Los Angeles a changed man. I saw it instantly from a distance, not knowing what I saw. The kind of a change that doesn't happen often in a person's life, decisive and irreversible.

In L.A., he had met Warren Beatty; they bonded instantly and became best friends. They were two egomaniacs, and with the new friendship came Shirley MacLaine and rich, beautiful Hollywood movie stars, drugs and alcohol, a world that was over-the-top. It was a world of superstars he had never known before, many realms higher than de Kooning and Pollock and the Abstract painters. Robert Rauschenberg was a famous artist, and the movie stars knew his work and treated him as their equal. Was this what I sensed with my intuition on the morning of July Fourth weeping in the park?

In Hollywood, Bob's big ego met its match and he was hooked. His big ego saw the other big egos as reflections of himself, and he wanted more. Steve and I, and everybody else, were to be left behind. No matter what bad qualities Bob had, his being a great artist trumped them all. His work was so great that, indeed, nothing else mattered.

Life went on as usual: we were lovers, but gradually over the months we began drifting apart. Bob missed many opportunities to be together. In November 1967, he started making it with the artist David Bradshaw, and it became an affair. David replaced me as Bob's lover. They were together for about a year, all while David was having a love affair with Deborah Hay.

In January and early February 1968, I called Bob every day, and I never got him on the phone. I left messages with Dorothea or on the machine, and he'd take days to return my call, with an excuse he couldn't see me, or else he'd come over and we'd make love. The sex was always great. But then I wouldn't see him for two weeks.

On February 12, I called Bob and got the machine. I never called him again.

RUN-INS

In February 1972, at an opening at the Museum of Modern Art, on a landing going from one floor to another, I bumped into somebody. "John!" I looked up, and to my surprise, it was Bob.

"Bob, how are you?" We hugged and kissed. We had not seen each other in four years, and were both pleased to run into each other.

"I'm really happy to see you, John," Bob said formally and gently. "I want to invite you to dinner at Elaine's."

Elaine's was New York's chic celebrity hangout, frequented over the years by the likes of Mick Jagger, Janis Joplin, Norman Mailer, Henry Kissinger, and Jacqueline Kennedy Onassis. What an exciting turn of events!

We walked to Fifth Avenue to get a taxi, looking in each other's eyes.

"Elaine's is on Second and Eighty-Eighth. John, do you want to go to Elaine's, or . . ." Bob kissed me, stuck his tongue in my mouth, and we deep-kissed in the freezing cold, bundled in our clothes.

I finished his sentence. "Or go to 222 Bowery?"

We took a taxi downtown. I might have known that the invitation to Elaine's was a ploy to get me to fuck him. But I still loved Bob, had no bad feelings, and why not. I liked fucking him.

We drank bourbon, smoked joints, and talked about what we were doing. We both had many accomplishments over the past four years, and Bob appreciated mine. We got through the talk quickly, because we wanted to fuck. Bob was always great sex. When you love somebody it is always good sex. I smelled Bob's smell. His nipples were as big as I had made them. We came, and then rested in each other's arms for an hour. Bob went home, the same pattern as four years before, and I felt a tinge exploited. It never happened again; but I still loved him.

IN 1983, I was performing in Paris at the Pompidou Center in the Polyphonix 5 poetry festival, organized by Jean-Jacques Lebel. I had performed in the festival before, but this year was particularly illustrious, with many great poets, and was held in the Grande Salle, the large, steep amphitheater in the Pompidou.

In the morning, I heard that Bob Rauschenberg was having a big exhibition opening that evening. As the day passed, Bob's show was the buzz of Paris. I had not seen him in eleven years.

At my sound check at three in the afternoon, François, a young curator who was a pleasure to talk with, said, "John, Bob Rauschenberg is having an opening party tonight. I look forward to seeing you there."

But Bob was completely off my radar. My tour was booked, my dance card was full, and I did not want to make any plans that might allow demons in to obstruct me and my performance. I knew better.

"You must come," said François, writing the address on a piece of paper—somewhere in Montmartre.

"But I perform tonight, and there's a dinner after," I said. It was the last thing I wanted to do.

"Bob's party will go on very late, and I'm sure you are very welcome anytime."

It was a little confusing: fifteen years after we broke up, by chance on June 10, 1983, my big night in Paris was also his big night in Paris.

I acted cautiously and did not make any decision. What unknown factor, nightmare, would that demon bring into my life? I did not want any trouble.

But with the paranoia came a warmth from thinking about someone I loved, a happy feeling remembering the love of my life. The Grande Salle was packed with young people, and the haut monde of the poetry and art worlds. This was a time in my life when I had become a great performer. I performed so often that I had developed skills using my voice and breath, through trial and error, and was able to strongly connect to every person in the audience.

That night, I gave a particularly dazzling performance of "Life Is a Killer," "Stretching It Wider," and "Exiled in Domestic Life." I performed with a tape-recorded musical accompaniment, so each poem was a rock 'n' roll song, with David Van Tieghem on drums, Pat Irwin on guitar, and Philippe Hagen on bass—the earliest version of what would become the John Giorno Band. A thousand adoring fans screamed and applauded, and I brought down the house.

After the show, at a dinner party on rue Quincampoix, about thirty people celebrated the very successful night. We ate and drank, had a good time, were all happy and exhilarated.

In a half-conscious zone, there lingered Bob Rauschenberg, like a dull toothache, something you would rather not have, but you can't get rid of. If I didn't go to the party, was I a coward? I had the address in my pocket.

In New York, our paths never crossed. I was in the world of William Burroughs and poetry, punk, and drugs, happily; and we were rock stars. Bob Rauschenberg was in another glorious parallel heaven or god world. 222 Bowery and 475 Lafayette were only several blocks apart, but a million miles away. They were satellite universes.

At one in the morning, drunk and tired, a little crazed on the adrenaline of the night, I went to Bob's party. Françoise Janicot, with whom I stayed on quai de Bourbon, accompanied me, which made me feel safe. We took a taxi, but the venue was very difficult to find, and we had to walk up and down the streets of Montmartre. It was a full moon, and the moonlight was thick. We got there at 1:45 a.m. I was exhausted, but I had embarked upon this mission. I had no expectations and just wanted to get through it, hopefully happily.

It was late, and the party seemed to be winding down. Leo Castelli welcomed me and we kissed on both cheeks.

I walked into a large drawing room with a crystal chandelier, where people were dancing. Bob Rauschenberg stood alone in the middle of the oak floor, looking at me with his piercing eyes. I walked toward him, and when I had almost reached him, he started laughing and laughing, in a sinister way.

"Hi," I said.

Bob didn't say anything. He lunged forward and hugged me, and we kissed. He put his wrinkled mouth onto mine. He was drunk, and so was I. When Bob was drunk, he had the cunning and precision of a poisonous snake, and was just as deadly. He continued laughing and laughing with demonic joy. It was very disconcerting. He still hadn't said anything, and when I tried to say something, he would only laugh with malevolent glee. He grabbed my hand and started arm-wrestling me, harder and harder until it became a real fight, became a duel; and it was the last thing I wanted to happen. Bob was laughing insanely as we reeled around, crashing down on the floor. It was the most horrible thing that ever happened to me. There was no kindness, no love.

We got up, and I felt humiliated, was in a state of shock. I somehow managed to graciously extricate myself and went back to Françoise.

Ileana Sonnabend came up and said, "Hello, John, how are you?"

"Good, thank you." We kissed. A few minutes later, I said to Françoise, "Let's go!"

I vowed never to see Bob Rauschenberg ever again.

But then, five years later, I did. Early one January afternoon, hungover and depressed, I turned left off of Bowery onto Great Jones Street, tugging the furry hood of my parka over my face to keep out the gale-force wind and razor-blade snowflakes. I collided into somebody, our foreheads banging and our noses touching.

"Sorry," I said, not looking and about to go on.

"John! Hi, John! It's Bob."

My eyes were tearing from the cold, and I saw through the tears that it was Bob Rauschenberg. "Bob! Hi!" We hugged and kissed. "What a surprise in the dazzling cold!"

Bob was with his new lover. He introduced us.

"I'm taking pictures," said Bob. He held a small digital camera.

Bob seemed genuinely happy to see me, which made me feel happy. In his beautifully aging face and body, I saw what I had loved, recognized it for an instant. It was still there. There was nothing to say, and the cold was a good excuse for me to keep moving.

The author performing at the Pompidou Center

IN THE SPRING OF 1992, there was a blank page in this memoir with the title "Bob Rauschenberg," a place mark for the chapter I couldn't write. Kirsten, a student intern, was endlessly retyping the manuscript as I wrote, correcting and adding to it.

One night, at a black-tie dinner following a performance by Merce Cunningham and John Cage at SUNY Purchase, Kirsten found himself face-to-face with Bob Rauschenberg, who was getting drunk at a crowded table. He waited for the right time to approach, Bob invited him to sit, and then Kirsten mentioned that he was helping me with my memoir.

"There is a chapter about you, but he hasn't written it yet," said Kirsten.

"What?" Bob said.

"There is a chapter about you."

"What?" Bob said angrily.

"There's a chapter called 'Bob Rauschenberg.' He hasn't written it yet. There's a blank page with the title."

"You tell John that if he writes about me, I will sue him," Bob exploded.

There were ten people at Bob's table. John Cage threw his head back in laughter. The composer David Behrman chuckled. David Whitney said, "He'll wait until you're dead." Everyone laughed louder.

"I will come back and haunt him," said Bob, furious.

Two days later, Kirsten came to work at 222 Bowery and told me the story. It seemed very funny. "When he's dead," I said, "won't he have better things to do than to waste his time haunting me?"

PART THREE

I FIRST MET Jasper Johns in June 1962 on a hot sunny afternoon at the corner of Bowery and Houston. A car had pulled over and was letting Jasper and David Whitney out as Jill Johnston and I were walking past on our way to her loft. Jill knew Jasper. I had met David before and had seen Jasper at parties and gallery openings. My heart was pounding when Jill went up to Jasper, said hello, and introduced me. Jasper was beautiful.

Throughout the 1960s, I ran into Jasper at parties at Billy Klüver's house, at Jill's loft, at the Judson Dance Theater, at the Leo Castelli Gallery, and so on. It was a challenge going up and talking to him. He had a brilliant mind, and the conversation always took a profound turn. He was known not to tolerate the slightest sloppy thought and could make a sharp retort and humiliate whomever he was talking to. He did it to me a couple of times, and I saw him do it to others often. I had to be careful, but Jasper was a great pleasure to talk and be with. I had a secret crush on him and looked forward to the odd times I ran into him.

In February 1968, Peter Schjeldahl, who had published my first book of poems a year before, said, "Jasper loves poets and poetry. He has done collaborations with Frank O'Hara and Ted Berrigan. I think Jasper should collaborate with you."

"What a great idea!" I responded, incredulous that he would suggest such a thing. I supposed he meant my use of the found image connected to Jasper's artwork.

A month later, Peter said, "I ran into Jasper at Leo Castelli's party, and I said, 'You should collaborate with poet John Giorno,' and he liked the idea. He said you should call him, and gave me his telephone number to give to you."

Over the next several months, Peter asked a number of times if I had called Jasper, and I hadn't. I was incredibly busy with the start-up of a new project, Dial-a-Poem, scheduled to go live in December. I was also writing poems, making sound compositions of them with Bob Moog, and making silk-screen poem prints, and

I had other poetry projects. And, of course, I was still suffering and scarred from my breakup with Bob. Subconsciously, I wanted to escape from the art world.

But more than any of that, in the late summer of 1968, I was reconnecting with one of the most important people in my life, with whom I had a lot of unfinished business.

THIRD MIND

"There is something very bad going on," William Burroughs said in his gravelly, drawling voice in September 1968, fresh from covering the riots at the Democratic Convention in Chicago. He pitched a little forward in his chair and looked at me with his needlepoint gray eyes. "Very bad indeed! Evil, evil, evil! You can't imagine how bad it is."

William was staying in Terry Southern's apartment, an old carriage house on East Thirty-Eighth Street between Lexington and Third Avenues. The place was chic and cool, but also small and dirty. I knew the look well: a pricey, 1950s-style furnished apartment with beat-up furniture and no air conditioner. The ashtrays overflowed with cigarette butts, and the ashes on the table mixed with the vodka spilled from our drinks, making a black muddy slosh that dripped on the floor, and dried there, day after night after day. Books and newspapers were scattered about. Garbage was knocked over on the kitchen floor.

But the dump was radiant, glowing with the clarity of William's mind. It was a brilliant mind, profoundly realized, which gave him a physical, magical power. "I advance the theory," he said, puffing a Player's, "that in the electronic revolution a virus is a very small unit of word and image that destroys. Once an image is put into circulation, it is impossible to anticipate or control its path. It is out of control!"

I sat on the couch and William sat in a chair, our knees almost touching, and as we looked into each other's eyes, I said, "The absolute nature of mind is beyond all concepts. Discursive thoughts are viruses, words obscuring the true nature, and imprisoning the consciousness."

"Of course," said William. We smoked a joint.

"Or maybe words are also the vehicles for karma to travel and manifest from one life to another, making more karma."

I was thirty-one years old, and William was fifty-four. I was busy those days working on poems, sound poems, and performance pieces. But with William in New York, my plans changed, and my schedule and heart opened up. When I first met William and Brion Gysin in January 1965 in New York (and spent nine months with them), Brion had been an overpowering presence, and his magnetizing qualities made him the center of attention. William liked hiding in Brion's shadow. Now, during these three weeks in 1968, William and I were alone for the first time, and gloriously together. We had been waiting for this. There was no Brion, no other friends dropping by, no endless discursive conversations. We were drunk and stoned, and I was exhilarated. Not in my wildest imagination could I have dreamed of being anywhere more perfect than right there. And I was in love with him.

What William liked to do, several times a night, was pause, then position us three feet apart so we could stare into each other's eyes, letting our minds rest in silence, allowing our thoughts to drift unheeded for several minutes. It was William's idea of the union of two minds, resting in its empty nature. This was similar to Buddhist teachings, which William very much understood. It was very powerful, because William believed in it so strongly. I had seen him do this with Brion in 1965, and I had done it with him then as well. He called it making a third mind.

"William, we are not making a third mind," I told him. "We are making one mind beyond all concepts. This is a greater accomplishment. A third mind is still in the relative world."

We were so happy being together. And I was overjoyed that he liked being with me. William leaned forward in his chair, looked at me with his noiseless eyes, and said, "Terry has a Luger."

"What?" I didn't understand. He said it again and I still didn't understand.

"Terry has a Luger. A German Luger!" said William, impatiently. "In his bedroom. Come, let me show it to you." We went up the dark wooden steps of the narrow, steep staircase to the bedroom.

William slowly opened the drawer, slipped his bony hand in under the cashmere sweaters, and pulled out a gun. "It's a beauty!" William was enchanted and caressed it. "A real beauty! A Luger."

"Wow! It's fabulous!" I was surprised. The gray gunmetal glowed, and the classic German design was somehow shocking. "A Luger is a German officer's gun?"

"I love the feel of it in my hand! . . . Yes." There was deep satisfaction in William's voice. His hands wrapped around the large handle, and with arms extended, he sighted and aimed at the wall, making exclamations of pleasure. "Pow! . . . I love the feel of it in my hand! Try it." William handed me the gun.

I held it, not knowing what to think. I was not familiar with guns; but it felt pretty good. Maybe I was supposed to feel the negative energy. The German officer to whom it belonged probably killed many people with it, I imagined. That was not so good, and bad karma can travel with objects. I decided not to discriminate, and relaxed, enjoying the purity of its power. "It's very wrathful, and so beautiful. It is empowered steel."

"I know, I love it," cooed William as I handed it back to him. Two guys playing with a dick, and it felt great. Why not!

William handed it back to me. I squeezed it in my hands, and said softly in his ear, "That gun's got blood in its hole."

Surprised by my words, William leapt a little into the air and let out a squeaky giggle. "What did you say?"

I leaned closer to him, and repeated in a deep, intimate voice, "That gun's got blood in its hole."

William smiled.

"I can feel the Nazi officers and their cold, sweaty hands."

"No, not at all!" said William, slightly disdainful of my ignorance. "The Luger was their World War One gun, and the Walther P38 was their World War Two gun."

"Are there bullets?" It was exhilarating. Playing with a gun with William Burroughs, with the Grim Reaper himself.

"I haven't found any. They're hard to get in New York," William said knowingly. "The Walther P38 was a much superior weapon, a semiautomatic, which gave a great advantage . . . But I love the Luger." William raised the gun again, arms extended, hands wrapped around it. "Pow! Pow! Pow!"

The black rider and the silver bullet. I was breathless. The silver bullet was William's mind. I knew that William had shot and killed his wife, Joan, in Mexico City in 1951, in a tragic accident. A catastrophe that overwhelmed him, caused him enormous suffering, and generated his life work as a writer. Yet I trusted William and had complete confidence. I was not in danger.

The Luger became a little ritual for the first week or so. After a few drinks and joints, William whispered, "John, Terry has a Luger. Come, let me show you."

I would feign surprise. "Let me see." And we would stagger up the precarious staircase to the bedroom.

Sometimes, I'd have to fake it, because I wasn't interested in guns. I had to think of something to get myself up, pornographic images. Guns were boring and I didn't feel anything; but I humored him because it made him happy. William's eyes, with their dry, gray clarity, would look directly into mine. For a moment, our two heart-minds locked together, and somehow became one, in a vast expanse, luminous and empty. We would hug each other, press our bodies and chests and minds together, and then head back downstairs to continue drinking, smoking dope and cigarettes, and talking.

ONE NIGHT, we talked about Jack Kerouac, whom William had recently seen, drunk, at the Hotel Delmonico just before his live television appearance on William F. Buckley's *Firing Line*.

"I told Jack, 'No, don't go; you are not in any condition to go. This is a disaster in the making. You shouldn't go, you're drunk!'"

"Did they ask you to be on it?"

"I was asked to be there with him! Not on it at all! Not on the show." I could tell that William was offended at not being asked, even though he did not want to demean himself by doing it. "Buckley asked Jack about Allen, and he said, 'That Jew!'" William stretched out the word *Jooou*. "Buckley was sort of encouraging him in this madness . . . The producer said he was a drunken moron. It was a disaster!"

William puffed on a joint. "The next morning, Jack came to my room, and poured himself a water glass full of whiskey." Even William, a drinker himself, was appalled at the idea. He asked Jack's brothers-in-law, who had become his de facto handlers, if Jack was always like that.

"They said, 'Yeah, I'm afraid so. He's got a great talent, but he's throwing it away.' They said there was nothing they could do. He's drunk the whole day."

Jack visited with William briefly before the brothers-in-law hustled him out. "'Got to get moving, Jack!' That was it. I went down to the street and saw them off." It was the last time William saw Kerouac.

I remembered that past spring, when I had run into Jack Kerouac myself. Ted Berrigan was taking care of Jack during his New York visit, and rumor had it that he wasn't doing well.

Suddenly, Jack, Ted, and I were on a corner of Third Avenue and Seventh. Jack was wearing a flannel shirt and a brown corduroy zipper jacket with the collar up against the chill. He was just a nice, overweight guy, with a hangover, who was smiling and gentle, with warm eyes. We had a surprise, intimate moment together, like we'd had when I first met him back in 1958.

"This is John Giorno! A poet. And the star of Andy Warhol's movie *Sleep*," said Ted, bellowing positive energy, high on speed. "The best movie I've ever seen! Him sleeping for eight hours. The greatest movie in the world!"

"I've heard about it," said Jack, smiling at me.

"John wrote a poem called 'Pornographic Poem' with the lines 'Seven Cuban army officers in exile were at me all night . . . in every conceivable position.'" We were all laughing. "'With two big fat dicks up my ass at one time.' I couldn't believe it! The best line is 'I was in heaven.' The greatest . . . !" Ted was straight.

"I read it in *C*," said Jack.

I got a buzz. Jack read my pornographic poem! Maybe it turned him on.

"It's a 'found poem,'" I said modestly.

Ted and I told Jack about a reading of "Purple Heart," where I used a fog machine to fill St. Mark's Church with smoke.

"A brigade of firemen in wet black rubber suits with axes raised appeared in the fog in front of me. They were so beautiful."

"Anne Waldman stepped up to the fire chief and declared, 'This is a poetry reading!'"

We stood on the street corner in the chilly morning. Jack's face was beat up and bloated. He and I looked in each other's eyes for a long moment. Love arose in each of our hearts. There was a sexual energy and unexpected possibility. We rested for a moment in the glimmer of our hearts.

But getting through to Jack, seeking a more sustained connection, seemed doomed to fail. My life was complicated enough. I didn't have time. I said goodbye. I had a day of appointments, and was already half an hour late.

"I've always thought that Jack has a gay side that we don't know about, or nobody talks about," I said to William, recounting the story of our intimate moment the first time I met him at the party in 1958. "If there had been no people there, he would have stuck his tongue in my mouth."

William and I lurched to the kitchen of Terry's shabby apartment in the sweltering heat and got ourselves another round of vodka and tonics. We rubbed our shoulders together sideways, like cats spooning. Occasionally, I gave William a big hug, he liked that, and his bony body hugged back awkwardly.

I thought about Jack Kerouac. When I first met him, he was gorgeous, hot-blooded, radiating glorious energy. Now, just ten years later, Jack was a mess—fat, numbed by alcohol. Things had changed. Kerouac was finished, and I was at the beginning of my life, in the center of the world of William Burroughs and the greatest minds of my generation. And for no good reason. As a young poet, did I deserve it? Or was it the luck of the draw? Or my karma? Or was I just a beautiful piece of meat?

WHEN WILLIAM AND I got together for drinks, at some point we had to address the question of dinner. We either ate in, or we went out, or we didn't bother to eat at all, which I liked best.

But sometimes, if it wasn't too late, we staggered and swayed in the delicious, warm night air, from Thirty-Eighth Street four blocks north to Horn & Hardart, one of the last of the original fast-food restaurants, inside a beautifully run-down, near-empty art deco building. William, who had gone there on junk in the 1940s and written about it in *Junkie* and *Naked Lunch*, loved the place. But if it was closed by the time we got there, which it often was, I was relieved.

If not, we went inside, bypassing the sandwiches behind small, coin-operated glass doors, to the hot food counter, and carried our trays to a Formica table. "There are only two Horn & Hardarts left in New York," William would extol. "And the food is so good. This pot roast is excellent. You get your money's worth here." He was quite serious. The pot roast and mashed potatoes were institutional.

I couldn't wait until we finished. There was never anybody interesting eating there, and to me, it felt barren. Empty, but for the hungry ghosts, I thought. But I always tried to make William feel good, turn the moment into something entertaining for him, because I really liked him. I hoped he saw some of his junkie ghosts at neighboring tables.

If we ate in, William bought some food and I cooked—almost

always steak, frozen french fries, and peas. But by the time we remembered dinner, it was late and we were drunk and stoned. Usually, we were busy talking when I broiled the steak, and the fat would catch fire, filling the apartment with smoke. The steak would be charred outside and bloody raw inside, the french fries still frozen in the centers, and the peas overcooked. Cooking made such a mess. But it was such a joy being with William, I was happy to do it.

He agonized over the recent assassinations of Martin Luther King and Robert Kennedy: "This country is out of control!" And then I chronicled my misadventures at the student strikes up at Columbia back in May. One night I had been performing my poem "Purple Heart" for a peaceful crowd, and the next night I was trapped in a sudden melee, being chased, then beaten by three cops.

"John, I didn't know!" William exclaimed, putting his hands to his chest. He loved it.

"The interesting thing is, I didn't feel any pain at all. No pain, not even for a moment. I think the first blow to my head was so strong, it sent me into shock, and triggered the endorphins. I went down soft, and lay there, and they kept whacking and slamming me for five minutes. I just relaxed, thinking, Why doesn't this hurt? They are hitting me and it doesn't hurt. I noticed my head was wet and I thought, It's not raining and my head is wet. Blood!"

"John!"

"My face was pressed in the cool dirt and grass and I looked up sideways, and there was the bronze statue of the goddess Columbia. I lay at the bottom of the cascade of marble steps, where ten years before I had graduated, and now the police are beating me senseless. My tenth reunion was a blood sacrifice. A ritual offering in the marble temple. It was glorious. It was like opera, unexpected and complete fulfillment."

"Did you get hurt?" William looked concerned.

"I have thick bones, I never get hurt. I was taken to St. Luke's

Hospital, and got twenty-four stitches. I crashed for a couple of days, but no damage."

"How extraordinary!"

THE FIRST NIGHT we got together for drinks, as we were about to say goodbye, we grabbed each other, and hugged and kissed. We had never made it before. We pressed our bodies together, and it felt really good. William Burroughs was a very sweet lover. I was surprised.

"Let's go up to the bedroom," said William. We lurched up the narrow staircase. We kissed some more, took off our clothes, and got on the bed. William's delicate body trembled with pleasure. He wanted to be fucked.

I asked for some Vaseline. "Don't need any." With some spit on his fingers, he wet his asshole. I gently eased my cock into his thin, soft ass. I squeezed his tiny maroon nipples on the ghostly white skin draped limply across his rib cage. William did not like his nipples played with. He was pointedly into fucking.

He had a very small cock, thin, but very hard. As I fucked him with his legs over his shoulders, I played with his dick, and he took my hand away. The thought arose that William's cock was a clitoris. As we were looking in each other's eyes, I thought, Your dick is as small as a clitoris. You misogynist, if you knew that I'm thinking that your ass is a cunt and your cock is a clit, you'd explode with anger.

It was very funny. William Burroughs, the hermaphrodite, with dual interchanging genitalia, straight out of *Naked Lunch*. And so different from the mythical, tough-guy Burroughs persona. I almost giggled with joy. It was fabulous and grotesque. I was making love to the Grim Reaper himself. I was fucking the Grim Reaper.

I remembered that William had extrasensory powers. He could, at times, read my mind. I quickly dissolved the thought that kept arising, as I didn't want to upset him or make him angry, because the great magician might destroy me, strike me to dust. He was moaning, and whining in a high-pitched voice, *"Ohhh! Ohhh! Ohhh!"*

Pale light from a streetlamp streamed through the window, mixed with the humid air, and gave William a rat-gray funguslike complexion. As we fucked, his sweat was cold and clammy, smelled ever so slightly rancid, and tasted bitter. The taste of a junkie, the glorious perfume of wrathful gods.

I was fucking a living skeleton, his flesh hanging off the bones. William was a spirit of the dead. In union with death, it was glorious; and I didn't allow myself, even for an instant, to be frightened.

His black eyes glittered and looked into mine. Black holes that sucked up and destroyed galaxies. I was spinning in an orbit around a black hole. Confident, I was in a strong orbit, in denial that the worst was inevitable.

As William was cumming, I dissolved all my thoughts in absolute meditation. I rested my mind with his mind in great emptiness and bliss. Our minds mingled in one taste, in the vast, empty expanse of primordially pure Wisdom Mind.

I was just getting started and it was all over. But it didn't matter, as I loved William, and he didn't get this pleasure often. "Why would anyone want to go to bed with me!" he'd say. "I look like someone from Bergen-Belsen!" For me, being able to share a secret blissful moment with William was enough.

I wanted to thank William for being a great hero of gay sexual freedom. I wanted to reward him for his noble efforts. He had the most appalling taste, attracted to puny, bad street boys from London and Tangier. Not very fulfilling relationships. And I liked to fuck tirelessly anyway. I wanted to offer him bliss.

After cumming, William immediately cleaned up with a towel and sat on the edge of the bed, ready to get on with business—appreciative, but not affectionate. A light sleeper, he didn't like anyone sleeping over. We talked for a while. I put on my clothes, we hugged, and I went home to 222 Bowery.

We fucked every time we got together, which was several times a week.

One night, Allen Ginsberg joined us for dinner. I always preferred being alone with William, and not with Allen, but at least Allen helped me cook. Again, the broiler fire, smoke, blackened/bloody steak, french fries half icy, pot burned, and Brussels sprouts as overcooked as the peas. We had a good time.

After dinner, Allen started kissing William. They had been lovers, years before, and for old times' sake and duty, every couple of years Allen made it with William. I thought, Oh, no, I have to have a threesome with Allen. William kissed me, which I loved; then, I had to kiss Allen. It was the first, and only, time that Allen and I kissed. There was no way out. His bushy beard and dried, cracked lips initially repulsed me, but he was very affectionate and loving.

Despite our differences, I liked Allen and Allen liked me. But he was my nemesis, always interrupting something important for me. It was a complicated karmic pattern, I would see years later, that followed us from lifetime to lifetime. And in this life, we usually only made it worse.

Upstairs, we rolled around naked on the bed, a little awkward at first, but then laughing and having fun.

"Let's go slow," said Allen. He knew how quickly William came.

Allen sucked my dick, very tenderly. We were kneeling on the bed. Then, I had to reciprocate. Sucking Allen Ginsberg's dick: a fate worse than death. But there was no way out.

William was becoming impatient. He was the star of this show. With William's legs up over his shoulders, Allen entered him. I was on my knees and hugged both of them. Allen pumped once, and William squirted a load of gray, watery cum. A glorious, blissful orgasm, in an instant. We rested. Allen and I were very respectful of the sacred quality of the moment.

William cleaned up immediately, as always. Allen and I were not interested in getting each other off.

We got dressed, kissed, and said goodbye. Allen and I took a taxi downtown, happy with each other. We had a new bond between us, a pure transcendent connection. Even though, I knew intuitively, it meant nothing.

ON OUR LAST NIGHT of drinks together, before he flew back to London, William talked about his piece on the Chicago convention and riots. Young kids confronting conservative authority, daunting and uncompromising, a triumph. "These young people are challenging the political establishment!" he marveled.

This was just what he and Allen and Jack had written and dreamed of, I reminded him.

William became Shakespearean. "Seeds planted years ago bearing magnificent fruit."

He wasn't happy to be returning to London. There, his eight-year affair and creative collaboration with a young computer and math genius had just ended. "I'm thinking of moving to New York," he said. "Coming to live here."

I didn't quite believe him. William living in New York, that was electrifying!

He looked in my eyes. "I've had enough of London. More can be accomplished here than sitting on that godforsaken island, with a nineteenth-century queen." We laughed. William was a nineteenth-century queen. "Can you imagine ten thousand people in front of Buckingham Palace, shouting, 'Bugger the Queen!' I can't."

My heart beat faster. If William lived in New York, we would see each other all the time, like lovers. We could continue this incredible, unfinished exploration. What inconceivable good fortune! But life was a killer, and didn't give such great things. I knew not to hold my breath.

In the aftermath of William's visit, I felt the energy of our connection still coursing through me. He had activated my soul, energized my radical political self. As insular as we had been, he had opened my eyes to the world. It felt good and right, that William energy, but it was dangerous.

TRYING TO GET IT RIGHT

Just before William returned to London, Peter asked again, and I bit the bullet, picked up the telephone, and dialed Jasper's number. He was sweet and kind. Yes, Jasper remembered Peter's suggestion that we collaborate, and perhaps we should get together and talk about it. We made a date for tea.

One afternoon soon after, Jasper came to visit my third-floor loft. "Should I make tea? Or would you prefer a scotch?" I said. "Yes, scotch, thank you," said Jasper. We both broke into laughter.

We had lots of friends in common. I knew his art world and John Cage, and he knew some from the downtown poetry world, and we gossiped about them. The collaboration came up briefly, a long poem as a short book, but I didn't pursue it. If it happened, it would in its own time. I was in awe of Jasper.

We drank more scotch and smoked a joint, and then another joint. And then we leaned forward simultaneously into each other's arms, hugged, and kissed. We made love and it was wonderful.

I called Jasper two days later, and we made a date for drinks and dinner at his place. Jasper lived in a bank building on the corner of Houston Street and Avenue A. It was built in 1905 in neoclassical style, with one enormous fifty-foot-square room with a forty-foot-high ceiling, and four gigantic opaque windows facing north and east. There was a second room off the far corner, twenty by thirty feet, which was a library with a daybed, and at the far end was a staircase going upstairs to Jasper's bedroom, which had formerly been the bank president's office. Half the gigantic room was Jasper's studio. The living room was in one corner, a kitchen in another corner, and a dining room table in the middle of the far right wall.

On the studio wall hung a white encaustic painting of the alphabet that Jasper was working on. It was awesome that one of his great paintings was being made at that moment. On the far right wall, just before going into the library/daybed room, was a white encaustic painting of the American flag.

Jasper drank scotch and I drank vodka and soda. We were brilliantly engaged in each other's conversation. I had brought some joints, and we got stoned.

"Would you like to see some prints I've just done?" said Jasper.

"Yes, please," I said, following him over to the dining room table.

"I've just come back from Los Angeles," said Jasper, "working with Gemini Gel."

I knew Gemini Gel from my days with Bob, but felt it best not to follow that line of thought.

"These are the trial proofs."

He spread out the prints—each one a numeral, 0 through 9, transitioning in succession from primary to secondary colors. They were dazzling and would go on to be considered among Jasper's greatest works. "Wow! They are magnificent!"

When it came time to eat, Jasper said, "We could go out to a restaurant. Or I have leftovers from lunch. What do you feel like doing?"

"Leftovers," I said. "Going to a restaurant always becomes so tedious."

We couldn't wait to make it with each other. After nibbling on some food, we went upstairs to the bedroom and made love.

The next morning, I said, "You know I have the Central Park Poetry Events happening on Friday, Saturday, and Sunday. It's quite a big production, and I'll be busy all week. I won't be able to see you until next week. I perform on Saturday night." I didn't expect him to come.

"Yes, next week," said Jasper, smiling fondly, amused with my endeavor.

Jefferson Airplane had given me the idea for the Poetry Events. The rock band had given a great free concert (with the Grateful Dead and Butterfield Blues Band) at the Central Park Bandshell back in May, and all they'd done was call up New York City to get permission. So that's just what I did. I told the city I wanted to have a poetry festival, and they said, Wonderful, come get a permit. And I organized it like a concert, too: stage manager, crew, a rented sound system with big speakers, and a van to haul it. Poetry as rock show.

The event was free. So to pay the poets, crew, and production costs ($3,000—a lot in 1968), I raised the money from foundations and rich art collectors.

For the poster, Les Levine photographed me and the poets at the Bandshell and in the Central Park Zoo on a steamy summer morning. He used a fish-eye lens, which had just become available that year: the cutting edge of art and technology.

Les Levine and the author at
14 East Seventy-Seventh Street, 1968

THE CONCEPT WAS LOOSE: poets performing any way they wanted to. And while I liked a couple of the poets I chose, I found some boring, and at least one was an arrogant pain in the ass. But I was trying my hand at poetry politics, including everyone fairly, each poet representing a different part of the poetry world.

Vito Acconci was amazing, as always. The New York poet Anne Waldman performed with a rock band and experimental movies. Fluxus poet Jackson Mac Low performed *Young Turtle Asymmetries* and *Word Event for George Brecht on this name Central Park*, with another poet, a painter, a chorus of five, and slides. During one reading, artists spray-painted cardboard boxes in fluorescent patterns. During another, four sailors performed the naval code of signals. As the producer, I inherited all the technical problems and hassles of each of the pieces.

I performed *Johnny Guitar* using a sound tape, made in collaboration with Bob Moog. Center stage, I had a large, black column with thirty lights—red, blue, yellow, and green—that danced with my words, thanks to the light organ that Fred Waldhauer had created for me. Six red spotlights surrounded and illuminated the audience.

To expand sensory involvement, automatic aerosol dispensers around the edge of the audience sprayed the arbitrary smells of strawberries and chocolate. At other performances, I'd given away grass and Sunshine LSD, but since I was working with the municipal Department of Cultural Affairs, I didn't do that this time.

I had wanted William to perform, but he had to leave for London. So I got the idea to present a recording, a cut-up of a found cassette audio that he had just recorded in Chicago.

We opened the Saturday night performance on September 28, 1968, with *Grant Park, Chicago, August 28, 1968 by William S. Burroughs*. It was exactly one month after the riots; we were fresh and hot! The cut-up sound transformed the antiwar rally and police aggression at the Chicago Bandshell. Blaring through New York's bandshell, it subverted the evil powers that be that William and I had just been railing against.

"Outdoor Poetry Assaults Senses" was the headline of the *New York Times* review. "Questions about the nature of poetry could not be avoided last night, and the night before, and the night before that, in the band shell on the mall in Central Park, where nine poets went way beyond accustomed forms in presenting their work . . . With sound, light, color and odor, it was clear that Mr. Giorno regards poetry as a total experience of the senses." It was a long review, going on at length about my work and reviewing each poem, and ignoring everyone else, except Emmett Williams.

Despite the unevenness of the performances, in the relative sense of the New York art world and the downtown poetry scene, we had made it. And we were now hated even more by the New York school of poets and conservative literati, who did not approve of poets behaving in such a vulgar fashion.

It was a total triumph, and we were just beginning.

Poster for *Johnny Guitar*

ON THE MONDAY after the final performance, I got together with Jasper at the Bank. When we had talked about the Poetry Events before, he did not quite approve of William's cut-up but was intrigued and supportive. But that night, Jasper was beaming. He had read the rave in *The New York Times*.

By the middle of October, we were steady lovers.

I was amazed at this unexpected happening in my life. In our small art world of 1968, Jasper Johns was the greatest living artist. Bob Rauschenberg was too crazy, Andy Warhol was too over-the-top, the Abstract painters were dying gods, and minimal and conceptual artists were still forming. Jasper had caught the golden ring. I rationalized my good luck: that I had not hustled him, that Peter Schjeldahl had nagged me for months to call him for the collaboration, that Jasper said yes to scotch when offered tea, and that when we kissed we both moved toward each other at the same time. We were so compatible, physically and emotionally. My daily life as a poet fascinated Jasper, and I loved watching his daily life as a great artist unfold.

Watching and feeling Jasper's mind as he interacted with whatever happened was an enormous pleasure—when he forced himself to work on a painting; seeing what he chose to do and not to do, and why. I was being taught how to use my mind by being with his mind. I also felt there was a blessing radiating from Jasper's mind, that the great artist made great art with the same energy as the spiritual practice of Buddhism. I appreciated my good fortune.

Jasper and I never talked about Bob. I wondered how he felt about me having been with Bob, and how this related to the scars from the deep pain caused by the end of their relationship. Maybe we shared similar scars, and it was a comfort. Bob and Jasper were the classic lovers and partners of the 1950s, and their relationship was the most important in Jasper's life. Bob and I were lovers between 1966 and 1968, and Bob was the most significant partner in my life, even though I was much less significant to him. I didn't think of myself as an equal, so it didn't matter. Jasper was kind and loving, and I really appreciated him after all my difficult lovers and promiscuity.

We never talked about Andy Warhol either. His name almost never came up in conversation. We didn't talk about how Jasper felt about my fluky accomplishment of being the star of *Sleep*. Or Andy being called the father of Pop, when Jasper was called the grandfather of Pop, which made both of us cringe, given that Jasper was younger than Andy.

ONCE WE WERE TOGETHER, Jasper and I both tried hard, but cautiously, to get it right and make it work.

Each night, I would arrive at the Bank at 7:00 p.m. Jasper had a scotch and I had a vodka and soda. I rolled a joint with our second drinks. We talked about what we did that day, and both of us were tired from doing it. Between talking, we hugged and kissed, and experienced the happy feeling of being lovers.

Our morning routine was: we woke up about nine, and stayed in bed cuddling, talking, expressing deep affection and having sex; our best time together. We had a bath in the brand-new, traditional Japanese hot tub that Jasper had just had installed, and was very pleased with. We sat in the water facing each other or with our bodies together. It was therapeutic and healing.

I put on my clothes, said goodbye, and left, while Jasper dressed. Downstairs, I'd have a sip of orange juice from the container, and I always stood for a moment in the open kitchen, gazing at the giant bank room, the sun streaming in from the south windows.

I would often see John Cage sitting at the dining room table. He slept over in the library when Merce Cunningham was on tour, as he didn't like being alone. John got up early, and sat working with his typewriter or on a musical score. We'd cheerfully say hello, exchange a few words, and laugh, and were always happy to see each other.

Sometimes, I accompanied Jasper and John up to the Duchamp town house on East Eleventh Street. Since Marcel's very recent death, Jasper and John were bending over backward for his wife, Teeny, happily overdoing their devotion, catering to the widow of their earthly god. It was always a treat to be in that home, the space where Duchamp had worked and lived, the residue of his life force in the dust that saturated furniture and walls.

Most mornings, however, my mind was on work. Out the door, I walked on Houston past Katz's Deli to Bowery, and down to Prince Street. I worked every day for two hours on a poem, and then the poetry projects, the most urgent of which in late 1968 was Dial-a-Poem.

DIAL-A-POEM

I had gotten the idea for Dial-a-Poem back in May, while talking on the phone. I heard the person I was talking to with great clarity, and it came to me that the voice was the poet, the words were the poem, and the telephone was the venue.

Previously, the telephone was a personal connection, one to one, "you call me and I call you." But now, I imagined, the telephone could be a medium for mass communication: a phone number for everyone to call, with a recorded poem for them to hear.

The idea hinged on answering machines and the early technology allowing a single number to receive multiple calls. But that wasn't all. I imagined not just one recorded poem, but many, which the callers would hear at random.

Getting a sponsor for the project was easy. The Architectural League of New York (ALNY) was known for supporting and presenting cutting-edge installation events, and I had worked with them before.

And I had no problem finding talent. I had to really like each poem and each poet in order to include them. The success of this endeavor, I knew, would depend on the greatness of the poems, the wisdom they offered callers. I got tapes from William, Allen, and Brion to start, and tapes of my own sound compositions. With a new Sony tape recorder, I invited the rest of my inaugural group to record in my loft at 222 Bowery: John Cage, Jim Carroll, Aram Saroyan, Bernadette Mayer, Anne Waldman, Ted Berrigan, Ron Padgett, David Henderson, and John Ashbery.

Dial-a-Poem announcement

THE BIG TROUBLE was the New York Telephone Company. When I told them what I wanted, they said, "Yes, but we haven't ever done this before." In 1968, the only answering machines that could do such a job were large metal boxes, thirty-six inches long and a foot wide, cased in a heavy, gray metal; they recorded a two-minute message on a cylinder disk. I needed ten of these, to include as many poems as possible. And all ten machines had to be linked together, so that each call would trigger the next machine. That meant ten telephone lines, too, one for each machine, all sharing a single telephone number.

In November, engineers started installing the equipment in a small rear office of ALNY's headquarters, on the top floor of the American Federation of the Arts' Upper East Side brownstone. But the primitive technology made it a constant struggle. They were able to patch the ten machines together, but the triggering devices kept breaking down. It was the engineers' problem, and happily not mine, but I was thrilled it was under way.

The press release for Dial-a-Poem read: "Duchamp once said, 'What I really want to do is send art over the telephone.'" I was very happy to discover that quotation. It also described Dial-a-Poem as a "continuous poetry reading extending the poet's work through technology to a huge audience all over the world. The use of the telephone as a new form of 'publication' is an opportunity for the poets to achieve world-wide exposure and for their poetry to be heard rather than just read."

The magenta announcement card was mailed to two thousand people on the Giorno Poetry Systems mailing list, timed to arrive the week before Christmas. That got things started.

212-628-0400.

In mid-December, people started calling. And with each call, they randomly got a different poet, reading for two minutes. William Burroughs read from *Naked Lunch* and *Ticket That Exploded*, and was the very best. John Cage read from *Silence*, and was so entertaining. Callers often found John Ashbery boring and hung up after ten seconds. I included an excerpt of Frank O'Hara reading from *Lunch Poems*, recorded just before he died in 1966. Allen Ginsberg chanted a mantra.

Every morning, I rushed up to ALNY and changed the tapes. Using a reel-to-reel tape recorder, I sent the selected poems into each of the ten machines. Each poet had ten or more selections/poems, so every call, every day, there were new poets and new poems. The relationships between the poets, how each poem juxtaposed and counterpointed the others, were very important. Ten voices sang at the same time. I had a large grid chart and could see at a glance what poets were on what days with what poems. It was an audio collage of voice and content.

The unending variety of great poetry nourished an insatiable desire for more, and people began calling again and again. And after the American Federation of the Arts sent out a ten-thousand-piece mailing, the phones really got busy.

The heavy-duty machines couldn't handle the volume and the two-inch vinyl cylinders wore out quickly, so upkeep was an endless worry. But on December 24, 1968, Dial-a-Poem was fully functional.

WHEN I ARRIVED at the Bank on Christmas Eve, Jasper had left-overs from lunch waiting. As we drank wine and smoked joints, the past came back clearly: I had spent Christmas of 1966 with Bob Rauschenberg. In '63, I was with Andy on the eve of *Sleep*; the 1950s Christmas holidays were a series of black-tie dinners, and before all of that, there were the abundant holiday dinners of my childhood.

I wondered if my relationship with Jasper would end in disaster—as it had with Andy and Bob, and, it seemed, with everybody else.

On December 28, Jasper and I drove eleven happy hours in his pale yellow Jeep to spend New Year's in Nags Head, North Carolina, with Jasper's good friends Laura and Bob Benson. Bob and Laura were both artists. Laura was the daughter of a famous socialite father who owned polo ponies.

We arrived at nine-thirty at night. The four Buckminster Fuller domes of Laura and Bob's house designated the separate rooms, and within the hour, we were tucked in bed in ours. The next morning, we opened our sliding glass door to the smell of brine, drifts of snow clustered in the dune grass, waves pounding the empty beach, and the vast blue sky.

"I called Dial-a-Poem, before we left New York," said Laura over breakfast. "Congratulations! What a wonderful work!"

"Thank you."

"I shouldn't say this," she continued, "but the one thing I can't stand is the sound of Allen Ginsberg's voice. He was singing a mantra, but even when he reads, it is like nails on a blackboard."

"Allen is Allen," I said, laughing. I was familiar with her brand of WASPy snobbism, but I knew what she meant. His voice was pretty irritating.

Jasper was a Southerner, and it was interesting to see him relax in his own element. He was 250 miles from where he grew up in South Carolina, and seemed as though he felt at home.

At Kitty Hawk, we stood by the man-made hill where the Wright brothers had pushed off in December 1903 and glided in the air for the first time. "It must have been the same weather when they flew," I said. "Sunny and freezing." It seemed like an auspicious sign for us.

At Cape Hatteras, we saw the iconic lighthouse. Jasper had a profound connection to the "Cape Hatteras" and "Cutty Sark" sections from Hart Crane's long poem *The Bridge*, published shortly before Crane jumped off a steamship and drowned in 1932. Crane had inspired Jasper's early sixties paintings *Land's End* and *Periscope (Hart Crane)*, both of which included a hand reaching for help from a sea of paint. And "Cape Hatteras" had been Crane's ode to his own long-gone inspiration, Walt Whitman. As I watched Jasper at the lighthouse, he seemed to be deep in thought, re-

visiting these connections. Like Whitman before him, Crane had affirmed male love, longing, and loss in his work through oblique allusion. And so did Jasper.

Jasper Johns

BACK AT THE BANK in early January, I jumped up from bed and put my clothes on. *The New York Times* was doing an article on Dial-a-Poem, I told Jasper, and I was due at the photo shoot in two hours. Jasper had a big grin on his face. He liked that I had a success. It was a continuing amusement to him, and this made me happy, because I was giving him pleasure.

The *Times* photographer was a puffy, grumpy man in his fifties. There was a silence, and he said quietly and cynically, looking me in the eye, "You're John Giorno. It's your turn now. Over here."

It was chilling. There was scorn in his voice. I was the no-good kid who had been chosen, or maybe he saw I was gay, just the next piece of trash. It had a strange effect on me. I had no idea what this article would bring, but somehow, he seemed to be saying, I didn't deserve it.

On January 14, the *Times* ran a quarter-page review by Richard F. Shepard. When I left Jasper's at nine-thirty that morning, I didn't know, and by the time I got uptown pandemonium had happened. The review had included the phone number, and hundreds of thousands of people were calling. It was a phenomenal success.

"The telephone company has warned us about the high volume," fretted Joanne Lupton, director of the Architectural League. It was causing a disruption in the Upper East Side telephone exchange, which has the capacity of giving out 250,000 busy signals at one time, and we were almost approaching that number. "If we do, they will cut us off."

It was extremely exciting.

Twenty-four hours a day the phones rang continually. From seven in the morning to midnight, all the lines were busy all the time. We received fourteen thousand calls a day, the maximum number possible with the ten lines and the technology. The first weeks, we received millions of calls and gave millions of busy signals.

My new routine after leaving the Bank and returning to 222 Bowery was going to check on the Dial-a-Poem installation around eleven. First, I took a count of the latest number of calls, making a tally of each line on a ledger sheet; then I changed the tapes. Every day, I met with Joanne and was updated with the latest news, about new publicity, interviews, photo shoots.

Jasper was amused daily by the continual success of Dial-a-Poem. There was something almost every week in *The Village Voice* by Howard Smith, and in the *East Village Other* and other underground press. Bea Fitler, whom I knew through Andy, did a feature in *Harper's Bazaar* on Dial-a-Poem. I was in "Talk of the Town" in *The New Yorker*, the *New York Post*, and the *Daily News* with quirky stories, in *Newsweek* and *Life* magazines with photos, in *The Christian Science Monitor*, and on the BBC, and interviewed by Gary Moore on Voice of America. The real joy of the publicity was that after these articles came out on the newsstands, the telephones rang out of control. It was rare for such fame to happen to anyone, and I was just a young experimental poet.

One morning, NBC's *Today* was scheduled to play a taped segment about Dial-a-Poem at about 8:20 a.m. Jasper woke up at seven and turned on the 18-inch black-and-white TV at the foot of the bed, so we wouldn't miss it. I had a headache from being overworked and stressed, crashing from the half an amphetamine pill every few days, and drinking too much. It was comforting being held in Jasper's arms, my face buried between his neck and shoulder, feeling his smooth and muscular body, as we waited.

Dial-a-Poem

THE PATTERNS OF THE CALLS were interesting. Heavy activity started at seven in the morning, as people woke up, and increased as they arrived at work. By five minutes after nine, when people were at their desks, Dial-a-Poem cranked up to over maximum, and gave off vast numbers of busy signals. It was a way of escaping work. At ten-thirty, during coffee break, at lunch, and at the three-thirty coffee break, it cranked up to maximum again. It dipped at five as people left work, picked up at six, and was running maximum from seven to nine as people were home, alone and relaxed. There was a heavy swell of calls at ten-thirty, with people coming home from dinner, then another swell after midnight, at one-thirty, three-thirty, and four-thirty, as people returned home from the bars. These patterns happened every day. It was a poignant expression of the need and loneliness of people. There were little red lights on each machine, which blinked off when answered, and on when that line was hung up.

This dazzling light show flashing on and off mirrored the moment, frenzied during the day, with swells of activity in the very early morning.

It was a joy for me, choosing which poets and poems, thinking about how they related to one another, what bigger story they told. They presented a full display of all the emotions, anger, desire, and ignorance—something for everybody. People called many times, to see what else was on. If they didn't like the poet, they hung up and dialed again.

One morning, I arrived at ALNY, and all the phones were dead. No blinking lights. A total breakdown. I called repair, who said that we had been disconnected. I called the telephone company. There was a complaint about obscenity, so they had monitored the recording, deemed it obscene, and disconnected Dial-a-Poem.

As it turned out, among the massive publicity we had received was an article in *Junior Scholastic* magazine, telling children to call Dial-a-Poem. Two twelve-year old boys in Queens loved it. They kept calling every day when they got home from school, sometimes hanging up right away, if they didn't like it, and calling right back. And when they liked something, they giggled and laughed, with their two ears pressed to the phone.

One afternoon, the mother of one of the boys grabbed the telephone from him and listened. She heard Jim Carroll reading a piece called "The Celia Sisters" from *The Basketball Diaries*, in which two sisters, fourteen and thirteen years old, walk down the street at night, and one pisses squatting on it, on their way to the beach, where they give blow jobs to all the guys. The mother was furious. She called the telephone company and started this mess.

A catastrophe! And automatically, a cause célèbre.

It was true: as a curator, my personal favorites were poems with sexual images, particularly gay ones. There weren't many poets who worked with sexual energy and images, and I was proud to spotlight them. So, as much as I wished this had not happened, I felt I had no choice but to go into full war mode, mobilizing support and making a strategy. I phoned my artist friend Ken Dewey, who had been named that year as the first director of the newly formed media department at the New York State Council on the Arts (NYSCA). Ken went ballistic, and said quietly, "John, I'll take care of it."

He mustered the NYSCA lawyers, who notified the telephone company that this was a censorship issue, and to connect Dial-a-Poem immediately, or there would be a lawsuit. Freedom of speech. After some determination, the telephone company buckled and reconnected us the next morning at nine. What a relief! They didn't kill us.

I had phoned Howard Smith immediately when we were disconnected, and there was already a story in *The Village Voice*, which was picked up by *Rolling Stone*, WBAI, and the Pacifica radio network, as well as the underground press and media across the country. Since the controversy had a happy conclusion, the Dial-a-Poem phone number was printed everywhere, and we received hundreds of thousands more calls.

In mid-January 1969, Vito Acconci came to 222 Bowery and I recorded him reading six poems. Vito was the poet I liked the most. His poetry magazine *0 to 9* was the best. His concerns felt similar to mine. He was trying extremely hard to understand what poetry was. We were both trying to see poetry clearly, unencumbered by traditions. We had the freedom of being the sum of, but not *of* any particular tradition. We and others were the beginning of poetry changing its skin.

With Dial-a-Poem, we transcended Marshall McLuhan's "The medium is the message." We were the medium *and* the message. And the real message was wisdom sound. Over the next years, Dial-a-Poem would usher in a new era of telecommunications, bringing poetry to millions of people. In 1970, Dial-a-Poem would open at the Museum of Modern Art in New York, and later do so at museums and galleries across the world. I actively encouraged people to start their own Dial-a-Poem in their hometowns. And Dial-a-Poem inspired an entire Dial-a-Something industry: Dial-a-Joke, Dial-Sports, Dial-a-Horoscope, Dial-a-Recipe, Dial-a-Santa-

Claus, Dial-a-Soap, Off-Track Betting results, Lotto results, and phone sex. But even as 900 numbers became big business, I refused to turn Dial-a-Poem into a commodity. Poetry would always be free.

Dial-a-Poem announcement

TRANSFERENCE

In February, Jasper and I flew to the Caribbean island of St. Martin for a ten-day vacation. We stayed in a small hotel next to a rickety fishing pier. The place had not changed since the early 1930s, with tin-roofed houses and colonial poverty. In its seediness, it had a Lauren Bacall and Humphrey Bogart glamour.

We were supposed to have a suite but instead had a dank cement cell on the second floor overlooking a rutted road and a dreary beach. The place had been recommended by a friend, who said it was beautiful. "I have been misled," said Jasper, a bit somberly.

"It isn't even quaint," I said.

It rained every morning, which made it cold, and after five days, it never crossed our minds to go swimming. Instead, we drove around and explored the island. From the thick jungle on the French side to the cruise-ship port town on the Dutch side, heavy and depressing with stupid shoppers. A delicious, drunken dinner in the one high-end "French-island" restaurant. A poolside dinner at a tourist hotel, loud merengue, trashy Americans.

At a little gift shop, I bought beautiful bright magenta sunglasses and a white embroidered blouse, connecting to my female sensibility, trying too hard to be cool. Jasper disapproved but didn't say so. Behind a row of poor farmhouses, surrounded by locals, we watched two roosters with sharpened talons tear each other apart.

I was acutely aware of the colonial privilege implications of our being there, but I also saw it as living in a British novel, empty and without substance. I contemplated my life, thought about the passing of the last ten years: from the Beats to Andy, being politically radicalized by Burroughs, in love with Rauschenberg, now Jasper. The anger of the Vietnam War and politics were getting worse, like a cancer. I felt compelled and propelled to somehow continue with poetic political action. But for my poetry to really mean something, I had to connect to the culture, more broadly, more deeply.

Jasper held up the brand-new Polaroid camera he had bought but never used. "I would like to make a photo."

I agreed eagerly.

He took two pictures of me standing in front of the sea, a palm tree, and the distant mountains. One good, and one bad, which he threw away. He laughed and handed me the good one.

THAT SPRING, my impulse to engage with the world tugged me, ever so subtly, away from Jasper. Sequestered in the Bank, he ate his lunch—prepared by his African American cook—by himself most days, every week or so with a group of ten friends. Meanwhile, I threw myself into direct political action, putting my media skills to use for a giant peace parade on April 5—a culmination of my radicalization that William Burroughs had begun in 1965. And I even took my poetry into the streets, too.

On a sunny, brisk early spring day in midtown Manhattan, I laced up a pair of roller skates and took off down Fifth Avenue. From Tiffany to St. Patrick's Cathedral and the New York Public Library, then up again and down again, I handed out mimeographed poems to whomever I made eye contact with, whoever seemed to want one. I was performing to each individual person in the theater of the street. My body, the poet's body, was directly involved in transmitting the poem. It was a strenuous performance, a glorious exhilaration.

Crossing my path on those fifteen blocks of Fifth Avenue were about twenty others in our group—including Vito Acconci, John Perrault, Scott Burton, Anne Waldman, and Hannah Weiner—all of us expanding poetry, performance, and art with the street as our venue.

Three hours later, I was tired, having given away all the poems. I took off the skates in front of the library, taxied down to the Bowery for a nap, shower, and joint, then headed over to the Bank. Hearing my stories of roller-poetry, Jasper got a big joyous grin on his face. "Oh, Giorno!" he said.

The author distributing poems
at a Street Works event

A MONTH LATER, our Street Works project had grown to include thirty-nine downtown poets and artists, spread out around West Fourteenth Street, performing incredible large-scale pieces and minor forgettable actions alike. The sum of the parts was powerful.

And in late May, our final site-specific public action, and my most extreme. Late on a Sunday afternoon, I took half a pill of speed and joined a hundred other artists out on the streets of SoHo, the downtown neighborhood of cast-iron loft-filled buildings that many of us called home.

I called my piece "Stop the Cars, Stop Vehicle Pollution, Stop Air Pollution." It was an ecological protest against air pollution, which in 1969 was at its worst, when acid rain burned our eyes to tears. I handed out bags of roofing nails to five friends and we all got to work. At first, we sprinkled them in the middle of the side streets when there was no traffic. I made sure that at least some of these nails stood upright, their wide heads on the cobblestones. We fanned out through the neighborhood, picking up new bags of nails that I had stashed at strategic locations. And finally, when it got dark, I threw handful after handful of nails across Canal Street in between traffic lights, and watched what happened.

Cars ran over the nails, driving for only a few blocks before their tires went flat. In the Holland Tunnel, there were dozens of cars with flat tires, and dozens more backed up outside. Hundreds of disabled vehicles fanned out across SoHo and beyond.

In the midst of the confusion, I approached a police officer and asked, "Excuse me, what is happening?"

"A nut is nailing the streets," said the cop.

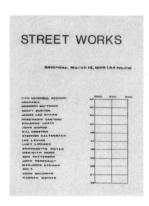

My performance piece was a brilliant success, I thought, falling into bed on the Bowery, aching with exhaustion. I was too angry, too selfish to think of the chaos and suffering I had caused, the lack of real benefit to anyone.

Street Works poster

ONE NIGHT IN THE MIDDLE of the Street Works project, I was at a dinner party for Wynn Chamberlain's birthday, and he wanted us all to take acid. I wasn't in the mood and resisted, but he pressed.

"Oh, come on, John," said Wynn. "You can handle it."

I gave in, broke a pill in quarters, put one quarter in my mouth, and swallowed.

Midway through the evening, I stopped enjoying the conversation. I began to feel increasingly separate from the people, a bit lonely, and waited for it to end so I could slip into bed with Jasper.

It was after two in the morning when I was able to extricate myself, very stoned, from the party. I took a taxi to the Bank, on Houston, and opened the big brass door with my key. The huge main room was flooded by the streetlights. I walked through the back room alcove and up the stairs to Jasper's bedroom. I took off my clothes in the dark, slipping into bed. I gave Jasper a hug, cuddled next to him, and went to sleep.

I woke a short time later, very stoned on the acid. I was wide-awake, and I tried not to move for a long time, worried about disturbing Jasper. I knew from past experience on LSD that when the mind is very active, it's best not to lie down, but to sit up in meditation posture, to rest the mind and not follow my thoughts.

I very quietly got up and went into the bathroom, which was quite large, and sat next to the hot tub on the white tile in the blackness. My mind was very active, and I tried to do meditation practice, even though I didn't know exactly what that was. (I had not yet been formally trained and had only read about it in books.) I let my mind rest, not following the thoughts as they arose, and the thoughts vanished. My mind seemed a gentle white light, not quite blissful but no longer racing. I was aware that all my thoughts were illusions or delusions caused by the drug. And I had to wait out the rattling effect it had on the nervous system.

The bathroom door burst open, the bright lights went on, and Jasper yelled, "What are you doing in here?"

"I took some LSD, and am just sitting up in meditation," I said.

"What!"

"I was at Wynn and Sally's for dinner, and we took some LSD. I'm a bit stoned, and just wanted to sit up."

Jasper was trembling with rage. "Come to bed!" I turned out the lights, and returned to my side of the bed, not touching him.

It seemed very bad that this had happened. A person on LSD is highly impressionable; feelings and events become imprinted in the mind. Jasper's anger rang like a death knell. I wondered what the result would be.

The next morning Jasper was grumpy and a bit distant. I made a big effort with kindness and loving affection, and it took about twenty minutes to win him over. Finally, Jasper turned and smiled with a big happy grin, and everything was forgiven. I spent the day at home, recovering from the drug and from the shock of Jasper's anger. Or maybe I just buried it.

LESS THAN TWO WEEKS LATER, the critical, defining moment in my relationship with Jasper finally arrived. It was the Saturday of the Memorial Day weekend, around four o'clock. He and I were in the Bank, having spent the afternoon reading, relaxing, and talking. It seemed that Jasper was peacefully contemplating something. Out of the blue, he said, "It is nothing more than the transference of power from one generation to another."

I was shocked. For the first time, Jasper was establishing a position, and it was the opposite of my view. For eight months, we had talked endlessly about what I believed was the somewhat enlightened times in which we lived—the change, freedoms, and individual liberations that had occurred in the culture from civil rights in the 1950s and '60s, protesting the Vietnam War, gay rights and feminism, psychedelic and mind-expanding drugs, and meditation. Jasper knew I felt deeply connected to all of it.

So what Jasper said—"It is nothing more than the transference of power from one generation to another"—rang like the sound of a big bell.

"You know, I think differently," I said. "Of course, every generation rebels against their parents' generation. But this time it seems different. The enormity of what is happening. In any case, it will have beneficial results, and change the world."

I was depressed hearing Jasper's pronouncement, but even more depressed by the thought that he might be right. And I had feelings of kindness for what he must be going through. Jasper always placed himself in a neutral position. Was it Buddhist equanimity or nihilism? What bothered me was that he was seemingly unable to appreciate aspiration and positive change, which required compassion. Was this the deathblow to our relationship?

A WEEK LATER, after a somber dinner of quite good leftovers from various lunches, Jasper and I were at the Bank drinking and smoking joints. Jasper was being slightly disapproving of some things, which pushed my buttons. I had a problem with depression, and it was easy for me to go over the top, which meant an internal feeling of spiraling to the bottom. I felt I had to hide my depression, because I thought it was caused by drugs and alcohol, and didn't yet realize I had a chemical, hormonal imbalance. I mistook it for intuition, and it clouded my judgment.

It seemed Jasper and I were incompatible. We were in love, and our minds had a deep nonverbal connection; but externally in the world, we disagreed about almost everything. I had ignored that from the beginning, but it was beginning to wear me down.

"Maybe we should break up?" I said. "We disagree about everything. Maybe we're not meant to be together." There was a shocking moment of silence. I could not believe I had said the words. Jasper's face wrinkled up and he began to cry. I rushed over and hugged him, and I starting crying, too.

We straightened up. I sat down and said, "It was a mistake for me to say that. Please forgive me! Please forget it. We leave in a few weeks for Nags Head, and a glorious summer on the beach."

Jasper looked at me for a long, sad moment and nodded his head yes. It was heartbreaking. I didn't quite verbalize it but knew intuitively in that moment that I had rejected Jasper just as Bob had done. Was being rejected the habitual pattern of Jasper's life, one that would cause him boundless suffering?

A WEEK AFTER Dial-a-Poem finally ended its twice-extended nine-month run, Jasper and I made our much-needed escape. He had rented a beach house on Nags Head for two full months. As Jasper drove us away from the bank building across Houston Street, we turned and looked into each other's eyes and smiled. We were very happy. It was a new beginning on the beach. Jasper had an enormous, radiant smile, and was at his best—full of love and positive feelings.

Our house sat on rolling white dunes overlooking the ultramarine surf. For weeks, we did just what couples in love are supposed to do at the beach: woke up in each other's arms, had morning sex or just groggy hugging, ate big breakfasts, walked on scorching sand, tumbled around in the waves, ate, drank, smoked, and fell asleep in each other's arms.

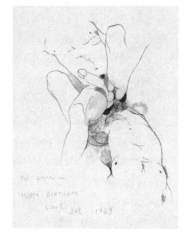

Every three or four days, I took a quarter or less of a Dexamyl pill to jump-start my energy in the sleepy, hot, numbing South, then focused on my poems for two intense hours. I was also working on a collaboration with the artist Joe Brainard, a pornographic cartoon.

Jasper read a lot.

Joe Brainard's birthday present to the author

ONE DAY, as we were driving out of the parking lot of the supermarket, Jasper asked, "Would you like to go looking for mushrooms?"

"Yes!" I said, surprised. "You mean like John Cage?"

"Well, yes," said Jasper, smiling. "I've been with him."

"Yes, I would love to," I said.

I assumed he meant we would make a plan to do it in a few days, but we were going now. We drove down a 1930s tarmac road bordered by a poor scrub tree forest. The land was completely flat, which made it introverted and depressing.

Jasper pulled off the road onto a dirt and white sand clearing in the woods. "Let's go mushrooming."

"What!" I said surprised. "You mean there are mushrooms here?"

We walked through a dwarf pine forest and scrub trees, petrified from the endless beatings by storms from the ocean. It had rained the night before, and lots of mushrooms, many different kinds, poked up through the moist pine needles and leaves scattered on the forest floor.

"Those are eatable," said Jasper. "Chanterelles."

"Should we take them home and cook them?" I asked.

"I wouldn't risk it," said Jasper. We both laughed.

It felt like a spiritual moment. I did my best to be in it, doing a Zen Buddhist meditation, watching my breath going in and out, counting the breaths one to ten, and resting the mind. I think it felt spiritual to Jasper, too, but I didn't know what he was doing with his mind.

There was a bright red mushroom. "Look at that!" I said. "It must be poisonous. It's so gorgeous."

"It sure is."

I told Jasper about a time the previous year on Allen Ginsberg's farm in upstate New York when we found *Amanita musca-*

ria mushrooms in the forest. Allen had a renowned mushroom book, and we verified it. The book explained you could extract the psychedelic juices by squeezing the mushrooms with your hands and collecting the milky juice in a bowl. I volunteered, and then immediately washed my hands. It was in the evening, and I went to bed shortly after, and got a bit high from what had been absorbed by my skin.

A week later, Jasper and I went looking for mushrooms again. It was very hot and dry, and we didn't find any. We never did it again.

Jasper was happy because he felt at home in the South, where he was born. He loved it. Hot and humid, there was the smell of warm breezes. Gentlemanliness emanated from him, and a feeling of well-being. I could feel him feeling it, and since I loved him, I took great pleasure in it.

Jasper was always reluctant to work on paintings and drawings. Maybe he felt that it took a great effort, and had developed a natural physical hesitation. About a week after we arrived, in the late afternoon, I saw a crumpled wire hanger on a table and the sketchbooks he had brought were moved to a different place.

He's working! I thought, with a feeling of triumphant fanfare. The coat hanger was one of Jasper's classic images. I didn't dare open the sketchbook. I waited two days, and asked, and he showed me the drawings.

On July 11, Clarice Rivers arrived for the weekend. Clarice was married to Larry Rivers, and an old friend of both of ours. She was exuberant and funny, and with her twilling Welsh accent told us endless stories about our many mutual friends.

"What are you working on?" Clarice asked.

Jasper showed her the sketchbook with the pencil drawings of the bent hanger as well as crosshatch and herringbone patterns.

"I'm going to do etchings for Tanya," Jasper said. Tanya Grosman had a lithography press, where Jasper did many etchings and prints. He had just mailed Tanya a postcard of the stone marker at the site where the Wright brothers pushed off on their first flight, which we'd visited on our trip to Nags Head the previous winter.

I thought again of the relationship between Jasper, Hart Crane, and Walt Whitman. "Cape Hatteras," *Periscope (Hart Crane)*, and *Land's End*, and Whitman's "tenderest lover of man." The indeterminate interpretations of Jasper's paintings echoed the shifting meanings in Crane's and Whitman's poems, and they all mourned the failure of homosexual love. But Jasper never talked about it.

About a week after Clarice left, Laura Benson, whose vacation house we had stayed at the previous winter, had us for dinner. "Don't you want to stay and see the astronauts walk on the moon?" she asked us afterward. That afternoon, Apollo 11 had landed on the moon, and Neil Armstrong was scheduled to take his first steps on the lunar surface on live TV in just a few hours. Back at our place, we didn't have a TV.

"No, I don't want to see it," Jasper said, and off we went in the yellow Jeep.

His reaction seemed a little strange to me. The first humans to set foot on the moon was a once-in-a-lifetime event and should be of some special interest. I knew he hated national, televised spectacles and tragedies, which were a cultural and political invention of the lowest order, and the rivalry between the United States and the Soviet Union for the conquest of space was loathsome to him. I completely agreed with Jasper. William Burroughs believed the media spectacles were ways to control people's minds.

But I thought a man on the moon was a splendid accomplishment, and should be appreciated. With my innate Buddhist meditation, I tried not to react. If that's what Jasper wanted, I went along with it. But I was a tiny bit disappointed.

The next day we visited Laura and Bob again, and I saw the replay on TV. I was amazed. Jasper saw some of the coverage and was, happily, at least a little curious, and smiling.

It seemed the root problem of our relationship—which had caused the crisis in the months before—was that Jasper was not connected to life and the present moment in the way I wanted to be. I had loved seeing the live coverage of Jacqueline Kennedy walking behind the coffin at JFK's funeral, and the men on the moon were pie in the sky. Even as this started to come into focus for me, I tried not to allow any negative thoughts toward Jasper, dissolving them as they arose, because it would have spoiled our time together. Maybe I sensed we were doomed, and I wanted to appreciate the last moments of profound love we shared.

IN EARLY AUGUST, Anne Waldman came to Nags Head for a four-day weekend. Jasper had encouraged me to invite friends, and Anne was the only one I thought appropriate. Jasper had not met her, but he knew her poems in *The World*, the magazine of the St. Mark's Poetry Project. He loved poets.

We had a wonderful time, chirping gossip, swimming in the ocean, smoking joints and drinking, visiting Laura and Bob, cracking open steamed bay crabs. It was a welcome relief from our solitude.

After she left, the vast heaviness of the ocean and emptiness of the sky in Nags Head became reflected in our minds, calming us in a sweet numbness. But I had, I realized now, an intractable dilemma. I was the cause of all the trouble and problems in my relationship with Jasper. I was the one who was attached to the 1960s culture, and who was deluded in believing that psychedelic drugs had magical powers, that poetry, art, and political action could change the world for the better. I felt exiled in domestic life. Jasper just wanted a sane, simple, fulfilling relationship with a man he loved.

On Friday, August 8, I left Nags Head for what I thought would be a ten-day trip to New York. "Why do you have to go back?" asked Jasper.

I reminded him that I was organizing a poetry festival at Wave Hill in Riverdale, the Bronx. It was a complicated setup and I had to meet with technicians and sound people beforehand.

Jasper seemed a bit sad. I tried to be cheerful. "I'm back here in one week, and then we have another week."

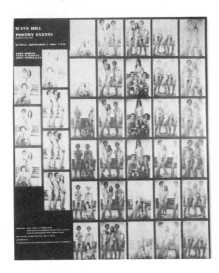

He drove me to the Durham airport.

As soon as I got home, the festival's patron called with bad news. The whole event was canceled, all because of a tiny bit of nudity in the poster.

Poster for Wave Hill Poetry Events

I WAS OUTRAGED and disappointed, but had plenty to fill my time in New York: six weeks of unanswered mail, work on Dial-a-Poem, which was opening in Chicago the next month, dinner with my parents in Roslyn Heights, and so on.

Then, three days before I was supposed to return to Jasper, Wynn called and invited me up to Rhinebeck for the weekend. I hesitated, but he assured me he'd put me on the train on Sunday so I'd make my flight to North Carolina the next day.

"You must come," he pressed. "We're all going to a rock concert in Woodstock."

The three-day festival was all over the news. Organizers couldn't get a permit in the town of Woodstock because the expected crowd was so huge, so at the last minute, they had relocated it to a dairy farm miles away. The endless publicity only inflamed people's desire to go.

As soon as I got to Wynn's, I took an hour-long nap, and by

seven that night, I was crowded into a station wagon with Wynn and Sally, their one-year-old twins, Sam and Sara, and three of our friends. We drove from the north on small country roads, while most people were coming up from the south on the New York Thruway. Traffic was intense in one direction, a bewildering number of cars jamming the roads until eventually it all came to a dead standstill. There were streams of people walking in one direction. We parked off the road, and followed them. It was drizzling.

"We should take our bearing," said Sally. "Remember where we've left the car."

"Who wants to join me?" asked Wynn, holding out a handful of tiny orange drum-shaped pills. Everyone reached for their acid.

Erring on the side of caution, I decided to wait until we got there. I wanted to see where I was going.

After a mile of walking, we arrived at the festival grounds—a huge bowl-shaped cow pasture with a stage at the far bottom. Before we got there, crowds had broken through sections of the chain-link fence, and now waves of people were flooding through the gaps.

"Let's go," said Wynn, and we joined them. The concert had begun and Joan Baez was singing.

As we neared the edge of the bowl, Wynn and most of the others veered away from me. This was good, because Wynn was a control freak and I wanted to escape from him. Now I was stuck only with Bill Berkson, the straight poet from the second-generation New York school of poets, whom I was beginning to feel estranged from. He walked to the right, and I eased away to the left, and got rid of him, too. The crowd was already so enormous that we were swallowed up. I never saw them again. I was ready for the festival. Now I had to get high.

I walked a little farther and came to the Hog Farm, the commune that was setting up its soup kitchen. Recognizing a guy carrying a giant soup pot, I asked him where I could score some LSD or mushrooms, and he pointed to a skinny guy with long hair.

I swallowed a capsule of psilocybin mushrooms, and it was on. Within hours, the ever increasing crowd grew to more than four hundred thousand people. That night and the next day were a blur, but it all felt incomprehensibly wonderful. By Saturday night, it *was* incomprehensibly wonderful.

For all the great moments of Woodstock, the very best for me was late Saturday night into Sunday morning. Janis Joplin sang her heart out in the dead of night, then Sly and the Family Stone, the Who, and finally, an exhausted Grace Slick and Jefferson Airplane as the hot sun rose up over the horizon. It was one of the most extraordinary things I've ever experienced.

In my ongoing disagreement with Jasper, the festival seemed proof of the new openness, the alternative culture, of consciousness expanding. Four hundred thousand people were the proof in the pudding. It wasn't that Jasper was wrong. I knew intuitively that Jasper was right, that it was just a generational transfer of power in a new form, polluted with traditional corruption and motives. But it was what I had to work with. Feeling the voice of my time was how I made poems. I had to go with it, not with Jasper. Just like his not wanting to watch the moon landing, my embrace of Woodstock felt like another fatal wound in our relationship.

On Monday morning, the fourth day of the festival, I woke having slept alongside the Hog Farm, had some tea, got high, and felt beyond stress, as if I possessed a great clarity. It was sunny, and the air was fresh.

I wandered about wondering what to do. Most of the people had gone, and there were only about twenty thousand people still there, many of them sleeping. The last morning performances had begun, and Jimi Hendrix was scheduled to play soon. The empty fields were littered with trash.

When I was walking near the backstage trucks and cars, I saw Bill Berkson standing in front of me. We were surprised and relieved.

"How are we going to get back?" I asked.

"I was just going to ask you!"

I asked somebody who was waiting near a car, and he said he could take us, but was waiting for a friend. I walked back to Bill and asked somebody else on the way, and they said they could take us. Bill also found someone who would take us. We ended up taking the ride that was leaving first.

Bill and I sat next to each other in the backseat as we drove away. We could not quite believe what had happened, what great luck it was to have been there. We were driving fast with the windows open on the New York Thruway, going back to New York, numb with exhaustion and radiantly clear.

I ARRIVED in my third-floor loft at 222 Bowery at 1:30 p.m. I lay down on the bed for ten minutes and rested my mind.

I got up, called Jasper, and explained that I had been to the Woodstock Festival, which no doubt he had read about in *The New York Times*. He was not pleased at first, but I explained with a lot of enthusiasm how wonderfully extraordinary it was, and he became happy, laughing, and accepting that I had gone.

"Jasper, please forgive me," I said. "I am a physical wreck from everything, and can't make the plane at four-thirty this afternoon. I have to rest and recover, I'm drained. You come back in one week. Please forgive me for not coming. I'll see you in New York next week."

Jasper seemed understanding and positive.

In late August, he drove back from Nags Head, on his own. We were happy to see each other, sleep together, and everything seemed to return to normal. But as the fall got busy, we saw less and less of each other. William Burroughs made an unexpected five-day visit from London. In Chicago, I organized a candlelight vigil with Abbie Hoffman in support of the seven men on trial for the riots at the Democratic Convention. In Washington, I joined four hundred thousand people for a rally against the Vietnam War.

The night after that demonstration, I had a dinner date with Jasper back in New York. At first, I phoned him to say I would be driving back a little late, but there were massive traffic jams, and I called again to say I wouldn't be there until after midnight. He was hurt again, I could feel it.

On Halloween, the night Dial-a-Poem launched in Chicago, I had dinner with Jasper at 7:30 p.m. I didn't know it would be the last time.

He canceled our next date, a month later, and the next one after that, and that was it. I came to the realization that we had broken up. It was heartbreaking, as I loved Jasper, but also inevitable. I never called him again and he never called me. I knew when Jasper made up his mind there was no going back. I was not happy, but relieved, and sadly went on, and before me was another lonely abyss.

IN THE SEPTEMBER 1969 issue of *The World*, there was a poem by Anne Waldman about the summer. It included a long description of her visit with Jasper in Nags Head, making no mention of me. Anne had never met Jasper before and she was there because of me. Yet she had eliminated me from her story about Jasper. In years to come, I would grow familiar with this pattern of hers, but at the time I was a bit shocked. It felt all too familiar: as I had been with Andy, and then Bob, I was being edited out of my lovers' stories.

PART FOUR

THE PATH

In the early 1960s, I did not know how to meditate. Sometimes on LSD or on psilocybin mushrooms, my mind was like the Buddhist metaphor of a drunk rampaging elephant, because I was having a bad trip, due to my grasping and attachment. Sometimes I was having a good trip, and it was wonderful. Everything arose from the mind and I had to work with the mind.

I stumbled on meditation out of necessity. Somehow, going to the Zen Center on Park Avenue was not an option, but I knew about the Zen practice of watching the breath. I imitated the Buddha in statues and paintings, as well as photographs of people meditating I had seen in magazines. I sat in meditation posture, eyes closed, and relaxed the mind. I found that if I did not follow my thoughts, let go of them, but without rejecting them, they dissolved; and I felt good, and sometimes there was a clarity and bliss. Following my thoughts was like falling down the stairs, and my mind was bruised from grasping at the thoughts. I didn't know what I was doing, but there was no alternative.

In 1970, after my relationship with Jasper was over, and while Dial-a-Poem was at MoMA, I spent a lot of time with Allen Ginsberg at his sixty-acre farm near the upstate town of Cherry Valley. The farm was home to the Committee on Poetry, a group of about fourteen or more of us in the summer, and four or five in the winter. I visited every three weeks or so for three or four days. We were experimenting with living together, a poetry commune of sorts.

At this time, Allen was very important to me, as a guru. I felt he was a bodhisattva, because he helped so many people. He had been to India in 1964 and was the only one who knew anything about meditation. I asked him lots of questions about Buddhist meditation, Tibetan and Zen.

I didn't understand that Allen was Hindu—that was his karmic propensity. I didn't know there were such big differences between the Buddhist and the Hindu. Allen was a politician, and considered Buddhists a part of his constituency.

Marietta Green, a friend of Allen's who had spent many years in India, was staying at the farm one time when I was there. A Tibetan Buddhist, Marietta got along really well with me. Secretly in our bedrooms, she taught me Tibetan mantras—Guru Rinpoche, Chenrezig, and Tara—and how to recite them with prayer beads. I was happy that my path finally pointed in a direction and my propensity was Tibetan Buddhism. Sitting in meditation posture, I rested the mind, repeated the mantras, and hoped for the best.

One day in August, on a bright, sunny morning, Allen and I were standing on the farmhouse porch, drinking tea and talking. A cool, fresh breeze fluttered the green leaves and blew on us, before another extremely hot day. We had all taken LSD the day before and were still high.

"What is the Buddhist view of . . . ?" I asked Allen. Then, I asked another question, "The nature of mind is . . . ?"

Allen screamed at me, "Arghhh! Stop asking me all these questions! Why don't you go to India and find out for yourself!"

Allen's voice was angry and loud, spit flying, and the sound struck my face like a sharp slap. I was stunned. Thunderstruck. In the sensitive state of tripping on LSD, I saw stars. My first reaction was to be hurt, then angry. But in the next moment, all I felt was joy. My heart opened up with a warm, bright light.

"What a totally great idea!" I said. "Go to India, and find out! Allen, thank you!"

It was the right thing to do, but how would I afford it?

Earlier that year, I had received a request from the Factory to lend Andy Warhol's *Bellevue II* (rolled up in my parents' attic since 1966) for a touring show of his work. When it came back, I hung it in my loft at 222 Bowery. It was a great painting.

Everyone loved seeing it, and word got out that I had it. For weeks, Les Levine kept telling me about Peter Brant, a collector who wanted the Warhol and would pay $30,000 in cash.

It was wonderful living with such a great, powerful thing, but my life had moved on. My obsession with my friend Marcia's suicide had vanished, and I was no longer involved with Andy. I was tempted. Thirty thousand dollars in cash, out of the blue, seemed like a gift of the gods, a belated reward from the 1960s, a big windfall. I thought, Why not spend it playfully, generously, and joyfully?

I sold the painting to Peter Brant. He gave me $15,000 in cash and said he would give me the balance in one week. He never did. I got Les to pester him. He said he didn't have the money, but he would give me another artwork worth more than $15,000 in payment: Claes Oldenburg's *Candy Counter*, 114 painted plaster candy bars. Les said I should take it, but then I couldn't sell it for years, because it wasn't in the original candy counter case. I was furious with Peter Brant, a really rich guy abusing a poor poet.

Suddenly, everybody knew I had $15,000 (a bunch of money in 1970) and it went quickly: $5,000 for an over-budget movie Wynn was making, $3,000 to a dope dealer friend. A message came from Andy that he would paint my portrait for $15,000—even he was trying to get the money!

Not long afterward, when the Factory superstars accused Andy of exploiting them, of using their talent and then getting rid of them without giving them any money, Andy said, "John Giorno is my highest-paid superstar. He got thirty thousand dollars." In 1995, *Bellevue II* was bought by the Stedelijk Museum in Amsterdam, for $1 million. In 2000, it was worth $5 million, and in 2006, $20 million.

But in 1971, all I knew was that this suicide painting of Andy's, a relic of my old life, was now a ticket to my new life.

I decided to end the poetry projects I was working on, and not start any new ones, to make a clean break. Dial-a-Poem's run at MoMA was ending in November. I was determined to finish the last program I was producing for WPAX/Radio Hanoi and Abbie Hoffman (rock 'n' roll and radical news for soldiers in Vietnam) in December. It took me until April 1971 to wind everything down and completely disengage. But then I was ready to go. On May 21, I flew to London on my way to New Delhi. I spent ten days visiting with William Burroughs, who lived on Duke Street in St. James's. We got together every other night or so, got drunk, smoked a lot of cigarettes, and talked. We liked being together and focused a lot of energy on each other.

"There is very little grass and hash in this god-awful place," said William.

He had only a hot plate to cook on. One night I fixed bacon and eggs and another night we ate peanut butter and crackers. Occasionally, we staggered out to dinner for Angus steak and potatoes. It was a cold, wet May, and everything was a little off and uncomfortable. William saw very few people in London, and he struck me as desolate and lonely.

Using a reel-to-reel tape recorder, I recorded William reading excerpts from *The Wild Boys*, a novel he was working on, for future poetry projects. I didn't have anything in mind. This was before William became a consummate master of huge audiences. He gave a naïve performance, frail, awkwardly innocent, but still brilliant.

William loved that I was, in his words, "going to India on a spiritual quest." And Tibetan lamas were cool.

I bought a cheap ticket, one way London to New Delhi, on Aeroflot. That meant I had to spend eight hours in the Moscow airport, before changing planes. In the airport, fat Soviet officers waited in their funny-looking Cold War military uniforms. I was in the bardo, in a Hollywood movie, and awaited rebirth.

I WENT TO INDIA to find the empty nature of mind. I had had enough of being a victim of my own mind. I knew there was a way out, a release from delusion and suffering. Everyone was a Buddha. From psychedelic mushrooms and LSD, I was aware that there were many other realms of existence, of which I knew nothing. How to realize it? Reading books did not do it.

Ever since my suicide attempt in 1959, intuitively I had felt an affinity with the Tibetan lamas who were refugees in northern India. And since there was almost no help from anyone, I had to trust my intuition, which was dangerous for someone with a depression problem. For those of us who went to India in the early years, when not many people had yet done it and there was no path—before the dharma came west and became readily available to everyone—it was a little scary. Every step was like walking blindfolded through traffic.

There were no acceptable alternatives, no other choices. Not to do it was to fail or die. And it was a joke, like Don Quixote charging windmills at night, delusion. But there was no way out. Unspoken: it was a noble effort, a secret heroic action, a pure spiritual search challenging profane America. I had to do it.

The author in India

SINCE BEING FORCED into exile by the Chinese Communist conquest of Tibet, the great masters had settled in Himalayan towns in northern India, former British hill stations where the colonial raj had gone during the summer heat and monsoon. Hundreds of thousands of Tibetan refugees suffered enormously, enduring near starvation, disease, bad living conditions in refugee camps, and harsh discrimination.

But life went on, and the Tibetans worked hard and prospered. The lamas gave teachings and did practice, bought houses and built monasteries. Wonderful dharma communities arose in the beautiful villages under the majestic snow mountains. The lamas, great enlightened beings, were hidden treasures waiting to be discovered.

As soon as I arrived in India, this was where I went. In Almora, an old British hill station resort, I rendezvoused with Sally and Wynn Chamberlain. Also there was my old friend Nena, now married to Bob Thurman, who was in India on a Fulbright.

We lived a beautiful, privileged life in a Himalayan paradise. We took Sunshine LSD and smoked a lot of grass. A stream of Westerners came through on their way to visit their gurus along the thousand-plus miles of Himalayan snow mountains from Darjeeling to Dalhousie. Everyone was like me: at some early but pure stage in their spiritual development.

One lama I found scholarly, grand, and boring. Through another lama, doing the death prayers for Sally's just-deceased brother, I got my first taste of Tibetan ritual: a room filled with statues and paintings, hundreds of burning butter lamps, sacred bell and *dorje*, manuscripts, incense, and *tormas*—small, colorful figures made of barley flour and butter representing the Buddha.

I was especially drawn to the meditation practices of a Nyingma lama and two young monk attendants, who were on holiday from school, and I asked them a lot of questions. To communicate, I began to study the Tibetan language with a monk. But I was lonely, and I kept reciting the mantras that Marietta had taught me in Cherry Valley. I prayed for my path to unfold.

ONE BRIGHT, SUNNY MORNING after I'd been in Almora for two weeks, Bob Thurman came into my room and said, "We're going to Dharamsala to visit His Holiness the Dalai Lama. Do you want to come?"

I was very surprised. In 1971, the Dalai Lama was a living Buddha, the god king of Tibet, remote and mythical, and as inaccessible as Shangri-La. This was decades before he won the Nobel

Peace Prize and became a pop icon and the great Buddhist teacher of the world.

"Yes, thank you!" I had come to India to experience Tibetan Buddhism, and it hadn't really happened yet.

"We leave in three days."

With his wife and two kids, we drove in Bob's Volkswagen camper, named Nandi, to Delhi, and across India up to Dharamsala. It was an excruciating drive, lasting four grueling days. One night I couldn't sleep because of the flies and mosquitoes, heat, and filth. Somebody gave me a tranquilizer called Mandrax. It knocked me out cold and I slept for twelve hours. I was a living corpse, transported by Bob and Nena across the lush rice fields of Haryana province. It was a mistake, and I missed mother India; I was carried across India in a cocoon, protected in a shroud of ignorance.

That night, we climbed back up into the Himalayan Mountains. I woke up and was reborn. It was a full moon, the Buddha moon in June of the Buddha's enlightenment under the Bodhi tree in Bodh Gaya. The moon was enormous, golden and luscious, and hot as a rising sun. A very auspicious sign, an awakening. We were going to see the Dalai Lama the next day.

"And tomorrow is the Dalai Lama's birthday," said Bob.

"How old is he?"

"His Holiness will be thirty-six." We were very happy, gleeful with anticipation.

We stayed in the Dalai Lama's official guesthouse, and the next morning we went to see His Holiness. Monsoon rains had come and things had cooled off. His residence was in a forty-acre compound surrounded by a fifteen-foot-high chain-link and barbed-wire fence, which also housed his government in exile. Indian soldiers stood guard everywhere to protect the Dalai Lama, which gave the appearance that he was their prisoner. Beautiful jungles spread out on top of a massive rock mountain with the panorama of the snow mountains beneath a vast blue sky.

His Holiness lived in a modest palace. We were taken along a garden of dahlias, zinnias, and marigolds to his private living room. The Dalai Lama welcomed Bob Thurman and all of us with great openness, friendliness, and affection. The private audience lasted for three hours. The Dalai Lama really loved Bob, wanting to know everything that had happened to him. Bob spoke perfect Tibetan and they talked with intensity and love. Then His Holiness wanted to know about each of us; and we gossiped. There was lots of laughing. His Holiness radiated a great warmth and blessings.

I gave the Dalai Lama a white scarf and a book of my poems called *Balling Buddha*, published the year before. The pages of the book were different bright colors—red, yellow, blue, green, purple—and His Holiness skimmed through them admiringly. Every once in a while, he picked the book up again, let the rainbow spectrum of pages flip through his fingers, and said, "Ahhh!" I was ecstatic.

Tea was served in proper English teacups from a Georg Jensen sterling silver teapot. Bob received teachings. His Holiness gave an empowerment of explanations and commentary. Everyone was very happy, although the Thurmans' little daughter, fourteen-month-old Uma, cried a lot. I became invisible, sat three feet back, did not interfere, and kept my mouth shut. Occasionally, His Holiness looked at me long and deep, then burst into laughter and asked Bob, "Who is he?"

The Dalai Lama was the incarnation of Chenrezig, the Buddha of compassion. I silently recited his mantra: *Om mani padme hum*. I was in the mandala of Chenrezig, becoming one with the deity, and it was very powerful. I repeated the mantra over and over again. Devotion was, maybe, a first step.

I wanted to take refuge with His Holiness, formally becoming a Buddhist, but it seemed a bit pushy and premature, and I didn't ask. I looked into his eyes and recited the refuge mantra.

When the teaching was finished, the Dalai Lama placed his Tibetan manuscript on the square saffron cloth, asked Bob and me to each hold a corner of the cloth, and folded the book tightly.

A physical experience with the Dalai Lama! When we said good-bye, His Holiness picked up my book of poems, tucked it in his arm, and walked with us down the hall. He turned and faced us. The Dalai Lama was holding my book above his forearm, framed by the maroon monk's robes, big and bright, like a billboard, at his heart center. The words *Balling Buddha* gave me a jolt, as did the fact that in the book there were lots of gay pornographic poems. I gasped blissfully. Thankfully, he didn't read English.

The author in India

A MONTH LATER, my intuition told me to follow the Nyingma lama and the two monks back to their home and school in Sarnath, a sacred ancient city, the site of Buddha's first teachings after enlightenment. To go down to the plains in the middle of monsoon season, with the heat, rain and flooding, and disease, was madness, but my heart told me to do it.

After an excruciating ten-hour trip in a third-class bus, I arrived in Sarnath just after sunset and was hurriedly taken to walk around the Dhamekh Stupa before it closed for the night. Hundreds of Tibetan monks with prayer beads recited mantras, walking fast and swirling up dust into the hot air that mixed with the clouds of incense and smoke from the butter lamps. The full moon hadn't risen yet. It was an auspicious moment for my arrival.

Some 2,500 years before, the Shakyamuni Buddha came to

Sarnath, four weeks after his enlightenment under the Bodhi tree in Bodh Gaya, and gave the teachings there. The Buddha from compassion first turned the wheel of dharma, and taught the four noble truths. In the darkness, I got a glimpse of the ruined monasteries and temples. Stubs of broken bricks, like witches' fingers, stuck out of the ground. But this was the Buddha's home, where he actually had lived.

The next morning, returning to the Stupa, I walked triumphantly down the road to the Buddha. My prayers had been answered. I was coming home. The air was hot and steamy. There were palm, banana, and mango trees. A soft breeze, sweet with honeysuckle, was exhilarating. I could scarcely keep from bursting with laughter and screaming for joy with the wonder of the moment. In a long Indian skirt wrapped around my waist, I walked down the dirt road, my yellow brick road, in the bright, clear, sunlit morning under a vast blue sky.

The Dhamekh Stupa, built by King Asoka about two hundred years after the death of Buddha, and enlarged in later centuries, had miraculously survived the ravages of humans and time. Most of the sculpture, friezes, and stone carvings that covered it like a skin, I was told, had been stripped and looted by the British during the colonial period. What remained was the solid, red-brick mass towering over the flat Indian plain.

I entered the ancient city of Sarnath and walked among the ruins, fragments of the brick foundations that had been monastic buildings, stupas, temples, and dharma palaces. There was nothing there. Just a few bricks and decaying stone that sank into the earth. A great shock! Horribly sad—it was a wasteland. I didn't know what I'd expected. It was a completely lost city. Nothing of the Buddha remained. There was nothing to hold on to. I relaxed for a moment and there was a brief moment of clarity; then I became incredibly depressed. Sudden withdrawal. A blinding moment of absolute disappointment.

Of course, I knew there were the great blessings inherent in the place. But blessings were not enough. It was something like a death experience, the realization that you are dead, and everything was lost. "I made a big mistake. I shouldn't have come," I said to myself. "I don't know why my heart is broken."

My face crumbled and floods of tears poured down. I wept uncontrollably. I sank down to the ground and cried more. There was nobody there. I got up and ran to hide, toward the deer park behind a big mound. I fell on the slope and wept big fat tears into the dirt. I let go. Screaming grief. I pressed my face and body into the grass and earth to become invisible, writhe and convulse stronger, and cry harder and deeper. Deep loss, absolute and inexplicable.

I knew the worst always happened, but the bottom line was: I didn't want anything, I didn't expect anything, and I knew I wouldn't get anything. I didn't come to find the cause of suffering, nothing so corny, although I was unhappy and lonely all the time. I didn't come to get enlightened, nothing as pretentious as that. However, I was deeply shocked to realize that there was absolutely nothing there. Shocked, like when you fell down the stairs and saw stars—for an instant, there was white light and bliss, and then pain.

It was a great teaching from the Buddha, a small enlightening experience, but I had misinterpreted it. Finally, I picked myself up and wiped my tears. The Buddha lived in the minds of the Tibetan lamas, I realized, not in the broken stones.

I rented a room in a Dharamsala monastery, on the second floor, facing the Dhamekh Stupa a few hundred feet away. My bed was a wood table with a straw mat that gave me sores on my hip bones. "I don't know what I'm doing here!" I said to myself, trying to sleep. "What have I gotten myself into?" Completely afraid, just this side of insanity in the middle of nowhere, knowing nobody. I smoked ganja and it made it worse. There was no way out, because I could not admit failure and return to New York. I knew that doubt was a big poison and an obstacle.

Usually by the next morning, everything was okay. And most often, everything was a joy. I did more meditation and had the good fortune of being a beginner. Letting my mind rest, I counted the breaths, in and out, one to ten, and over again. Watching my breath and watching my mind.

The only thing I had to hold on to was my devotion to the Buddha and Guru Padmasambhava, founder of the Nyingma tradition, and my trust that I would be shown the path. "I will not give up." With two other students/friends, I translated the Nyingma, laboriously, word by word, sentence by sentence, writing it down in longhand in a lined notebook. Every afternoon, I studied the Tibetan language and made simple conversation with a sweet and beautiful nineteen-year-old instructor. At night, I copied sections of the ancient Tibetan manuscript that we were going to read the next morning. This was my first serious Buddhist study.

At the Institute of Higher Tibetan Studies, I learned alongside forty Nyingma monks. They ranged from fifteen to twenty-three years old, but because of their lack of worldly experience, poor vegetarian diet, and unexpressed sexual development, they looked much younger, unbelievably beautiful and fresh, with brilliant minds and joyous intellects. And in decades to come, they would become the next generation of dharma teachers around the world.

India was an ocean of contamination and disease. The slightest mischance and there was fever and dysentery. You were served tea in a cup that had been washed in a bucket of water contaminated with hepatitis; or bad food, which looked good but you ended up with a parasite. After a few months and illnesses, I built up an immunity and tolerance.

I didn't have sex for six months. I didn't even jerk off. I had not come here to masturbate thinking about some delusion from the past. I happily accepted it as the pure celibacy, beyond vows. But every time I squatted to shit, over a pipe in the floor, I got a half hard-on, then shot a load of cum. Without my hand touching my dick and with almost no sensation, I ejaculated. This always amazed me. It was wonderful having all the sexual energy, and using it in meditation, study, and devotion. Instead of always being horny and always wanting to make it, I was learning to let go and be less attached to desire.

Once a week, a friend named Dhammadipo and I took a bicycle rickshaw, riding for hours through flooded rice paddies, past wallowing water buffalos and squawking peacocks, to the filthy city of Benares. Here, we ran errands, bought *Time* magazine and chocolate squares, and smoked opium for endless hours among a scene of musicians and artists living in houseboats on the Ganges.

On the August full moon, we wandered down to the ghats, where the dead were burned. The monsoon-flooded river had covered all but one of the ghats, which was jam-packed with roasting bodies. Stacked next to one another, like a parking lot. It smelled like a suburban cookout. We slipped into the ghat, squeezed between the railing mud wall and the burning wood logs, and watched. Three feet in front of me, a woman's body, wrapped in a red sari, writhed in the flames. The muscles burned, and got taut. A man burned unevenly, his leg stuck up in the air, not far from my head. He was completely charred at the thigh, but his calf and foot were untouched, and a rather handsome bronze color; and blood dripped down and hissed on the red coals. A man called the Poker tossed the charred bodies back on the fire, pushed them down when they sat up straight, and stuck his poker into the top of the head, so the skull didn't explode when the brains boiled.

If nothing else, it was a rite of passage; and the opium helped me meet the challenge. And it felt wonderful. I simply observed a charnel ground, without discrimination. There was no aversion. I watched my thoughts as they arose, and let them dissolve. And I hoped I would not get captured by a demon spirit.

The next day we rode back to Sarnath, exhausted and shattered. My mind was clouded for two days. I regretted these excursions, as an obstacle to the teachings and meditation. Tibetan Buddhists did not use drugs and did not approve, but drugs were very much a part of the American culture, and I enjoyed them. It was a weekly dilemma.

WHEN ALLEN GINSBERG invited me to Calcutta, out of the blue, I hesitated for three full days, then finally agreed. He was returning to India for a festival with the Living Theatre, and I tagged along on part of his whirlwind trip. A one-minute photo op at the Howrath Bridge; an opium den just before it was raided. A devastating trip to a camp for Bangladeshi war refugees; the brutality of being pulled in a rickshaw; a moment of meditation by a pile of burning bodies.

Allen looked like a speeded-up cartoon character, his overly pleated long white skirt coming undone, tripping him up as he ran around bellowing Hindu mantras and playing his harmonium, and sweating profusely. He was a mess. On the one hand, I felt strongly that Allen was a bodhisattva with great compassion for the suffering of all sentient beings, and I honored him in the role of his servant and attendant. After all, it was because of Allen that I was there. On the other hand, he was fat and full of ego, an embarrassing, uncool dad.

At the end of it all, he flew with me back to Benares and forced me to bathe with him in the Ganges, where garbage, bloated dead cows, and half-burned corpses floated past, and tens of thousands of Hindus washed away their defilements. My skin was tacky, like butterscotch, and I had to wait until late that night back in Sarnath to take a shower.

The author, Allen Ginsberg, and Wynn Chamberlain in Calcutta

SARNATH FELT LIKE HOME, at a very deep level, and I always wondered if I had been there in a past life. When I learned of the city's history—it was invaded in the twelfth century by the Mughal army, its monks slaughtered—I understood.

I had lived through this experience myself during a hallucination I'd had with Brion Gyson in 1965. Amid the siege of an ancient city, I was hiding inside the head of a giant stone Buddha. A projectile hit it, and everything collapsed around me. Falling with the statue, I somehow managed to escape being crushed by the stones, but invading soldiers threw a net over me and killed me with swords and spears. They had broken the body of the Buddha, and destroyed the dharma. A catastrophe beyond comprehension.

The city was Sarnath, I realized now. I had once been a murdered monk.

As attached as I felt to the place, when a smiling Dhammadipo came into my room one day, inviting me to Darjeeling to meet his teacher, I did not hesitate. The teacher, His Holiness Dudjom Rinpoche, was a great Nyingma lama.

"Yes! That's what I've been waiting for!"

Some time before we left Sarnath, a bolt of lightning struck the Dhamekh Stupa. A five-foot-square chunk of brick, stone, and mortar ripped off from the top and fell crashing down to the ground. A very auspicious sign. The lamas said that it was predicted in the ancient texts, as a sign of bad times.

A big pile of brick rubble lay on the path. We knew they were blessed relics, and tried to step over them as we walked the path, but we kept tripping on them. It was monsoon season, and the rains washed away the bricks and mortar crushed under our feet. The Indian government and the museum were supposed to remove and preserve it.

Perhaps the rubble released extra blessings. One day, I reached down and picked up a broken piece of ancient brick and mortar. I wrapped it in a white scarf and took it with me.

The author on Jessore Road in Calcutta

FINALLY, IN SEPTEMBER 1971, I arrived in Darjeeling and met my root teacher, the one who would show me the nature of mind. His Holiness Dudjom Rinpoche was viewed as a completely enlightened being. He was a genius, celebrated as the greatest scholar of his time, a completely accomplished yogi, and a *terton*—a person who revealed meditation teachings hidden away centuries ago to be brought forth at the right time. His Holiness was head of the Nyingma tradition of Tibetan Buddhism.

Dudjom Rinpoche was smiling and gracious, radiating a feeling of joy and kindness at whatever happened around him. I received teachings, took refuge, and began formal meditation practice. He also spontaneously gave me Dzogchen teachings, the highest lessons on the empty true nature of mind, and how the mind can attain awareness of its true nature. Because he was speaking from the direct experience of an enlightened being, he gave me confidence that I could achieve it.

Rinpoche lived with his wife and family in houses in Darjeeling and in nearby Kalimpong. In the Himalayan snow mountains, the hills were covered with tea plantations and tropical flowers, a heaven world. There were many great Nyingma lamas who had settled in Darjeeling after fleeing Tibet in 1959: Chatral Rinpoche, Kanyur Rinpoche, Dilgo Khyentse Rinpoche, and Trogawa Rinpoche, among others. This was my coming home to the nature of mind. I left India a month later, and began integrating Tibetan Buddhism into my life, knowing that this was where I would soon return.

His Holiness Dudjom Rinpoche
and the author in Darjeeling

ON WEDNESDAY, NOVEMBER 8, 1972, I performed a piece called "The Day After the Last Election" at St. Mark's Church. The day before was Election Day and Nixon had won. It was a depressing time. It seemed like the success of the conservative forces was destroying all compassionate work.

It was an elaborate production, including movies by Bob Fiore (of Vietnam war crimes testimony), Les Levine (of that summer's Republican Convention in Miami), and Patty Oldenburg (of her in the kitchen with her new boyfriend). I presented sound compositions of three poems, including "Balling Buddha," recorded in a studio on a sixteen-track board, with complicated voice modulations and multilayers of sound. And to induce a higher awareness of the poetry, I gave out LSD, joints, and free wine. Everyone was stoned.

It was a great triumph with a standing ovation. Allen, who didn't like my poems but was always very respectful of success, offered: "The poems are interesting."

"Thank you." I hugged him. He did the best he could.

As the crowd danced to Grapevine, an all-women rock 'n' roll band, a friend named Nanao approached. He was a great Japanese poet whom I had gotten to know on the farm in Cherry Valley, a Buddhist monk and an expert meditator, with a high degree of realization. He was about fifty years old, thin, and in the dim light, his dazzling eyes looked at me.

"John, you don't look well," said Nanao. "You should see a doctor. It is important."

I went to bed thinking of Nanao's words and I woke up the next morning still thinking about them. For the past year, since an injury in India, my left testicle had become enlarged to the size of a lemon and rock hard, and it hurt a little all the time. I had to do something. I got dressed and took a taxi to Bellevue Hospital.

The emergency room sent me up to Urology. "We are checking you into the hospital immediately," announced the examining doctor. "There is the possibility of testicular cancer."

The worst was always true. "Well, yes, very good. But I have to go home and I promise to be back in two hours. I left a kettle on the stove."

Back at 222 Bowery, I crawled into bed and took a long nap. When I woke up, I thought about what to do and called a few friends. Everyone agreed that Memorial Sloan Kettering was the best cancer hospital in the world.

Three days later, I checked in. A young resident named Dr. Kaiser and Dr. Marks, the head surgeon at Sloan Kettering, operated on me. They cut off my left testicle. It was easy, a chop. It was not such invasive surgery. Many friends came and visited and we laughed and laughed.

The pathology report came back saying that I had four cancers. The first one, nine out of ten people die within five years. The second one, nine out of ten die within ten years. The third one was 50 percent within five years, and the fourth was not so bad. They advised a second operation, cutting out fifty lymph nodes to see if the cancer had spread.

The second operation was horrendous. The lymph nodes were along the inside of the spine, and to get to them, the five doctors went in through the front. They cut a twelve-inch gash down the middle of my stomach, opened me up, moved aside my liver, kidneys, intestines, and whatever else was in the way, and surgically removed the fifty lymph nodes, stuffed everything back in, and sewed me up. It was the most excruciatingly painful, extreme suffering that I ever experienced. During the first thirty-six hours, even though the nurses were shooting me with morphine and Demerol, it felt like a burning log was eating away at my stomach.

To get through the suffering and horror, I did a Tibetan Nyingma Buddhist meditation that I had learned in India but not yet practiced. I was a novice, but out of desperation, as I was wheeled into the operating room, it came to mind. It was called the Chod. I visualized my consciousness as a *dakini*, a beautiful female Buddha; and symbolizing the death of ego, she cut off the top of my head with a curved knife. The skull became a huge bowl and she chopped up the body and stirred it around, and it became an ambrosial stew, supremely delicious. I offered it to all the Buddhas, and with compassion to the beings of the six realms: gods and warring gods, humans, animals, hungry ghosts, and those in hot and cold hells.

The operation was a complete success. I recovered quickly. The biopsy came back negative, the cancer had not spread. Tibetan Nyingma Buddhist friends came and did meditation and mantra practice in my room and in the halls. Many friends and poets came every day. Allen Ginsberg came with his harmonium and sang Hindu mantras. Everyone laughed and had a good time and every day was a party.

"I look like a Thanksgiving turkey stuffed, trussed, and sewed up with black thread," I said. It seemed funny, and I laughed, which made the stitches hurt, which seemed even funnier, and made me laugh harder, gasping for air with tears running joyously.

I healed in a short time, much to the surprise of the doctors. "We don't know what you're doing," said Dr. Marks, "but keep doing it."

The nurses said, "John, say your meditation for me!"

Patients, quite sick, moaned from their beds, "John, say your meditation for me."

Memorial Hospital was charnel ground. People with cancer came there to die. The room had six beds. Two men in my room died: the man in the next bed, and a few days later, the man in the bed across from me. Around three in the morning, as he lay dead, his consciousness still there, the room filled with something inexplicable and strong, before they took the body away and I went back to sleep.

I checked myself out of the hospital after ten days, four days early. I just wanted to get away and heal myself, before they decided to do something else.

Three days later, I flew to Wyoming for a meditation retreat and seminar with Trungpa Rinpoche. These were the first tantric, or Vajrayana, teachings he gave in America, a very special moment. It took place at a ski resort in the Grand Tetons. There was lots of snow and it was extremely cold. It was very healing to my body and mind.

One afternoon, about ten of us, both men and women, took steam baths, hot and moist and foggy, and we ran outside naked and rolled in the snow. My body was so hot that the snow felt warm. My boiling body was caressed by the feathery touch of the snow. I rolled over and over in it, surrounded by the spectacular Grand Teton Mountains. It was a god world and it was glorious. And opposites were true: good was bad and bad was good, and cold was hot, pure empty display and great clarity.

We went inside the steam bath and got hot again. The red scar on my stomach from the operation still made me look like a stuffed turkey, with big scar marks from the black stitches. We ran out again laughing and naked, and collapsed and rested and rolled over in the snow as if on a featherbed, and bunched up snow for a pillow, resting under a vast, empty blue sky.

I believed that loneliness had caused the cancer—the nagging loneliness that had been in my heart all my life. Each of my great loves had been a sort of torture when it was happening, and each ended in disaster and abandonment. Loneliness almost killed me. In coming years, I would have scientific proof: medical studies linking loneliness with compromises to a person's immune system and the ability to fight diseases. But even without science, I believed instinctively that the pain from the loss of each lover had impaired my immune system, and had caused the four kinds of cancer. There was no blame. I caused my own suffering, my desire, and my grasping mind.

Unspoken, below the surface, it was very depressing. I had based my life and work and practice on the concepts of liberation through love and sexual freedom. Transcendence and emptiness, sex and great bliss were spiritual accomplishments. I was fighting the battle of gay liberation in a homophobic world, and I was a heroic champion of the golden age of promiscuity. Wisdom arose in life as metaphors, and having my ball cut off symbolized the complete failure of everything I believed, hoped, and aspired to.

In 1973, Something Else Press published a book of my poems called *Cancer in My Left Ball*. The poems were written between 1970 and 1972, as the cancer began, grew, and was cut out. They reflected the state of my mind, resulting in the cancer in my body. They were a collage of found images from everyday life—TV, magazines, newspapers, anywhere words appeared—that came into my consciousness. The images were metaphors and my mind was the mind of America. "It's what we're dying of America!" I wrote.

WITH MY CANCER in complete remission, I returned to Darjeeling in September 1973 and continued to receive teachings from my root teacher, Dudjom Rinpoche, starting with a strict three-month retreat at the monastery of another teacher, Kangyur Rinpoche.

It had been renovated in my absence, from a sprawling, run-down house to a magnificent traditional monastery. At eight thousand feet, the monastery was perched on a few acres of a very steep slope of pine trees, directly facing the towering Kangchenjunga snow mountain.

For those three months, I was in one of the new retreat cabins built on the slope above the monastery. In November, winter and snow came. My cabin was unheated and without electricity. I got a brazier and a big bag of soft coal, but it was difficult to start the fire outside and bring in the red-hot coals, so I was often in a toxic smoky room. Then there were the fleas.

Food was delivered outside my door from the monastery kitchen. Rinpoche's son Tulku Pema Wangyal appeared every other day in the evening and answered my questions, gave teachings, and explained the teachings I had received from Dudjom Rinpoche.

Kangyur Rinpoche's wife, sons, and daughters were all completely enlightened beings, wonderful and important supports for my practice. Kangyur Rinpoche himself was old and solid, a bit wrathful and miraculously compassionate. He was famous for his lung, or oral transmission, of all the Buddha's sutra teachings. He, too, was a terton, a revealer of hidden teachings. Sometimes, during teachings, instead of throwing rice as a blessing, he threw a banana or an apple, always a funny surprise, like a Zen slap.

Kangyur Rinpoche died at age eighty in January 1975 and attained rainbow body. The death was in the tradition of great lamas. After six weeks, his consciousness left the body, and his body was cremated on the roof of the monastery. There remained in the ashes many sacred relics: white and rainbow pearl-shaped pills, his tongue and heart joined together into stone—signs of his great accomplishment and powerful blessings to help us, his disciples.

By the late 1970s, Darjeeling's heyday as a Tibetan Buddhist hub was ending. The political situation in the state of West Bengal was difficult and dangerous, with Maoist rebels and armed fighting factions and machine-gun fire in the streets. The lamas moved one by one to Kathmandu or to the West (America, France, and elsewhere). For me, the golden age of Darjeeling was a great blessing.

THE BUNKER

In early 1974, not long after I returned from my second trip to India, William Burroughs moved from London back to New York, arriving on February 5, his sixtieth birthday. I was thirty-seven. He sublet a loft at 452 Broadway, a block up from Canal Street. He had come to Manhattan to teach a class at City College, once a week for a semester, for the money. He was attracted to New York by the energy, and the radical politics and counterculture seemed a fulfillment of his work. He was one of the movement's heroes, and his life in London had been desolate.

We got together and it felt very auspicious, the possible beginning of something new with him. We had drinks and dinner once a week. The next two and a half years were for me the time I was closest to William. We didn't have sex anymore; instead, we drank vodka and tonics and smoked lots of joints.

When we were stoned enough, we sat facing each other, looking into each other's eyes. We rested in a state beyond all concepts. Fearlessly. I didn't know exactly what we were doing. Something in our hearts rose up and out each of our eyes, and into the other's eyes, and down into each of our heart centers, giving rise to great clarity. Wisdom mind, beyond a third mind.

William controlled when we began and ended. In between was beyond discursive thought, beyond subject and object, empty and transparent, and luminous display. We relaxed. William said, "Wow!" The bliss of the clarity was better than sex. I did Tibetan Buddhist Dzogchen meditation; and William did something similar, of his own invention, with a natural understanding of mind.

ON FEBRUARY 14, Valentine's Day, I gave a dinner party at 222 Bowery to welcome William to New York. Six people would fit at the low round marble table in front of the fireplace for dinner. We were seven, so it was already a squeeze. Then William telephoned and told me, "Allen Ginsberg wants to come to dinner and bring a young friend." I had not invited Allen and I knew William preferred that, but he was put in the middle.

"No, it's too many people," I said. My private, personal dinner party was getting ruined by Allen. It was hopeless. "Allen can come, but not the friend."

Allen telephoned two minutes later. "I want to bring a young poet. He edits a magazine called *City Moon*, and has come all the way from Kansas to see William." There was no way to say no, a feeling of dread arose in me, and little did I know I would never be able to get rid of this young poet for the rest of my life.

Allen arrived with James Grauerholz, a tall, skinny kid from Kansas wearing a red flannel shirt and sneakers.

The party was totally great. I cooked an elaborate dinner, and everyone got drunk and stoned and was very happy being together. We toasted, "The St. Valentine's Day massacre!"

William was drunk and staggered a little, as he always did when he was drunk, looking more unsteady than he actually was. He knew how to take care of himself. "William, are you all right?" asked Allen. "James, perhaps you should accompany William home."

"Yes!" said James Grauerholz, seizing the moment. "I am happy to. Let me get a taxi and take you home!"

James and William got together the next night and had sex, and were lovers for two weeks; then they never made it again. James hated making it with anyone over nineteen. Instead, James became William's lifelong secretary.

William's loft on Broadway was sublet from a painter who was a friend of Bob Rauschenberg. On the floor, I was surprised to see a Chinese rug—1905, champagne color, nine by twelve feet, and quite a good one—that I had given to Bob when we were lovers in the late 1960s. The Chinese rug had been our living room rug in Roslyn Heights when I was a child, and I knew every inch of it. It had been stored in the cellar and given to me by my mother. I gave it to Bob for his bedroom, in a gesture of deep love. When we broke up, he apparently also got rid of my Chinese rug. In the two months that William was at that Broadway loft, it got more and more filthy and wretched with spilled booze, cigarette ashes, food, and dirt. Seeing my family's rug ruined daily on William's floor was a little sad. But what better end! It was like my life, and my magic carpet. I never told William or anyone else where the rug had come from.

In March 1974, the St. Mark's Poetry Project called asking me to perform in April. Someone had canceled, and I said maybe. Then they had the idea of teaming me up with William. Two poets always read on their Wednesday night series. They knew I was seeing him. I was very surprised. It had never occurred to me that I, a lowly mortal, could perform with a god. I hesitated for just one moment. "Why not!"

William and I performed at St. Mark's Church on Wednesday, April 24, 1974. The Sunday before, we used a performance at the West End Bar as a dress rehearsal. Although we didn't know it at the time, this began a practice we continued for the next twenty years of performing and touring together. I went on first, and got the audience hot, and then put them in the palm of William's hand, and he worked them masterfully, culminating in a standing ovation. St. Mark's Church was full, with even the balcony jam-packed. Some were my audience, but all were adoring fans of William.

It was William's first performance in front of such a large audience, ever. He gave a brilliant performance. He was a natural, and over the next twenty years he honed his skills, becoming one of the greatest performers.

Afterward, William and I got together at a loft he had just

rented on Franklin Street and talked about our great success. "Everyone was there, all the poetry and art world, the Pop artists, Bob Rauschenberg and Marion Javits. *Tout le monde.* You have had a triumphant return to New York," I said. William looked pleased.

The author watching William Burroughs read

IN MAY 1974, I went on a strict solitary meditation retreat for one month at Tail of the Tiger in Vermont. It was very disciplined and rigorous. I did the meditation practices I had received from His Holiness Dudjom Rinpoche. We were here to become enlightened and I wanted to go all the way. When I returned, I had dinner with William on Franklin Street, and brought with me all the glorious retreat energy. William was very impressed. It was just what he liked, vitality for him to suck in, like a black hole—he only took, never gave.

A painter and friend built him a Wilhelm Reich orgone box, a chair surrounded by metal and plywood, and covered with a bearskin, an organic material on the outside. It was a kind of sensory deprivation/meditation chamber. For a while William said he sat in it for twenty minutes in the morning. It was a noble effort that failed. But to me, William was heroic for having attempted such a thing. I was still a young meditation practitioner.

In an echo of our dinners in the fall of 1968, William would buy two chicken breasts, a pack of bacon, and frozen peas for me to cook. I'd be quite drunk when I got around to putting the chicken covered with bacon in the oven. We smoked joints and cigarettes, drank vodka, and had an intimate meeting of mind. In our long friendship, it was the best time I had with William, alone together, as he didn't yet have a retinue, both of us in some ways innocent and concerned with the true nature of mind.

IN DECEMBER 1974, I was having drinks with William at Franklin Street. He said mournfully, "John, I have to find another loft. The rent is being raised sky-high. I have to move, I have to find a place."

My heart sank. This was the very best time that I had ever had with William, here in this loft, and it was going to end. Then it hit me. My landlord, Sam Waponowitz, had mentioned that morning that a loft at 222 Bowery was coming up for rent.

I was surprised by the coincidence.

"It's on the second floor front, directly below my loft," I told William. "The same as mine, only the ceiling is fourteen feet high. It's the *piano nobile* floor. The painter who lives there is moving upstate."

"John, I'm very interested." William's gray-blue eyes looked keen.

The next morning, I spoke to Sam. William then telephoned him and made an appointment to see the loft. I stayed out of it. I was not going to be accused of having coerced William to move into my building.

Not long after they met, there was a little knock on my door. "John, great news! I'm renting the Bunker."

"What?"

"The one down in the back. I'm not getting the loft below you."

I didn't understand.

William explained, "The storage room, which used to be the locker room in the old YMCA!" He was referring to the rear mezzanine loft, which had been the locker room for the boys to take off their clothes before going down to the swimming pool on the floor below or up to the gymnasium on the floor above. It was used for storage by the chair store on the ground floor. The loft had been spray-painted, the six windows were completely painted over, and not a trace of daylight seeped in. William, a junkie, liked it dark and quiet.

He sat down. "It's four times larger than the one below, and quiet, very quiet. And a really good deal, only two hundred seventy-five dollars. I walked in the door and said, 'This is my Bunker.'"

I was thrilled.

Soon after he signed the lease, I gave a New Year's Eve dinner for William and a bunch of his old Beat friends: Allen Ginsberg, Gregory Corso, Peter Orlovsky, Lucien Carr and his girlfriend. We celebrated that William was about to move into 222 Bowery.

The Bunker needed some renovation. The artist David Prentice (who had been a studio assistant for Bob and Jasper) did the construction, building walls to make rooms in the large open loft space, including a bedroom for William and an office for James Grauerholz. The walls and floors were painted white, and it was well lit, so even though there was no outside light, it was always bright. There was one window that opened on a dark backyard. The renovations were not complicated but took a very long time.

Then James moved in with his boyfriend, "temporarily," and stayed for a year. Paying two rents while he waited, William kept saying, "Where is my Bunker?! I want to move into my Bunker."

"David hasn't finished the work yet," said James, happily ensconced with his boyfriend. Finally, in March 1976, William moved in and James moved out.

Every morning, William and I met or phoned, and talked about whose turn it was to buy the food for dinner, which I always cooked. Who was coming or would it just be the two of us? Would we eat upstairs or in the Bunker? Were we going out together to a dinner party? Were we going out separately, or maybe we just didn't want to see anyone? After the intense experiences in his Broadway and Franklin Street lofts, things became more domestic when William moved into the Bunker. It was wonderful.

IN NOVEMBER 1974, William, James, and I went on tour. We performed in San Francisco at Glide Church as a benefit for *Gay Sunshine*, a Californian gay-lib publication, then in Berkeley at the Pauley Ballroom. The next day, James arranged for us to rent an apartment for a week, a couple of blocks away, up in the Berkeley hills. We looked forward to the little stopover, fun and play, time off together in a different city.

Someone had given us psilocybin mushrooms. Generally, we didn't do such drugs together. William didn't like LSD, saying, "It makes me feel uneasy." But there were these sacred mushrooms. William had a compulsive addictive personality. While James had gone out to get the newspapers for our reviews, William said, "What do think, John?" and popped one of the capsules of ground psilocybin mushrooms into his mouth. I had one. "Why not?!"

When James got back, he took one. James was making it with a young guy named Greg whom he'd picked up at our reading two nights before. Greg arrived at the apartment, and took a capsule too.

The four of us sat around the kitchen table, waiting to get high. Mushrooms take about an hour to digest and take effect. Or vomit, as sometimes happens. William said, "I feel a little upset in my stomach." But we didn't get sick.

The shabby garden apartment, in a run-down building, belonged to an actor who was away on tour. After about an hour and a quarter, we said to one another, "Do you feel anything?" Which always means it's already happened. I was really looking forward to a transcendent, sacred trip with William, moving beyond duality, becoming a third mind, finding the union of great clarity and great bliss. These were rare moments. It was just about to happen, when the doorbell rang, and then rang again, like an electric shock.

James looked through the peephole. "It's Billy! Oh my god, it's Billy!" William's son, William Burroughs, Jr., had appeared unannounced.

Oh, no! I thought. He's the obstacle. At very important times, big obstacles always arise. There goes our great spiritual trip down the drain.

"Billy, it's great to see you!" said James, welcoming him warmly.

Ragamuffin Billy, in baggy clothes and a bit disheveled—but still looking good—came smiling through the door; William stepped forward and gave him a jerky hug. Then James and I hugged Billy, offering him loving kindness, helping him feel at home with his father. We made some tea and smoked some joints.

The most important thing, now, was William and Billy. We had to make sure everything flowed perfectly for them, allowing them enough space to be together, dissolving any obstacles that might arise. They seldom saw each other, so this was vital. Billy was living in Santa Cruz with his girlfriend, Georgette, who, William and James said somewhat disdainfully, was from a hippie rainbow tribe.

We were very high. It was funny that Billy should appear at the exact moment we were going over the top. Billy was famous for always interfering with plans, interrupting, changing things with his presence; and now he'd done so again. There was nothing to do but laugh joyously at the magical display.

"Billy, you look great!" I said.

His eyes sparkled and he was in relatively good shape. And, after on-and-off heavy drinking, then totaling his car, he was sober. For the moment anyway: Billy had an ongoing problem with drinking and drugs and always seemed to attract trouble. His life, externally, was an endless series of negative events, which gradually internalized. I often wanted to help him because he was William's son, and because he was suffering, but I didn't want to get too engaged. As William said, in general, "They will make you as crazy as they are."

Billy stayed for about an hour. It seemed to me like three hours or an eternity, but it was a very successful visit. William and Billy talked and moved about together with warm affection. We were thrilled that everything had gone so well, and we were really high.

Later, when Billy moved to Boulder, he would telephone me on occasion, asking for help. He thought of me as a neutral avenue to James and William. I knew what to do when I heard his voice. I'd go down to the Bunker, or wait for the right moment, and tell them Billy had called. James would wire him money immediately.

After Billy died, I saw a photo of the shrine in his bedroom in Boulder. Among the various sacred objects, there was a picture of me, cut out from one of my album covers. I knew he really liked me, but didn't realize the extent of his feelings. I was very sad after I saw it, because it meant that I had really let him down. I didn't feel guilt, just that I made another mistake, and I make them every day. I could have done more for Billy, but I was self-absorbed.

Once Billy left that day in Berkeley, William, James, and I relaxed in great clarity. What a relief! We got ourselves drinks and smoked more joints. We talked about our tour, about the difference between the San Francisco and Berkeley audiences, and gossiped about friends who had showed up for the performances.

When William said how much he liked my poem "Suicide Sutra," I was taken by surprise. I had just written it and only just begun performing it.

"Just think of all the ways to commit suicide," he said joyously. "Jumping off a cliff, oh my god, no." We were all laughing. "Of course, by hanging, you get off."

"You cum when you die," I said. We had all seen photos of hanged men with hard-ons. "Great bliss at the moment of death, that's pretty good."

"The very best way is," I said, reciting an excerpt from "Suicide Sutra":

There is a gun
in your hand,
a 38-caliber

revolver,
and it's pointing
at your face,
and you pull
the trigger,
and the bullet
shoots
slowly
toward
your head,
and the bullet shoots slowly toward your head,
and it smashes
into your face
and it smashes into your face
and it smashes into your face.

Everyone was laughing hysterically.

and blows
your skull
open
and blows your skull open,
blood
and brains and flesh
and skin
and hair,
fly into the air.

Tears of joy poured from our eyes, and we were doubled up with laughter.

You are
dying
you are dying.
and it's the same

and it's the same
and it's the same,
more horrible,
and you haven't gotten anywhere,
only here.

We were so high. We talked some more, then decided to rest. James and Greg lay down on the couch and cuddled. William and I went into his bedroom and lay on the bed together. We hugged and kissed, wrapped in each other's arms, experiencing infinite pleasure, white light and luminosity, as we dissolved into one another, pressing our clothed bodies together, resting in the union of bliss and emptiness. Then we lay next to each other and drifted off to sleep and fabulous hallucinations.

The next night, William and I went out for dinner at a Mexican restaurant. James and Greg stayed in and fucked. One of our visitors must have flicked a lit cigarette butt in the plastic wastebasket in the kitchen. As they made love in the bedroom, it smoldered and caught fire, creating a lot of toxic smoke that eventually crept under the door into the bedroom. The next day, the wastebasket was a solid lump.

After we departed, there were lots of complaints from the owner about how we had trashed the apartment, torched the kitchen, smashed the furniture, pissed on the walls, and spilled booze everywhere. This was not true. It was a dump when we got there. The disgusting apartment had been transformed by the psychedelics into a heaven world.

IN THE FALL OF 1974, somewhere in the middle of a long interview for *Gay Sunshine* in San Francisco, the editor Winston Leyland asked me about Allen Ginsberg.

With *Howl* in 1956, Allen had been my hero; and in the 1960s, he was a bodhisattva of compassionate activity, and I was very devoted to him. But in the 1970s, something changed. Most recently, in the summer of 1974, he and Anne Waldman inexplicably excluded me from the Jack Kerouac School of Disembodied Poetics, an experimental writing program at the Naropa Institute, even though I was there with them when they conceived it.

For years, my relationship with Allen had been full of subtle unconscious abuse, and by the time I sat down for that interview, I had had enough.

LEYLAND: What about Allen Ginsberg? How do you feel his fame has affected him?

GIORNO: I think it fair to say that he's a pushy Jew—speedy and aggressive—whose expertise at public relations ranks him equal to the brilliant boys on Madison Avenue . . . He is a genius at manipulating political power. He is a great politician. And that is wonderful . . . [But] I mean his guru trip in the 1960s. How can you be a guru, if you're not enlightened? . . . And he is ravenously desirous, gets angry at the drop of a pin, and won't listen to any criticism of himself. His brain is so quick that he will rationalize, or twist anything you might say. The only time you cut into his ego is when you say it in the media.

Of course, reading this now, I am horrified by my choice of words. I was in a low, low place, but that doesn't excuse it. Nevertheless, having eviscerated his personality, I then went after his poetry.

GIORNO: Allen Ginsberg hasn't written a good poem in years, and hasn't written a great poem in twenty years. When he wrote *Howl*, he was the voice of his time, mirroring what everyone felt in their heart. Now, he's just a good poet, which means he's a bad poet, and everyone listens to him because he's famous.

And I kept going:

> GIORNO: His music is awful and his blues melodies are worse. He hustles all these great musicians, Bob Dylan, Archie Shepp . . . and it's a joke, they laugh behind his back. But he's Allen Ginsberg and they are respectful, "Man, that's totally great." And after they leave, "Man, what was that!"

Occasionally, I tried, and failed, to be generous:

> GIORNO: His meditation is quite strong. And it's quieted him down. He's down to just working with himself and his own garbage, rather than bellowing out mantra over a microphone to a captured audience, which is beside the point . . . Allen used mantra as entertainment.
>
> LEYLAND: His mantras for the destruction of the Pentagon and that kind of thing?
>
> GIORNO: Mantra is for meditation practice, not for politics. Allen uses mantra to support ego. "I want this good thing to happen." It has good intentions, but it is not Buddhist meditation.

I was applauded for my heroic candor, for saying aloud what everyone said privately. Taking a risk for honesty, exposing a sacred cow. I did it fearlessly, with the delusion that it was a good positive thing. But it was poisoned by anger.

It took two years for me to feel the blowback.

IN 1976, I released a two-record LP called *Totally Corrupt*. Thirty-four poets read, used technology and music, and gave great performances, including Charles Bukowski, Ted Berrigan, Amiri Baraka, Ken Kesey, and Sylvia Plath and William Carlos Williams (both recorded before their deaths), along with many young poets. It was our tenth album. Selecting poets and poems, recording them or finding live recordings, and mastering and producing was all an enormous effort.

But the album cover was just as important. It was an artwork, and it gave me the most pleasure. The concept was photographs of a meeting of the members of the board of directors of Giorno Poetry Systems in William's Bunker at 222 Bowery. I asked John Cage to join us, since he and William were on the LP, along with Allen Ginsberg and Anne Waldman. *Totally Corrupt*. What a brilliant idea, and I hoped I could pull it off!

Les Levine set up lights and camera around William's dining room table, which, with its six orange upholstered chairs, would make the perfect boardroom table. John Cage arrived promptly at seven and immediately found the right chair for himself, laying claim to his location in front of the camera.

"John, can I get you something to drink? Tea, wine? William and I are drinking vodka."

"Nothing, thank you!" John laughed and everyone laughed.

We smoked a joint, and John declined graciously, laughing again. We laughed a lot, and what was being said was not so important.

As the others trickled in, I was transfixed by the exchange between John and William, two great princes meeting for the first time. They exchanged pleasantries and talked about a few old friends in the distant past. They had almost nothing in common, other than a clarity of mind and similar concepts of cut-ups and randomly arising wisdom. They both had great understanding of the empty nature of mind.

Having little in common made it more interesting. William was a junkie alcoholic. John didn't do that and had even stopped drinking wine. They were both gay men but with completely different tastes. John was in a long-term relationship with Merce Cunningham, but his work was asexual. William's work was pornographic and he had a taste for street boys. By 1976, neither, I think, was interested in doing it.

Then Allen arrived, late, having been delayed. Below the surface there was complicated, bad energy between us, but I was not going to allow anything to spoil my photo shoot. I tried to be relaxed, gracious, and forthcoming. We were all cheerful and professional.

As Les started shooting, we all became such big hams. A whole series of shots was taken with William wearing dark round glasses, looking like a mafia don. I was thrilled. During the shoot, William wrote notes on a yellow legal pad. Words that arose in his mind as we sat at the table talking about nothing and laughing— the nonsense "minutes" of our "meeting." When the shoot ended, John departed right away. He said to William, "I am very pleased to meet you." Everyone laughed. I hugged him. It was inexplicably joyous.

James Grauerholz, his boyfriend, Michael, and several other friends joined us for dinner. We had more drinks and smoked more joints, and I cooked fettuccine carbonara and filet mignon. James stood up and raised his glass, saying, "I want to make a toast to Allen, on his fiftieth birthday, tomorrow. To Allen!" We all toasted Allen.

And then, not long after dinner, the joy vanished. Apropos of nothing, Allen began to scream: "I hate your albums, I hate your album covers." He was vicious, trembling, spit coming out with his breath.

I was shocked and deeply hurt. There had always been problems with Allen, just below the surface, jealousy for one reason or another, from the first time we met with Kerouac in 1958. I knew Allen disliked my poetry, but I thought he liked the records, because I presented him prominently with many other great poets. And the cover shoot had been so brilliant, why had he chosen this moment to express his rage?

Allen's assault had the force of multiwarhead missiles exploding, sudden death. It was like getting whacked in the head by a mind fist. And now I was numb and depressed. It was horrible, my worst fears come true. I could not believe he had done it.

I should have guessed that Allen was also in a fit of jealousy, because William had moved into 222 Bowery, and I was, de facto, living with William. Allen was very possessive of William.

But of course, this wasn't the only reason. I realized that Allen was angry about the interview two years earlier. And I realized that I deserved it.

In the interview, I had said loud and clear what I thought reflected my mind and everyone's mind, and hoped that Allen would hear it and wake up. However, I regret having done it. I made a bad situation worse, caused more anger and more suffering for both of us. He heard nothing, and never forgave me.

Allen Ginsberg and I did not do such a good job of it in this life. We possibly carried forward bad habitual patterns from past lives. And we will, sure as hell, continue in future lives.

The Dial-a-Poets: *Totally Corrupt*

IN 1975, I went to Kathmandu for five months to visit Dudjom Rinpoche, who had moved there, to receive teachings and do a retreat. I also went on a mission. Emily Stevens, a friend and a Du Pont heiress, wanted to give her ranch in Wyoming to a Tibetan lama for a refugee settlement, and I was delegated to offer it to Dudjom Rinpoche. After several weeks, he accepted and decided to come to the United States. I said, "Rinpoche, you have to pass through New York to get to Wyoming. Please give teachings in New York." He said yes to that, and I went on, "I request that you start a meditation center in New York for the benefit of the many Nyingma disciples living there." After a week he agreed.

I had seen how many centers began, and I myself had helped some get started: those founded by Trungpa Rinpoche, the 16th Karmapa, Kalu Rinpoche, and Dilgo Khyentse Rinpoche. I knew the problems and troubles of a visit and a center, and felt I could do it. Emily's ranch didn't work out, but she gave Giorno Poetry Systems the money to buy a town house at 19 West Sixteenth Street, which became Yeshe Nyingpo NYC.

Eight days after the incident with Allen, His Holiness Dudjom Rinpoche, my guru and teacher, arrived in New York at my invitation for a five-month visit. Perhaps my unconscious motivation toward the dharma was again part of the recurring pattern of running away from the politics and poison of the poetry world.

Dudjom Rinpoche gave many great teachings to many people in New York, in New Mexico, and in Boulder, Colorado, where there was a formal visit with Trungpa Rinpoche. As William Burroughs was at Naropa for the summer, he and I gave a poetry reading together to a huge audience on July 21, 1976. I traveled on with Dudjom Rinpoche to California. In November, just after Dudjom Rinpoche departed, William returned to New York and the Bunker.

My life was very full with Dudjom Rinpoche and William Burroughs, two amazing beings, in two very different worlds but with the same concerns about the empty nature of mind.

I WAS IN KATHMANDU in 1977 for eight months, living in His Holiness's house as a member of the family, doing a retreat in my room, receiving teachings, and seeing him every day. I had a unique position among Western disciples. In December, His Holiness gave a Kha Wang, or big empowerment, of all his teachings that went on every day for a month, attended by many tulkus and twenty thousand people.

In 1978, when the cultural theorist Sylvère Lotringer asked me to produce a tribute festival to William Burroughs, at first I said no. After organizing these kinds of events for ten years, I knew it was a thankless task. Everybody had a good time but me. Then, James, William's secretary, somehow won me over.

Even before it began, this festival, called the Nova Convention, caused a stir. Brion Gysin came in from Paris, where he'd been talking the event up with Keith Richards. Keith told Brion he would give an unannounced performance on Saturday, December 2, but then the plan was leaked to the press and the night was quickly sold out with starstruck fans. So because he'd said no publicity, Keith refused to come. Out of the blue, Frank Zappa, when he heard about the problem, volunteered to read "Talking Asshole" from *Naked Lunch* instead.

When the throngs descended on the East Village's Entermedia Theater on Saturday night, all of the performers were greeted with the screams: "Where's Keith! Where's Keith!" Philip Glass and Brion endured it, and so did Zappa. I managed with my aggressive performance, playing with the empty nature of the emotions of anger and desire in full force, subduing the audience.

Despite that drama, the weekend was an explosion of talent. Laurie Anderson, whom I had included on an album the year before, appeared on stage in white tie and black tails, her ponytail shorn, and performed for the first time with the vocoder, for the first time to a crowd of thousands. John Cage and Merce Cunningham performed, the brand-new B-52s played at the Mudd Club, and Patti Smith played the clarinet in a new mink coat with the inside pockets cut. At a packed after-party at Max's Kansas City, William and I spotted a familiar figure with his collar pulled up, looking our way: Abbie Hoffman, who had been in hiding as an FBI fugitive since 1971. As he sidled through the crowd, we stood up to say hello. I gave him a hug and kiss, thanked him for coming, and he was out the door. Perfect theater.

When something happens that is very successful, I always have the optimism that it is the beginning of something and the best is yet to come. This is always wrong. It is always the end. We were celebrating the end of the glorious 1960s and '70s, and Burroughs was the fortunate icon around which everybody celebrated themselves. I wondered what it portended for the future, and got a heavy, negative feeling. Of course, what else. I did not know that my life, and each of our personal lives, would radically change. In 1979, the tragedies of the AIDS catastrophe that devastated our world would begin.

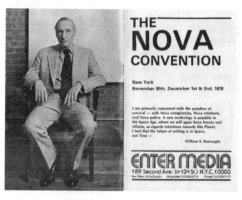

The Nova Convention poster

IN THE SPRING OF 1979, after James Grauerholz moved to Kansas, William got a junk habit, for the first time in the five years he'd lived in New York. He was shooting up with an assortment of people who thought it was really cool to come give William junk in the Bunker. William was the patriarch of heroin, and it was like offering apples to Johnny Appleseed. And it was not my problem.

The only reason William Burroughs did not get AIDS was that, being head honcho, he shot up first with a clean needle, and everyone followed after him. Many of the people whom William shot up with did die of AIDS.

While I did not discriminate against drugs and found no contradiction between drugs and Buddhism, heroin was not good for my meditation practice.

My life with William Burroughs at 222 Bowery continued, except that I was away a lot, with Dudjom Rinpoche (who had returned to the United States), as well as performing and touring. I liked it best when it was just William and me having dinner alone, and so did William. We appreciated quietly resting our minds together in emptiness. William was also getting an energy hit from the great blessings I was receiving from Dudjom Rinpoche.

William had lots of visits from friends, and people were brought by to meet him. The more aggressive ones pushed their way in quite often. I'd come down to the Bunker at seven and we'd sit in the orange chairs at the table, drink vodka, and smoke grass, laughing and talking with whoever was visiting.

Because there was a junk scene happening around William, people disappeared into his bedroom, I assumed to shoot up, and vomited with their head in the toilet. I'd cook dinner and serve it, and whoever was there washed the dishes, or I left them for William to do the next morning.

On December 31, 1979, I gave a New Year's Eve party. It was a little special, as we were turning decades, the 1970s into the 1980s. Even though my life centered on Dudjom Rinpoche, and not on the junkies in the Bunker, it seemed important to give my annual dinner to usher in another year on the third floor at 222 Bowery.

As usual, I wanted to invite six people—a select few who were closest to William and me—for an intimate dinner, and as usual Allen invited himself and someone else. Over the evening, the party became an enormous dinner for twenty-four people, and more afterward.

William shot up beforehand and we all devoured a plate of hashish brownies. In the third-floor fireplace, I broiled filets mignons coated with rock salt. At midnight, I made sure that everyone had a glass of champagne.

At five minutes after midnight, Anne Waldman said, "Let's do the I Ching."

"John, do you have an I Ching?" asked Allen.

I got the book and the three Chinese coins. Allen threw them.

We got P'i, Stagnation, Standstill. "Things cannot remain forever united."

"That's really bad," I said. "A very bad omen for the nineteen eighties!"

"'Evil people of the time of Standstill do not further the perseverance of the superior man,'" read Allen. "'The great departs, the small approaches. Heaven and earth do not unite, and all beings fail to achieve union. Upper and lower do not unite, and in the world, states go down in ruin. The shadow is within, the light is without; weakness is within, firmness is without. The way of the inferior is waxing, the way of the superior is waning.'"

"It has a positive end," said Anne, who took the book and read. "'The Standstill serves to help the great man to attain success.'"

"It's worse than I thought!" I said, and it was very funny. "William, we're in trouble!" I had a sinking feeling. This was a very bad sign. I wondered what bad times it portended.

About a quarter past midnight, Carl Laszlo arrived with the two Michaels. Carl was a Swiss art dealer, a survivor of a Nazi concentration camp; he lived in Basel and had a huge cocaine habit. The two Michaels were Michael Archangel, age twenty-one, and Younger Michael, age nineteen. These tall, blond, beautiful, heterosexual boys were Carl's servants and sex slaves. Carl, apparently, was a sadist. He made them fuck each other and watched, and had lots of whips in his bathroom. The boys had girlfriends. High on speed, each boy eventually committed suicide, one and two years later, by jumping out of the third-floor window of their bedroom in Carl's house in Basel.

I welcomed them and invited them to help themselves to dinner. Carl was a vegetarian and ate very little food. But seeing the medieval slabs of charred rare filet mignon oozing blood, Carl decided to have some. He took a big piece, and right away it stuck in his throat and he stopped breathing. He choked, coughed and coughed, and gasped, and fell down on the couch, and passed out.

We all stood around, stunned, watching. Maybe he was resting, I thought. "Carl has stopped breathing," screamed Anne. More minutes passed. Both Michaels tried doing the Heimlich maneuver, as well as squeezing and massaging the diaphragm, but it did not work. More time was passing and it was very serious.

"Call an ambulance," yelled Allen.

What a nightmare! It was New Year's Eve and I had a corpse on my hands. My loft was filled with drugs and marijuana smoke, and half the people were stoned on heroin, and Allen just said call an ambulance, which was 911, which was the police. *"Om mani padme hum,"* chanted Anne.

It was getting onto fourteen minutes and Carl lay there, his face blue and dead. Then, Michael Archangel did a reverse Heimlich above the diaphragm, and the meat went down Carl's throat and he started breathing. Joy filled the room.

I hugged and kissed Carl. "I'm so happy you're okay!" I hugged and kissed Michael. "Thank you so much!"

"Glad to see you." William, who never smiled, smiled, and looked like a ghoul.

Everyone started laughing. It was a close call. What a way to begin the eighties, I thought. In the first forty-five minutes, there were very bad signs!

After a short time, William retired to the Bunker. "Good night, John. Thank you." We hugged and kissed each other's cheeks, as we did every night.

The party went on for seemingly endless hours; people came and went. At three in the morning, a guy I didn't know—the beautiful nineteen-year-old boyfriend of my neighbor on Elizabeth Street, visiting from a college in the Midwest—came over to thank me for the party. "You have no idea what this means to me, to be in the real Beat world of Jack Kerouac. Being here with these guys for the first time, Allen and William and Gregory. It made a dream come true. It is the most important moment in my life." He reminded me of my younger self at the party near Columbia, about to graduate and meeting Kerouac and Ginsberg for the first time.

But that was so long ago. "For me it's a little different," I replied wearily. "I can't wait until it ends forever, until all this ceases, and I mean all of it, not just the party." I had gotten very depressed. Whenever I got exhausted or overworked, I fell into an extreme depression. I felt unappreciated. I had created the scene at 222 Bowery for fifteen years, invented it, paid for it, and cleaned up after, and everyone took it for granted. Everyone got what they wanted, and I got nothing. I felt exploited and abused.

At five in the morning, after every last person had left and I padlocked the gate, I finally went upstairs. What a relief! I stood still in a sort of blissful relaxation after extreme stress. And I got ready to go to sleep.

Five minutes later, the door opened and the beautiful nineteen-year-old boy from the Midwest came in. He had been on the upstairs landing. He and I fell into each other's arms, hugged and kissed, had wonderful sex, and went to sleep in an embrace. What an unexpected pleasure, a gift of the gods, out of the blue. At around ten, his boyfriend, who had waited without complaint on the landing all night, came down to collect him.

On New Year's Day, for our annual St. Mark's Church poetry reading, both William and I were a bit shaky from the night before.

DUDJOM RINPOCHE and his family arrived in New York in September 1979. I had started the Yeshe Nyingpo center with some friends—Vivian Kurz, Rudy Wurlitzer, Les Levine, and Terry Clifford—and many other devoted Nyingma disciples. Vivian and I managed the daily details, renovating the brownstone on West Sixteenth Street and creating the shrine room; the building became His Holiness's home and main residence. During the visits,

I arranged that every person requesting an interview had one, making His Holiness completely accessible. At the end of the day, an enormous number of people had seen him in twenty-minute private interviews, miraculously more than should have fit in. We arranged for him to meet poets, artists, and people in the art world, and he gave many teachings in many places.

The meditation center needed a retreat center for doing practice. I asked Emily Stevens, who had given us the money to buy this town house. Again, she insisted on giving it through Giorno Poetry Systems ("I know you and trust you"), but she enabled us to buy a property in Greenville, New York, that became Orygen Cho Dzong.

With these wonderful things happening also came problems. A center is a worldly operation, and people came with emotions like jealousy. A small group said, "Why does John Giorno have lunch and dinner every day with His Holiness and family, and we don't?" There were the political problems coming from a few people with agendas. Some people came to escape their failed lives, and were know-it-alls. The crazies brought endless distractions. The majority of the people were happy and joyous, and appreciative. The difficulties between His Holiness's wife, Sangyum, and his elder son, Thinley Norbu Rinpoche, were a big obstacle. In many Zen and Tibetan Buddhist centers in America, there were scandals and trouble, so I didn't take it personally: it was a part of the dharma growing in America. We were all doing something wrong, and what and why became a great teaching.

When Dudjom Rinpoche and family departed in December 1980, I withdrew from the center. I had accomplished everything I wanted to do. I was a poet—not a manager, a fund-raiser, or a medical doctor. Yeshe Nyingpo went on to flourish with its problems. I was free and went on happily doing my meditation for the rest of my life.

BAD TIMES

In 1980, I put together a two-record LP called *Sugar, Alcohol, & Meat*. Thirty-seven poets performed: William Burroughs, John Cage, Allen Ginsberg, Patti Smith, Kathy Acker, Ted Berrigan, and a number of young poets.

I asked Robert Mapplethorpe to shoot the cover photographs, in color. Black-and-white was what he was famous for. Twice, he asked: "Are you sure you want me to shoot color? I never shoot color."

"I know, that's what makes it interesting." I was being daring, and maybe missing the opportunity for great black-and-white photographs.

On June 3, Tuesday, at one o'clock, on an oppressively hot afternoon, William and I rented tuxedos for the shoot. I had my Brooks Brothers black tie from 1956, but I was not going to chance it being tight and looking funny. We took a taxi to a tuxedo rental store on Lexington Avenue and East Fifty-Eighth Street.

"William, poetry is show business and this is wardrobe."

"I know, getting all gussied up."

"The Ziegfeld Follies!"

We tried on several black dinner jackets until we found the right ones. I already had a formal shirt and black tie. William rented one.

Two days later, we shot the album cover in Robert Mapplethorpe's loft at 24 Bond Street. William, James, and I arrived at 6:30 p.m. John Ashbery was very late. William became annoyed as we waited. "I'm here, sugar. You're here, meat." And he said with great disdain, "Where's alcohol?"

"Yes! Once, Andy Warhol had said, when he was angry at me, 'You're just a big piece of meat,'" I recalled. We all laughed.

Robert had planned to shoot us separately, so we started. William was first. Robert requested no one else be there when he shot. John finally arrived and went second. And I went last. Robert made a personal moment of it, squinting his eyes, moving around, sizing up the situation. I was very relieved; I had pulled off this amazing thing.

After my shoot, Robert took classic black-and-white photos of William in black tie.

That fall, I gave a big party in the Bunker for the new album. Robert Mapplethorpe scarcely knew William and had never had dinner with him, so I tried to make it more casual and invited a crowd of all gay men. We sat in the orange chairs around the big table, smoked joints and drank vodka, and talked and laughed in the former YMCA locker room.

The Dial-a-Poem poets

WILLIAM MOVED TO KANSAS in 1983, but returned to New York, and the Bunker, regularly. To celebrate his first return, in 1984, I bought live lobsters on Canal Street. As a friend cooked them, William retreated into his bedroom, and later said mournfully, with a feeling of compassion for the lobsters that died, "I couldn't bear to be in the room."

I always have thought that William's attachment to guns was from a karmic predisposition from a previous life. We all have habitual patterns in this life, things we do over and over again, inexplicably, because they bring us pleasure and pain, whatever and why ever. If they are a very strong habit, when we die, our consciousness will take the habitual tendencies, along with the karmic package, on to rebirth in the next life. This is true for all of us, and I assumed that William, in many past lives, was attached to guns. And why not!

William was an infinitely kind, gentle, compassionate man. He liked the power and precision of guns, not that guns can murder and cause suffering. His wife Joan's death was an absolute catastrophe: he had killed someone, someone he loved at that. He had shot his wife, and even as an accident, that was very negative karma.

In February 1985, William wrote an introduction to his never-before-published novel *Queer*; we had discussed what went into that introduction over the years. He described Mexico City in 1951, that late afternoon about five, when he was walking through the winding streets on his way to meet Joan in a bar; and inexplicably, he started weeping, not knowing why, and continued walking, then started crying again, and then profound sadness descended. "A premonition," said William, "of something terrible."

> [T]he death of Joan brought me in contact with the invader, the Ugly Spirit, and maneuvered me into a lifelong struggle, in which I have had no choice except to write my way out.

The author and William Burroughs, circa 1980s

IN JANUARY 1985, I had given another dinner for William, who was in town from Kansas and about to turn seventy-two. James arranged the dinner, and said, "The concept is famous gay men around William."

The dinner was a little awkward, since William was shy with strangers and everyone was in awe of him. I served champagne, crab mousse, lobster fra diavolo, chocolate truffle pie, red wine, and many joints. Keith Haring and his boyfriend, Juan, had been up all night the Saturday before, dancing at the Paradise Garage. Juan was crashing and spent the evening in the hall, sitting on the steps, sleeping with his head in his hands. Laurie Anderson arrived over two hours late, when we were finishing eating, and she was the only woman I invited. For me, the best thing about the dinner was that it ended.

Keith gave William and me his beautiful catalogues and books, signed them for us, and invited us to visit his studio the next day.

We all had horrible hangovers. William didn't feel up to it. At 1:00 p.m., James and I walked to Keith's studio at 611 Broadway. Keith had just arrived, and was beginning his day. His studio assistants and helpers—beautiful young men—started appearing and working at things. Keith showed us his new work, which was totally brilliant. James and I stayed for about forty-five minutes. It was a joy being with him.

Keith said, "John, I have a present for you." He gave me a painting on paper, a red-and-black gouache of a man with a big dick at the head of which was a hand holding a baby. Keith's joyous celebration of life!

"Thank you!" I said. "Are you sure? Such a magnificent gift and we scarcely know each other. Thanks."

"I owe it to you," said Keith. "When I came to New York in nineteen seventy-eight, one of the first things I did was go to the Nova Convention. William and Brion and you completely changed my life. I want to thank you."

Keith Haring, William Burroughs, and the author

DURING DINNER the night before and at the studio visit, I couldn't shake the feeling Keith seemed a little familiar. Then it hit me.

In July 1982, at about eleven-thirty in the morning, I was taking the subway uptown. I had an appointment with my printer. I went into the Prince Street station and immediately into the men's toilet, as I always did. Rather than just stand around a boring platform waiting for the train, I'd go in the toilet, and all I had to do was take out my cock, wave it around, and some guy would go down sucking. It was more fun than waiting on the platform, and a great pleasure. When the train came, whether I came or not, I'd stuff my dick back in my pants, run out, and jump on the train.

That morning I was getting my cock sucked when a young, slightly homely but still cute kid wearing wire-rimmed eyeglasses put his arm around me, and we started kissing. His eyeglasses were getting crushed between our faces and he took them off. He was a plain boy with pale white skin, but with a very attractive quality. We were hugging and sticking our tongues in each other's mouths, while the other guy was sucking my dick. After a while, I noticed an unusual passion in the kid. He was making love with great energy and focus, affection and delight, different from the routine going on around me. The guy's heart was flowing love and I went with the flow.

I began to realize that the kid recognized me as the poet John Giorno. This was always disappointing, because it compromised the spontaneously arising play where there was no past, present, or future, only bliss continuously coming. I looked at him and wondered how much he knew, and whether he was a poet or an artist. My guess was that he was an art student, and went to the School of Visual Arts. None of this mattered because the kid seemed pure, and we were making love.

The toilet stank of cigarette smoke, disinfectant, and piss, which in the hot, humid morning bit the nostrils, almost making me gag. The underlying constant danger that a cop or plainclothes policeman could at any moment walk in the door and arrest everybody sharpened the clarity. When somebody entered the toilet, everything stopped, and he was checked out, straight or gay, trouble or okay. It took a few seconds for my intuition to say yes or no. I was lucky and never got busted. I was always in a state of constant desire, always wanting more, no matter what I was getting, never at ease, never relaxed, always looking over my shoulder; the danger heightened the pleasures.

We kissed, holding each other as tight and close as we could. We pressed our bodies together hard and strong, trying to push inside each other, so there would be one body, one dick, one heart.

The air was soaked with humidity, the toilet crowded with men. The kid and I were completely hyperventilating, our body temperatures burned, and we poured sweat. *You got to burn to shine.* We got to burn some more. Burning away all concepts, releasing the bliss trapped in our hearts.

The great thing about anonymous sex is that you don't bring your private life or personal world into it—it's just pure sex with abandon between consenting men. No politics and inhibiting concepts, no closed rules or fixed responses. It's spontaneous.

Five guys circled around us, jerking off. Somebody stuck a popper in my nostrils and the kid's, and we fell into each other's mouths and bodies again. Everyone vanished but the two of us. In the ecstasy of sheer stoned delight, we were in a dream of the formless divine.

Somebody straight came into the toilet, who didn't look cool, and we took a break. I asked the kid, "What's your name?" Not that I wanted to know, but simply to extend with generosity the openness we felt for each other. At that very moment a train roared into the station. The kid said his name, "Keith," in the deafening noise.

I unbuckled the kid's belt and pulled down his pants. I turned him gently around, slowly eased the wet head of my dick in his ass, and then slipped it in all the way in. I fucked the kid, gently at first, then gradually as hard as I could. Sweat poured off us in sheets. From the depth of inebriating darkness of the underground cave, stretching my dick to a black sky, I shot a big load of cum, straight and glorious. Perfectly arisen and accomplished, and perfectly dissolved back into primordially pure empty space.

After I came I rested in his arms for a while. The kid pressed his hard dick against me, and obviously wanted to cum, too. I sucked his cock and I wished he'd cum so I could stop. I got up and kissed him, and tried to jerk him off, but he gently pressed my shoulder for me to go down. He wanted to cum in my mouth. Now, giving blow jobs is not my specialty, and since I'd just cum, I couldn't have felt less like doing it, but he was special, and I wanted to give him back something he wanted. Gagging, I kept at it. The kid arched his back and started writhing, thrusting his hips forward and sinking his shaft all the way down my throat. He came in a flood. I got up and we kissed. In 1982, I knew very well about AIDS, but I thought, This kid is so pure, and has such pure intentions, how could he have AIDS?

We smiled and said goodbye, and I was out the door in a flash onto a train that had just pulled in going uptown. It was always a shock entering the straight world of a car full of grim people imprisoned in their minds, sitting dumbly with their suffering faces.

That very month, twenty-four-year-old Keith Haring had just

joined the Tony Shafrazi Gallery. In October, he would have his first one-man show in Manhattan, which turned a young, relatively unknown artist (he had been doing the subway drawings on the black empty advertisement panels for a year) into a world-famous superstar. Three years later, in January 1985, when Keith came to dinner in my house, his body had changed slightly. He'd put on a little weight, become more solid from self-empowerment, and gained an aura of power.

Later, I'd find out that Keith suspected he was HIV-positive in 1981, when he discovered early symptoms of what was then called gay-related immune deficiency. When we'd had sex, he was HIV-positive. Keith died of AIDS on February 16, 1990. I stayed HIV-negative, one of many miracles given my voracious sexual appetite. In the early '80s, even though people were dying, I stubbornly refused to take AIDS seriously, and kept thinking that AIDS was Legionnaires' disease, and that they would find a way to clean air-conditioning systems and it would go away, or it would turn out to be a minor health problem. I still went to the baths for great sex, because it was my habit. I must have come into contact with the AIDS virus many times, and somehow remained negative.

I have always remembered that anonymous kid for opening himself so extraordinarily, for allowing a great moment of transcendent sex, motivated by genuine love, trying to radiate enough blissful compassion to fill the world. The kid opened himself the way people don't generally do even with a lover, wife, or husband. Of the countless great sexual encounters in the golden age of promiscuity, that one always symbolized all the others. I believed we were the combat troops of love liberating the world.

After the studio visit, Keith and I became good friends. Anything I asked him to do, he did happily and tirelessly with devotion. He did the art for my LP *A Diamond Hidden in the Mouth of a Corpse*. He made paintings for the front and back covers, and did drawings around the photographs on the inside gate and record sleeves.

More than a year before Keith died, I asked him to illustrate one of my poems as a collaboration. I sent him two poems and he chose "Sucking Mud," a four-page poem dealing in a way with our AIDS sexual crisis. He had the four pages photocopied onto linen paper and made drawings in sumi ink with delicate lines and shading, unlike his usual work with bold lines. Keith finished the drawings right away, and over the months asked many times about where and when I was going to do the prints, and how it was progressing. We decided maybe they should be etchings, because of the subtlety of the halftones. I had no idea how to proceed. Jean-Paul Russell at Durham Press, whom I worked with making silk-screen poem prints, had done an edition of Keith's pornographic drawings, which had not sold well. I didn't want to seem as if I was forcing it to happen quickly before he died, because I knew the edition could not be proofed, printed, and signed in the six months before his death.

KEITH AND I never talked about the Prince Street toilet. He said in John Gruen's biography: "I firmly believe that sexual relationships—a deep sexual relationship—is a way of truly experiencing another person—and really *becoming* that other person." I agree.

Poster for *A Diamond Hidden in the Mouth of a Corpse*

AIDS TREATMENT PROJECT

On a beautiful spring morning in May 1979, I was walking down Bleecker Street near La Guardia Place, and I ran into Michael, a film critic and great guy who sometimes came over for sex.

"How are you?"

"Terrible," he said. "My roommate Steve, my ex-lover, just died. He died the most horrible death. In three months, he went from normal to being destroyed by this disease, which went into his brain. He died insane."

"Oh, I am so sorry. Was it cancer?" I asked.

"It was cancer, but something more than cancer. It was horrible." I had the feeling Michael was telling me something momentous, but I wasn't sure yet what it was.

By the early 1980s, it had gotten worse, and many more men died. It was being called the gay cancer, and heroin users were included in the mounting numbers of the dead. Once I realized I couldn't ignore this, that it wasn't going to go away, I became extremely depressed. Over the next decade, many close friends would die—Gregory Kolovakos, Keith Haring, Peter Hujar, Howard Brookner, Cookie Mueller—and for some I managed to be there with them at the time of their death, or shortly after. It felt like the ultimate failure of all our aspirations of love, sexual freedom, and drugs. The heroic effort and accomplishment of the gay liberation movement, the sexual openness and equality, came to nothing. Many sick people—seeing their imminent dementia and death—committed suicide, and weren't recorded as AIDS deaths. The toll this epidemic began to take in the arts community in particular was almost unfathomable.

I knew I had to try to do something, so in 1984 I decided to take direct action, and started the AIDS Treatment Project as a program within the nonprofit Giorno Poetry Systems. It began as an attempt to combat the catastrophe of the epidemic with all-pervasive compassion. When a person got sick, lost their job, or became disabled, they needed immediate help. And that help was most often in the form of cash. So I would send a check. Grants for emergency situations: back rent, telephone, utility bills, food, nursing, alternative medicine not covered by Medicaid, taxis, whatever was needed. The grants were $500, $1,000, $3,000, $5,000. Money was given with love and affection! When a person is sick, paperwork is the last thing they need to worry about; their replies of gratitude became a deeply moving record. In the interest of transparency, every year we released a joyful color brochure about the people who helped—all volunteers—and those who had received money, and how much. The intention was to encourage other people to do the same in their communities.

That first year, Bob Mould of the rock band Hüsker Dü, who had played on Giorno Poetry Systems albums, said he wanted to donate the band's royalties to the AIDS Treatment Project. I asked other artists who appeared on the albums—William Burroughs, Allen Ginsberg, Laurie Anderson, Patti Smith, Debbie Harry—and who could afford to, to do the same. And we put on some fantastic benefit concerts.

The AIDS Treatment Project felt like an extension of the golden age of promiscuity, when you made love to whomever you were mutually attracted to, even if they were strangers. I reached out to anyone who had AIDS, the same as if they were the beautiful people I cruised in the baths, bars, and toilets. I looked into our extended poetry and art world community for anyone needing help, or tried to help people who just crossed my path. During great anonymous hookups, I always had an affectionate, personal moment of connection after sex, and I brought this moment of affection to the people I helped with AIDS. I wanted to offer love from that same place, in the form of boundless compassion.

The AIDS Treatment Project did its job, as much as anything could help during such a cataclysmic time. In the 2000s, it morphed into the Poets and Artists Fund, and we began helping people with other medical problems as well. In recent years, we mostly help older people—people in their seventies, eighties, and even nineties, living on fixed incomes and battling illnesses.

The 1993–1994 annual report of the AIDS Treatment Project

IN JANUARY 1988, two Tibetan Buddhist lamas, whom I had met in Sarnath in 1971, came to tea at my loft. After William had moved to Kansas, the building had gone co-op, and I had bought my loft, the Bunker, and a third space, which I used as a painting and rehearsal studio, an office for Giorno Poetry Systems, and a guest bedroom. As I gave them a tour of the building, Khenpo Palden Sherab and his brother Khenpo Tsewang Dongyal, both disciples of Dudjom Rinpoche, who had died the year before, were surprised at how big the Bunker was. "John, we are looking for a space to give a large teaching," one lama said. I readily agreed and over the next many years, the Khenpos gave countless teachings in the Bunker. More than eighty people came to each teaching. Over time, the shrine evolved. And in 1989, we had our first fire puja for three days around January 1, to celebrate the New Year. The first puja in the morning was in the baronial fireplace in my third-floor loft, with meditation in the Bunker, which had been turned into a shrine room, in the afternoon. Khenpo Palden Sherab made a perfect, huge, blazing fire and fed it symbolic offerings of grains and other substances, which roared up the chimney. The flames leapt out of the hearth, into the smoke-filled room. The fire puja has happened every year for more than thirty years now.

From the late 1970s on, many great Western-bound Nyingma lamas came from India to Paris and New York on their way to California, or from Hong Kong to San Francisco and New York on their way to Paris. They knew they could stay in the Bunker, free, and I paid for the food and arranged for the guest cooks. The lamas had private visits and gave teachings. It was my extended family: since His Holiness Dudjom Rinpoche was head of the Nyingmas, they were all his disciples. It was my good fortune, as I received teachings and their strong blessings in appreciation. Many lamas went on to start meditation centers in America.

THE DEATH OF WILLIAM BURROUGHS

In September 1994, I was in Geneva, performing at the Festival de la Bataille in an eightieth-birthday tribute to William Burroughs. He had accepted the honor but never had any intention of attending. So the festival organizers invited me to perform as a stand-in for him.

Early in the show, William and I spoke on a live hookup over the telephone; he was in his living room in Lawrence, Kansas, and I was on stage in front of two thousand people. William was an old-fashioned gentleman and generally did not like talking on the phone. "I disapprove of visiting over the telephone," he would often say. He held the phone, metaphorically, at arm's length. We made small talk, which was awkward for both of us until we hit on the subject of William's cats: Felch, Spooner, Ginger, Mute, and Senco, whom I knew well. William read several excerpts from "Words of Advice for Young People"—a very funny piece that made people laugh and scream.

The audience was giddy hearing William's soft, gravelly voice booming out from the speakers, filling the space. Everyone adored the intimate moment. Each person made a strong heart connection with him. Including, formality aside, me.

A dozen poets and bands went on to perform. Lee Ranaldo of Sonic Youth made a collage of William's words and images. I performed "Life Is a Killer." It felt good. I thought of William's work and my work and our work together, over all of these past years.

How the hell
did I end
up
doing this
for a job?

IN THE FALL OF 1995, William and I visited Paul Bowles at the Mayfair Hotel on Park Avenue. Paul was in New York for a retrospective at Lincoln Center of the incidental music he composed in the 1940s, basking in a lot of attention and adulation.

"What is incidental music?" William had asked the day before, drinking vodka and Coke in the Bunker.

"Music that no one takes seriously," I replied. "Music that is not very good, by someone who is famous for something else." We laughed, because it was true.

"It's so slight, it barely exists," said William, smoking the joint that I had just passed to him. Neither William nor I had even the slightest thought of going to any concert.

We waited in the hotel lobby until Paul Bowles appeared through the front doors: at eighty-four, an old predator bird. He had a strong life force and was in excellent health, although he hobbled on a cane, and was followed by his Moroccan attendant with a wheelchair. I had not seen Paul since 1966—had not laid eyes upon him in thirty years. I was surprised at how strong his vitality seemed, like a rock. He was not about to leave this world anytime soon.

Paul had a three-room suite: two bedrooms and a sitting room. A film was being made about him by a young, handsome Canadian filmmaker. Paul sat perched on a couch. William and I sat on chairs around a coffee table. We were surrounded by the retinue and the film crew setting up. The conversation was polite, awkward, until Allen Ginsberg arrived, filling the space with noise and energy.

Paul was in a froth about a recent biography. It had uncovered details that painted him in a less flattering light than his own memoir had. "Now he says that I have lied. He accused me of lying," said Paul about the biographer, shocked and outraged. "I have never! Cover things up a little, covering things up that should be covered up. That's not lying, is it?"

"Of course not," said William politely.

Paul smiled, like an old hawk, and said, "It is not true!"

I was thrilled by what Paul was saying. I kept repeating everything he said, three times to myself, to remember. And I went to the bathroom several times and wrote it down. I felt like a terrorist. Paul tried to cover up everything interesting about their lives. I had to blow it up. I had to do it.

The young filmmaker was ready to shoot. He asked us questions about Tangier in the 1950s and New York in the 1940s. The responses were stiff and boring. Neutral remembrances, as we were on camera, and nobody wanted to be compromised.

I didn't understand this cool-hearted ritual. It was clear that William didn't particularly like Paul or have any spiritual connection to him. William was doing this because he was attached to the myth that had been created about them. And William, as much as he respected Allen's devotion and usefulness, always thought he was a slight nuisance. Allen was very political, which was why he was there, always at the hot spot. And Paul didn't really like anyone, except those working to help him in some way.

During the interview, there was talk about them smoking kif and hash, and eating majoun in Tangier. Off camera, William made a sign to me and I said, "Paul, would you like to smoke a joint?"

I had waited long enough; it was now or never, and I couldn't resist. "Whatever happened to Cherifa?"

Since briefly living next to Paul and Jane Bowles in Tangier decades earlier, I had remained strangely obsessed with mad, tragic Jane and her spurned lover Cherifa. In 1973, when Jane died, I had written an obituary in the St. Mark's Poetry Project magazine. Building on what Brion had teased Paul about in Tangier, the game that I wasn't sure was a game, I wrote about how I thought that Jane had been poisoned over a long period of time by Cherifa. Paul had read the obituary and did not like it all, and for years, he attacked me with venomous denials: everything I said was false. It was all lies, he insisted. In 1984, I actually wrote him a letter to apologize. I had made the mistake of believing Brion's lurid psycho-pathetic view of Jane and the world.

Then, a year later, Paul admitted in an interview that there was always the possibility of Jane being poisoned, and that all their friends talked about it, but that it was not true. I told this to William, who said that the likelihood of Jane being poisoned was great, given Cherifa's knowledge of it, "but Jane did not die of poison."

Now here I was bringing it up again. I was sure that, intuitively, Paul knew I was a traitor. Like a reptile put on alert, his eyes instantly glinted. He smelled danger. "I haven't heard about her in years. I haven't spoken to her in a very long time."

"Is she alive?" I said casually. "I'm just curious."

Paul reconsidered. "I don't know if she's alive. She was sick. Targuisti ran into her on the street two years ago. She said she had cancer. She said, 'I have cancer and the doctors in Casablanca have taken all my money.'"

"She must be very old."

"Very!" said Paul, smiling sharply. "I don't know if she's alive, or dead."

I thought back to the darkness of my time in Tangier, the savagery in that ugly apartment building. I realized that Cherifa and Brion, who had died in 1986, were probably demons.

A demon was an ordinary being who was very angry, from being deeply hurt. This person died with great anger and suffering, and in the bardo and rebirth was more angry and suffered more from it; in each of their successive lives, the consciousness was more and more angry, which caused more suffering, until this being was so distorted, it frightened everyone. People ran away. This caused more suffering, until this being became what was called a demon. And everyone wanted to destroy this person, kill, subdue, annihilate. A demon suffered more, and so needed more love and compassion, because underneath the anger and suffering was a very tender being, infinitely gentle; and inside this was something even more deeply hurt; and still further beneath was a consciousness that was more soft and vulnerable, and total openness.

A FEW WEEKS LATER, William said to me, over the telephone from Kansas, "Paul and I have very little in common . . . I am interested in people who are interested in the things that I'm interested in." Meaning drugs (namely, heroin), guns, magical powers, and wild animals in magazines and on television.

What was William's interest in me? It was, I understood, what I had realized from the great Tibetan Buddhist teachers I'd known and meditation practice I'd done. I could talk to him about death, and the process of dying. I also thought that William and I must have had strong karmic connections from past lives, as we had felt so at home together for over thirty years, and yet were so different.

William Burroughs, the author, and Ginger the cat

ON JULY 13, 1996, I arrived in Lawrence, Kansas, to take William to Los Angeles for the opening of his "Ports of Entry" show. My being there was James Grauerholz's idea, and a ticket was sent for me to come and serve as William's attendant, to keep him out of trouble. It was a role I was used to from being on tour with him. I was happy that James still included me, as he had gotten rid of many of William's old friends.

William and I were sitting in his bedroom in our usual positions, me on the bed, him on a wooden chair in front of a window that offered a view of the small pond outside, which was surrounded by the graves of his dead cats. Our drinks were on the windowsill, with an ashtray, roaches, and matches. Fletch, the fat black cat, was on the bed with me.

"This is the tenth anniversary of Brion's death," I said.

"I know," said William. "July thirteenth . . . And we arrive in L.A. on Bastille Day."

We were about to embark on another tour, and this was exciting. We had been on the road together for more than three decades. "Old troupers," William said proudly.

WHEN I ARRIVED for my next visit nine months later, William looked gaunt and white. His eyes were sunken in his head. "I just had a small heart attack. I don't feel good."

"Great! Wonderful!" I was very stoned from all the grass I had smoked on the drive from the airport to his house. I didn't understand what William was saying, but I managed to ask, "What did you say?"

"John, I just had a heart attack, a great pressure on my chest and arms." He made a gesture with his spindly hands, down his head and body, and described the overwhelming dead weight that had come down over him. "It was a small heart attack. Not a bad one, but a light one is a sign that the big one is gonna come. Phow!"

William continued, with great aplomb, "I even went in there and wrote down these words:

Seeing that death
a necessary end,
will come when
it will come!

"Famous last words!" I said admiringly. "Very good!" I could see William scrawling it in longhand with a ballpoint on a pad. "Very professional, famous last words!"

William was eighty-three years old and in relatively excellent health, despite the aches of age, methadone, the vodka and Cokes he drank starting at 3:30 every afternoon, the grass, the meat, the salt, and the ice cream. William had had an angioplasty heart procedure that had failed, and a triple-bypass heart operation six years before. It was time that trouble might begin, again.

That night, we drank a lot of vodka, smoked a lot of joints, and ate a meatloaf dinner. It was wonderful being with him again.

"I had this feeling once before," said William. "A long time ago, when I OD'd on heroin. A dead weight."

We went to sleep and William had a very bad night. Staying awake from nausea, moaning in bed, he finally vomited at four in the morning, just after taking his methadone. That made it necessary to take more, even though we didn't know how much he had vomited up. Only then did William fall asleep.

The next morning, James and I telephoned several of William's doctors and made the earliest possible appointment, a few days later. William recited the words of an English folk song about the plague, which he would sometimes do when he was drunk and stoned and the subject of death came up:

Is it not fine
> *to dance and sing,*
> *while the bells of death*
> *do ring*

Bring out your dead
Bring out your dead

Turn on your toe
Hey ny nee no

THE NEXT AFTERNOON, we drank vodka and Coke and smoked joints in William's bedroom. His diary, on a spiral lined pad, was open to the words he had scribbled the day before, Sunday, April 13, 1997.

> I feel wobbly like I may be dying—who lives will see—way I feel, now, don't know whether to call a doctor or the undertaker. It is not good. Fortunately my company are gathering—This may be it—Seeing that death
> > a necessary end,
> > will come
> > when it will come!
> Shakespeare, Julius Caesar—any case no fear—it could be tonight—I had the dying feeling an hour or two ago—It will return and heavier.

At the doctor's visit, William's cardiogram was okay, exactly the same as in 1993, though James and I planned to follow up with a specialist. We all agreed that this recent heart attack was a warning. That William must have a detailed exam.

We talked about dying. I always brought it up once, discreetly, every visit, to remind him, and make him familiar with what happens at the moment of death, for the glorious thing that it was.

William would say, "Bring me your dead, you ain't got anything better to bring!" Drunk and stoned, we would laugh and laugh.

I left for New York the next day.

FOUR MONTHS LATER, on Saturday, August 2, at 6:01 p.m., William Burroughs died of complications from a massive heart attack he had suffered the day before. Although he was in the hospital in Kansas and I was at a friend's birthday weekend in Maryland, I was with William's consciousness when he died, and it was one of the best times I ever had with him. You never expect that someone will actually die, but when they finally do—after the first brief moment of bright recognition and clarity—the person then causes you the last great inconvenience; their final, grasping act, as their fading consciousness sponges up your energy, thanklessly, exploiting your devotion for the last time. William was the most sublimely selfish person in the world for one last time.

The great demon king is dead. Absorbing the news from James over the phone, all I could think was: What a relief, it's done! I felt like yelling "Hallelujah!" Death is very powerful. The consciousness of the dead person reaches around the world to anyone who is thinking about them, radiating great clarity and great bliss.

Almost right away James and I began dealing with the practical details. What do we do next? The funeral. First, the undertaker. Then it hit me: what I had to do for William. I had to guide his consciousness through the dying process, go through the bardo with him. Nobody else was going to do it, and I doubted whether he could do it himself.

"Don't touch the body!" I said to James over the phone. "Let his consciousness rest in *great equanimity* inside his body for as long as it can . . . This is very important! Dying is a long, complicated process. After the breathing stops, the subtle winds continue moving for many hours through the channels. It is important to allow this to happen naturally. Ask them if they can leave the body in the hospital bed until tomorrow morning. Sometimes they say yes. I've done it."

"I'll ask," said James. "But what about . . ."

"Don't worry, it doesn't rot so soon. Or stink. You can leave a piece of meat out overnight, and it will get a little dry, and you might not want to eat it, but it's okay." We were laughing.

"Ask the nurses if they can leave William's body in the bed, with or without the bedsheet over his head, until early morning, or for as many hours as possible. Two hours are better than one, three hours better than two."

James called back a few minutes later, and said, "The hospital has agreed to leave him until the funeral people will come to take him away." James's voice almost cracked.

In Maryland, I bolted awake about midnight, with a clear head. I got out of bed and started doing whatever it was for William. I wasn't sure, I just let it happen. I got my mala (prayer beads), relic bag, and a cushion. Under the vast, black, starry Eastern Shore sky, I sat on the grass in the middle of the garden. Fifty candles were still burning in their lanterns from our earlier dinner party, an offering to the Buddhas for William. I sat on the cushion, dissolving my thoughts and relaxing my mind. I did several practices: formless meditation, mantra and visualization, and some breathing exercises to generate more heat and energy.

About twelve-thirty, things got intense with a sudden display of energy. I didn't know it, but at exactly that time, they were moving William's dead body from the hospital bed to the funeral home. William's consciousness left his body when they moved it. And in that moment, I said to myself, "Maybe I should do Powa for William, now!" Powa is the transference of the consciousness of the dead person to a pure field. Although I had some training in Powa, I hadn't planned to do it; I was neither a lama nor a meditation master.

But I followed my instinct. Doing Tibetan Nyingma Buddhist meditation practices, I absorbed William's consciousness into my heart. It seemed like a bright white light, blinding but muted, empty. I was the vehicle, his consciousness passing through me. A gentle shooting star came in my heart and up the central channel, and out the top of my head to a pure field of great clarity and bliss. It was very powerful—William Burroughs resting in *great equanimity*, and the vast empty expanse of primordial wisdom mind.

I did it.

Then it hit me that this was only the beginning of William's dying process. Oh, no! No escape from the worst! rang in my head.

There was no other friend with the spiritual skills who could help him. And it had to be done right now. I didn't want to do it for him, because William was always tricky. He was the black hole— everything goes in, nothing emerges. Thirty-two years after meeting him, I had learned not to want anything, or expect anything, and I wasn't disappointed. But now there was no way out. It was like jumping into dangerous water to save a drowning person, knowing that person is likely to pull you under.

When a person dies, the best way for the consciousness or soul to leave the body is out the top of the head; however, if the dead person is unable to do this, another person can do it for them. Normally, the consciousness or soul of the dead person leaves the body through one of the five holes: asshole, ear, nose, etc., determined by their karma. A Tibetan lama, or meditation master, can free the consciousness of the dead person by absorbing it and then ejecting it through the crown of the head to a pure land or Buddha field, where the consciousness can become enlightened or go on to rebirth, according to their karma.

There is no time and no space for a dead person. And without a body, the consciousness can travel great distances instantly. If someone in Paris or Los Angeles has a connection with the dead person, the consciousness can be in both places almost simultaneously, for a moment, and then back to hanging around its dead body.

In deep meditation, I took William's consciousness into my heart center. A feeling of light, like a small, pale comet or sperm surrounded by love, compassion, and wisdom, came in a muted, blinding flash into my heart, and up the central channel, and up out the top of my head to a pure field of great bliss and clarity.

There was a feeling of absolute certainty and relief. I finished my prayers. Then I was really tired. I returned to the house and went to sleep.

The next day, I flew to Kansas. As James drove me to William's house, he told me the whole raw story of William's death. William had been given blood thinners, which caused his lips and gums to bleed. He was in extreme pain, and was making cat sounds, with clenched teeth like a trapped animal, moving his head back and forth. *"Oww. Meow. Oww."* The nurse was having difficulty finding a vein for some new medication, and William stopped breathing. "His heart kept beating, but he stopped breathing." James choked up. I held him as he drove.

James continued, "When the funeral people came to take the body, I leaned over and whispered in his ear, *'Listen to me carefully, they're going to move your body now. But you can find me anytime.'"*

Even though I knew Dean Ripa would be at William's house, I was still surprised to see him. Dean was a handsome straight guy who lived in North Carolina and on rare occasions was known to be bisexual, but not with William. He was a snake dealer. He captured wild, poisonous snakes in the jungles of Central and South America and sold them to zoos and collectors in the United States. He was also a bad painter and bad writer. But he was very good-looking, and very into women. I tolerated Dean, because he was William's indulgence. He was like a character in one of William's early books.

Dean had been visiting William and was having drinks with him when William had the heart attack. Dean was staying in the guest bedroom, where I usually stayed. But after William's death, he took it upon himself to move into William's bed, giving me the guest room. For the next three nights, Dean thrashed around in William's bed, tossing and turning, disturbing William's mind with his own demons and nightmares. In the morning, the twisted bedsheets looked like a torment from hell. This was very bad for William. The bed of the dead person should remain untouched for at least three days, allowing the subtle energy, the residue of the life force and vitality, to breathe. Dean's demons were his own demons, not William's. But it was not for me to say anything to Dean; and James, in his grieving, could not ask Dean to leave.

I had a very good time, in my room next door, doing my meditation practice, transforming the energy in the house to one of bright clarity and serenity. This was an obstacle for William that had to be overcome.

But the house wasn't even the worst of it. At the hospital, James told me, when he and Dean had come into the room and found William dead, Dean became distraught, crying and yelling, and making a disturbance. Dean grabbed William's dead body and shook it, screaming, "Wake up! You can't die. Wake up. Goddammit." Weeping, Dean kept shaking him violently and slapping William's face. This is the very worst thing that can happen. William was just realizing that he was dead. And this idiot was beating him up. The dying process was being horribly upset.

A person realizing he is dead rests the mind or consciousness in great equanimity, in emptiness, with great clarity and bliss. This was a door or threshold of liberation for William's consciousness—the moment when enlightenment is possible for someone with experience in the nature of mind. William had been waiting his whole life for this moment. We talked about it often. Death was an opportunity for freedom from rebirth, and liberation from the suffering of the wheel of samsara. Dean had ruined it. How was this possible? A catastrophe! Thirty-two years before, in 1965, on LSD, Brion Gysin said, "William will make one big mistake at the last moment. Everyone thinks he's so cool. He'll make one big mistake and blow it."

But all was not lost. I was sure I could make contact with William's consciousness, and help him, guiding him through the intermediate state, or bardo. When you're working with the dead, you can't let doubt arise, because it allows doubt to arise in the consciousness or soul of the dead person, and doubt will bring you both down to hell.

So during those two days after his death, I stayed mostly in my room, doing my meditation practices for him, trying to maintain the good conditions and dissolve any obstacles that might be arising for him at that very moment in the bardo. I was confident that William had a high degree of realization, but he was not a completely enlightened being. I had to proceed fearlessly, with absolute confidence. William was resting in the union of wisdom and emptiness. And I had to keep him there.

Dying is a most terrifying experience—frightening beyond anything you can imagine. Hurricanes of fear and tornadoes of doubt rip the mind. Everything is lost, no friends and no protection. It's similar to entering a dense darkness, falling down a deep precipice, drowning in the ocean, being swept away by the great force of your karma. This is true for everyone, except great meditation masters and totally enlightened beings.

But William was not one of these, even though he had a strong understanding of the empty nature of all phenomena. William was lazy; he never really worked at it, he never conquered his mind. He preferred to write, and be drunk and stoned, a bimbo sponge. All of that helped him to a high level of realization, but it was not enough. For the last many years of his life, William complained that being in this world caused him great suffering: a very Buddhist view.

When it became too difficult to use a typewriter, William had started writing on notepads in a scratchy, dysfunctional handwriting. In his bedroom, on the small desk, there was a spiral pad half filled with scribbles. Three days before he died, on July 30, 1997, William wrote:

When you see someone who looks like the saddest man in the world. That's him.
How can a man who sees and feels be other than sad? To

see Ginger always older and weaker. The price of immortality, of course. Well you should have thought of these things.

The day before he died, William wrote:

I did. Thinking isn't enough. Nothing is. There is no final enough of wisdom, experience, any fucking thing. No Holy Grail, No Final Satori, no final solution. Just conflict: only thing that can resolve conflict is love. Like I felt for Fletch and Ruski, Spooner and Calico. Pure love. What I feel for my cats, present and past.
     Love? What is it? Most natural painkiller what there is. LOVE

The last word that William wrote—his last written word—was LOVE. That was pretty good.

During my hours of meditation process, there was a very strong feeling of William's consciousness pervading everything: my mind, and the walls and furniture. The space in the house glowed with clarity, a luminosity that arose as a result of him being free from subject and object, and free from thoughts.

And then, two and a half days after William died, I noticed that everything had changed. Everything seemed bright and optimistic, cheerful, even; different from the black oppressiveness. William's consciousness had awakened from the black state.

Dean left before the funeral. He deeply loved William and was oblivious that he was a demon. And there was no blame. We are each the victim of our own karma, victims of ourselves. Before Dean departed, he was sitting in the living room. I was walking to the kitchen to make myself some tea. Dean got up, and said, "John, I just want to say how much I appreciate everything you've done. Everything's really changed since you've been here. It was hell before you came. And now, everything feels wonderful. Thank you."

I thanked him, and we hugged each other. It was a big blessing when he moved out. William's bedroom was cleaned and became itself again. The space in the rooms took on a glow from William's wisdom mind. I wandered about the house, and out back to the pond, and fed the goldfish, as was William's pleasure. Not so much remembering, but feeling the many times I had been with him there. I was not sad, but full of love and happiness. This was our newest moment together.

It was time to pick out the clothes for William's corpse, as well as the things to go into his coffin and grave, accompanying him on his journey in the underworld. James, Ira Silverberg, a friend from New York, and I opened the closet door and began.

William's favorite gun, a .38 special snub nose, fully loaded with five shots. He called it "the snubby." William always said you can never be too well armed in any situation. He slept with it, fully loaded, under the bedsheet, every night for fifteen years. His gray fedora. He always wore a hat when he went out. We wanted his consciousness to feel perfectly at ease. His favorite cane, a sword cane made of hickory. A greenish-black sport jacket, which smelled sweetly of him. Blue jeans. A red bandanna. He always kept one in his back pocket. Jockey underwear and socks. Black shoes, the ones he wore when he performed. I thought the old brown ones, which he wore all the time, might be more comfortable. But James insisted, stating, "There's an old CIA slang that says getting a new assignment is getting new shoes." A white shirt. We had bought it in a men's shop in Beverly Hills in 1981 on "The Red Night Tour." It was his best shirt. Even though it had become tight over the years, he had lost a lot of weight, and we thought it would fit. James said, "Don't they slit it down the back anyway?"

Necktie, blue, hand-painted by William. Moroccan vest, green velvet with gold brocade trim, given to him by Brion Gysin twenty-five years before. In his lapel buttonhole, the rosette of the French government's Chevalier des Arts et Lettres, and the rosette of the American Academy of Arts and Letters, honors that William very much appreciated. A gold nineteenth-century Indian head five-dollar piece, symbolizing all wealth, in his pants pocket. He would have enough money to buy his way in the underworld. An old, worn silver coin.

James suggested another coin, one that had once belonged to the satanist Aleister Crowley, but I didn't think it was a good idea. The door to hell was already open for William, and he didn't need to be encouraged. James and Ira grinned mischievously, and said, "Yes!"

His eyeglasses in his outside breast pocket. A ballpoint pen, the kind he always used. A joint of really good grass. Just before the funeral service, Grant Hart, one of the founders of the rock band Hüsker Dü, slipped a small white paper packet of junk into William's pocket and said, "Nobody's going to bust him."

At the funeral home, I saw William's dead body for the first time. William Burroughs, the dead man. Clear, serene power radiating from his mind filled the space. Beside him, I did meditation practice, for more than four hours, and in the days that followed, alone with William's consciousness. After almost thirty-three years, for me to be there for him at death was the ultimate expression of love, beyond all concepts.

I had things to do with William's dead body. I wanted to put the mandala of Kuntuzangpo, the Primordial Buddha, at William's heart center, touching his skin. It is called liberation through touch. The funeral director had put a T-shirt on the body, even though William never wore one with a shirt and tie, so both layers had to be slit open with a scissor for me to reach the skin. I slipped in the three-inch circular photograph of the blue-black Buddha with white consort, yab-yum, surrounded by a mandala of other Buddhas, facing down, over his heart.

I put some oil in William's nose. And I poured some white sand into his left ear. The sand contained relics of His Holiness Dudjom Rinpoche, my teacher, whom William had met; and the blessings of Chenrezig, the Buddha of compassion. The oil and sand block rebirth in the three lower realms. Not to move his head too much, I funneled the sand in using a small piece of white paper. William was not a Buddhist, but he himself would say, "In situations like this, you can't get enough help."

I tied a red protection cord around his neck and slipped it down under his collar, so nobody would see. I pulled a chair right up in front of his corpse in his coffin and did my meditation practices. I did three practices of the Buddha Vajrasattva. First, the One Hundred Syllable mantra for purification, and to dissolve obstacles that might be arising for William at that moment. Second, Vajrasattva, as the wisdom deity. And third, Vajrasattva as the absolute nature of mind, which is free from all thoughts of past, present, or future—innate primordial wisdom.

AH

AH symbolizes the great emptiness, and is a sign of the ultimate true nature. It also symbolizes love, compassion, and wisdom. All indications were that William had done it, had successfully released himself. He was not a totally enlightened being, but he had a great understanding of the nature of mind. His consciousness was now beyond all concepts, beyond time and space. He'd finally done it. For almost thirty-five years, William and I had talked about the moment of death, and the possibility of liberation at that time from the cycle of rebirth and suffering. William had just died, and was there right now, finally after all these years. A great accomplishment. I was very happy for him.

I kissed him. A 1975 LP of us together was called *Biting Off the Tongue of a Corpse*. I kissed him on the lips, but I didn't bite off his tongue. And I should have. I kissed him some more, light and affectionate, the way he liked it, catlike. His cheek was hard and his skin was dead-man cold. I held his hand, the way I did when he was alive, to make him feel at ease.

My intuition told me that William was being reborn in a formless heaven world. It was what he really wanted. For how long depended on his karma. But this state is nonregenerating. It uses up what got you there. It uses up good karma and doesn't generate any—like when you have to pay the rent, and you don't have any money and get kicked out of your apartment and travel to a lower realm. In William's case, he generated so much good karma with the wisdom of his writings, he would be born human again, and in relatively good circumstances. Now, at that very moment, William Burroughs was transcendent wisdom light. And maybe he would stay in a formless heaven world for quite some time. William's corpse in the coffin was his relic body, a powerful sacred relic.

William Burroughs in his casket

THE NIGHT AFTER my work at the funeral home, in an old 1910 vaudeville theater where William and I had performed many times, about three hundred invited guests attended a memorial with William's body in the open coffin on stage. James made it into a modest midwestern homespun affair. I thought, perhaps, William should have a royal state funeral like Queen Mary or Princess Diana, the interstate highways lined with stoned people, and superstars who like junk, or even skinheads on speed, anything that gave a lot of energy to William. It would be in the spirit of his writing and his myth, which had changed the world. Instead,

James's eighty-year-old mother, whom William didn't particularly like, sang Protestant hymns in a withered, cracking voice.

I did not allow any negative thoughts to arise in my mind, even for an instant, because William could see them. The dead can see everything, even what you're thinking. Any thought I did not want William to know, I popped like a soap bubble. I had to be with him and guide him fearlessly, without a moment of hesitation or doubt.

I had telephoned two great Tibetan lamas who had given teachings at 222 Bowery, formally requesting them to do Tibetan Buddhist prayers for William. I heard them chanting mantra, ringing bells, and beating drums. And I could hear William say, "I need all the help I can get!"

The day we buried William, I woke up at 6:30 a.m. to get ready. I made myself a cup of tea. But instead of making William's breakfast, one boiled or one fried egg sunny side up, toast buttered with margarine, I helped with the small details of the funeral, with the same loving care as I had served him breakfast. After all those endless visits for all those years, making breakfast, and feeding the six or seven cats at nine o'clock in the morning.

On the six-hour drive to the Burroughs family grave in St. Louis, I had the feeling that this was the end of the completion stage of devotion. It was the beginning of the rest of my life with William dead.

Finally, he was dead; finally, I was rid of him. I was feeling better and better about it. I was surprised that William dying felt so good. It would be another two years before I could dissolve him from my mind, and maybe the karma never. Riding in an enormous white stretch limo, I looked out the window at the vast, clear, blue sky, and the undulating land of Missouri, endless cornfields surrounded by green trees. The highway rolled under us in space and time, exit signs and overpasses, and occasional billboards.

We arrived in St. Louis about 2:00 p.m. and drove by the

Pershing Avenue house where William was born. At the cemetery, about thirty people took turns performing a song or poem or saying a few words. The gravediggers lowered the coffin into the ground and covered it with dirt. We, each in turn, threw a handful of earth over the top.

ONE WEEK LATER, I flew to Buenos Aires to perform at a Jorge Luis Borges festival. During that week, grief for William became real, manifested itself, surfaced. It hit me, spontaneously, without warning. I started weeping, any time and place; tears swelled up and poured out. I became like Jell-O, and had to run away from the other poets, any place out of sight—the toilet or around the corner in an alley—and cry uncontrollably for thirty seconds. Jet lag and exhaustion, and the extraordinary feeling of great loss.

Then, at times, Buenos Aires took on the surreal quality of one of William's early books, *Naked Lunch* or *The Soft Machine*. Everything was a cut-up of art deco, Eva Peron and the tango, and slang. "Te cozi!" in Spanish means to get or grab, "I've got you!"; but in Argentine Spanish it means to fuck, "I've fucked you!" William was dead. Everyone was dead. His Holiness Dudjom Rinpoche, who was the most important person in my life, was dead. William, who was the most important secular being to me, was dead. Brion Gysin was dead. Allen Ginsberg was dead. Andy Warhol was dead. Vast numbers of friends and people dead from AIDS, the great minds of three generations dead of AIDS, and seemingly everyone I ever made love to in the golden age of promiscuity was dead. And then, even my father was dead, and all my family's friends were dead. Almost everyone in that world had died, decimated by a plague, cancer, old age.

There was no nostalgia, only a sense of relief. Much of my world was dead, but the world was also very much alive. I was very much alive. I was sixty years old and my energy was strong, as a result of the meditation practice, the blessings of His Holiness Dudjom Rinpoche, and my karma. I was doing my best work now. I inherited the earth. A reluctant king; thank you, but no thank you. We were approaching the end of the millennium, and about to begin a new millennium made of magical display. Life goes on.

William Burroughs in 1994

A FEW WEEKS LATER, while on tour, I was staying again in William Burroughs's house in Lawrence. I slept in his bed this time. It was very peaceful. This was one week after the forty-ninth day in the bardo, after his death. Maybe he was gone wherever he was going.

In my meditation practice, sitting on the bed where he had slept, I could go where William's consciousness rested. I felt very close to him. Even the grieving was over. But there was the low-level nagging sadness in my heart—that he wasn't in the house, and was gone forever.

I stood on the front porch near the rose trellis in the sunlight, at the end of summer. Only two of William's seven cats remained: Ginger and Mute, who were forlorn. Ginger was old and thin and frail. Five cats were dead and buried around the pond, outside William's bedroom window. In the pond, the big fat goldfish were thriving.

Sometimes when I lay on his bed resting with my eyes closed, there was a very strong feeling of his presence in his chair next to the bed, where he sat all the time. I counted my blessings from the great demon kings, for all the time I had being intimate with William, at 222 Bowery and in Kansas, and touring the world and performing together for decades, and just the two of us living an ordinary life.

EPILOGUE

I met Ugo Rondinone on March 11, 1998. He had heard me perform at the New Year's Day marathon reading at St. Mark's Church, telephoned, suggested we collaborate on a work of art, and came to visit at 222 Bowery. Ugo was working on a sculpture of trees wrapped in brown tape with speakers in the branches, and he wanted poems coming from the speakers. We talked about the possibilities. Ugo brought a bottle of red wine, which we drank at three in the afternoon. We had a good time talking about poets and artists, and learning about each other. A few hours later, I took Ugo on a tour of the three lofts. We were standing in the Bunker, between the kitchen and the big dining table with the orange chairs, where the countless great dinners had happened. We leaned forward slowly toward each other and kissed and hugged. And then we went into the bedroom and made love, falling asleep in each other's arms. We woke up, went upstairs, smoked a joint and had a glass of wine, and talked some more. We went to bed again. Ugo left at eleven, eight hours after he arrived.

We saw each other a week later, and again a week after that. Each time was a totally wonderful, intense experience. We would talk about poetry and art, our minds communicating compatibility, and then have fabulous sex. Ugo departed for Zurich in May and returned in September, and it was a great pleasure being with each other again. Instead of collaborating, we became lovers, although in the years that followed, we collaborated many times.

We very much connected as artists, and Ugo had an enormously positive effect on my work. He was a painter and sculptor, and had a natural understanding of poetry, using words in some of his work. I was a poet, and also made paintings, watercolors, and drawings as venues for my poetry. Ugo was a good editor, making very helpful suggestions when I showed him my poems. He also became my art teacher, encouraging me to go in new directions with my work, and never allowing me to make a mistake with my career in the art world. Even though I had been making silk-screen paintings of my poems since 1968, I was in the world of poetry, and opportunities for exhibitions came only from galleries and museums in Europe. After successes in Paris in the Polyphonix 5 festival at the Pompidou Center in the 1980s and an exhibition at the Galerie Almine Rech and Galerie Presenhuber in the late '90s, finally New York opened up, and I had shows at the Nicole Klagsbrun gallery, the Elizabeth Dee Gallery, the Sperone Westwater gallery, and MoMA. With Ugo, I was once again in the New York art world, like with Andy, Bob, and Jasper. Going to exhibitions with Ugo, seeing the art through his eyes, learning about its place in history was exciting, a great pleasure. I assume I've had a reciprocal positive effect on Ugo, as we are lovers, have lived our lives together, and sleep every night with our minds resting together.

Meeting Ugo was the beginning of a new life, less than a year after the deaths of William Burroughs and Allen Ginsberg, which had the profound effect of liberating me from the Beat Generation and the New York School.

In the twenty-two years Ugo and I have been together, I have written my best poems, done my best work as a painter and an artist, and found my secure place in the art and poetry worlds. Ugo and I are each other's muses. What a happy good fortune!

The author and
Ugo Rondinone

AS A POET, I am devoted to the people who love my work, my fans. I feel that my poems and performances had a profound effect on their minds, reflecting the wisdom already present there, helping them to recognize what they already knew. They thought they were hearing my poems, but my poems were mirrors in which they were seeing themselves. The best reward, and the reason to be a poet!

I have lived a blessed life with the freedom to work on what I want every day as a poet, artist, gay man, and Nyingma Buddhist. Poets don't make much money, and I have managed to slip through life by living marginally, which was a huge privilege. It enabled me to use all my energy for work. I was trying to see what a poem was, stripped of everything. The search led to clarity and emptiness, and words arising as wisdom.

Seen from 2019, poetry has again shed its skin, reinventing itself in form, as it does endlessly, and it is hard to fully see and understand the magnitude of the change. I feel privileged to have witnessed the form reinvent itself several times. One thing is certain: the last sixty years have been a golden age of poetry.

OLD AGE HAS BROUGHT with it several health issues. In August 2013, I had a transient ischemic attack, or an early-warning stroke. I recovered with no apparent damage, and was put on medications. The drugs and my aging decreased my ability to generate the big breath and heat necessary when I performed. I could not go over the top anymore.

In June 2016, I had heart failure. A viral infection collapsed the lower ventricles. The doctor said the virus had to be healed by my immune system.

The kind male nurse said, "John, your heart has just stopped three times: for twenty seconds, then ten seconds, and then for three seconds." I said, "It's beating now." I had no other thought, no fear—just doing what happens next, and it all felt good. Seven days later my heart booted itself up, like a computer. A stent was put in my left ventricle, which was 85 percent closed. My performances were even more diminished, and shortly after that I retired. What an enormous relief! The next problem is that I have an atrophying heart valve, which has remained unchanged for two years.

UGO BELIEVED THAT I was as important an influence on his generation of artists—Rirkrit Tiravanija, Pierre Huyghe, Michael Stipe, Ann Collier, Angela Bullock, Verne Dawson, Elisabeth Peyton, and others with whom I have collaborated—as I had been on artists of the 1960s. For years, Ugo considered how to present a poet and his archive as a museum exhibition. He finally came up with what would become "Ugo Rondinone: I ❤ John Giorno" at the Palais de Tokyo in Paris in 2015. Two years later, in honor of my eightieth birthday, it was restaged in nonprofit galleries across New York, with posters proclaiming it all over the city.

Entering the lobby of the Palais de Tokyo and under the High Line in New York, Michael Stipe's video "We All Go Back to Where We Belong" played continuously. The video was shot as a "screen test," as in Andy Warhol's Screen Tests. I was looking directly into the camera as Michael sang to me. It was R.E.M.'s last video, filmed in 2011. Scott King did the graphic design, logo, and lobby murals.

As one entered the exhibition in Paris, the first gallery was Ugo Rondinone's 2015 video installation of my performance of "Thanx 4 Nothing" on four huge screens, hanging on walls covered with black velvet, and on sixteen video monitors. Ugo had made a masterpiece video installation of my best poem.

The next chapter was my archive. For fifty years, I had saved everything—books, magazines, photos, and artwork—in thousands of cardboard cartons in my parents' house in Roslyn Heights. The archive was catalogued, and fifteen thousand scans printed on color paper were now pasted on the walls of the huge gallery. Ten tables displayed binders with all the documents organized by year, eighty for my eighty years. Paintings done between 1968 and 2014 hung on the walls.

The next chapter was dedicated to my collaboration with Andy Warhol: *Sleep* on a four-by-six-meter screen. Eric Satie's *Vexations* played, quietly filling the room. Five monitors on the walls showed the films *John Washing Dishes*, me washing dishes naked; *Untitled (John in Hammock)*, me sleeping; *Untitled (John in Country)*, me flying a kite with Bob Indiana; several other films; the photo booth strip photos; the large still frames from *Sleep* printed on Plexiglas; and other artworks.

Another chapter was Rirkrit Tiravanija's *JG Reads*, a work originally shot on 16mm film that captured me performing my poems from 1973 to 2008 for ten hours. There was Pierre Huyghe's installation video *Sleeptalking*. Françoise Janicot had a wall with one hundred photographs of me over fifty years. There were portraits by Verne Dawson, Elizabeth Peyton, Judith Eisler, and Billy Sullivan.

Another chapter was the wall paintings, sound poems, Dial-a-Poem. Another gallery showcased Giorno Poetry Systems with an installation of the fifty LPs and CDs of 250 poets, which could be listened to on tablet devices while sitting on the artist Angela Bulloch's beanbag chairs, accompanied by an Anne Collier photo installation of the album covers.

The last chapter was a celebration of my life as a Tibetan Nyingma Buddhist. We brought the shrine from 222 Bowery, which was installed on one wall, and on the facing wall was Ugo's bronze sculpture *John's Fireplace*, cast from the fireplace in the third-floor loft where the three-day New Year fire puja (fire ritual) has been performed for more than thirty years. On the other two walls were ancient tankhas and sculpture borrowed from the Musée Guimet in Paris and from the Rubin Museum in New York.

At the New York staging, a new chapter about the AIDS Treatment Project with the film *Loving Kindness* by Peter Ungerleider was featured at Hunter College's 205 Hudson Gallery downtown.

There were the T-shirts made from 1968 to 2017 at White Columns. The summer issues of *The Brooklyn Rail* and *BOMB* magazine were the exhibition catalogues, and works by Kendall Shaw and Joan Wallace were added to the show. While the Paris exhibition was contained in one space, in New York, it was organized in nine nonprofit institutions, which allowed more work to be included, and was the first time they all worked together on one exhibition. It opened simultaneously on the summer solstice, June 21, 2017.

When the exhibition at the Palais de Tokyo opened on October 10, 2015, some 11,500 people waited in line on opening night, and the museum stayed open until 3:00 a.m. I didn't perform at the opening, because the show was the show, but it was arranged for me to come back five weeks later to perform. I was scheduled to depart New York on November 14. The night before, Friday, was the terrorist attack and massacre at the Bataclan theater. I arrived in Paris on Sunday and the city was shut down and in a state of deep shock, grieving from the tragedy. I performed on Wednesday, the first day people came out of their houses and returned to work. I performed *There Was A Bad Tree*, and people started weeping and screaming joyously, which led to a crescendo of sorrow when I did *God Is Man Made*. It was the best performance of my life, because we, the people, were engaged with their suffering in a positive way.

ON FEBRUARY 10, 2017, Ugo and I got married. We had been together for nineteen years, and had talked about doing it since 2011, when it became legal in New York. I had asked Ugo to marry me years before, he said yes, and finally we did it. I was eighty, and Ugo was fifty-four.

We were married the day after a big snowstorm, a sunny, bright, cold Friday. The marriage bureau was crowded, the heavy snow the day before having shut down the city. Located inside a beautiful black-and-green marble art deco masterpiece, the office was filled with ordinary people, or each with their own beauty, waiting in line to do their mundane transactions. They were a reflection of their minds. Joy reflected in their eyes and bodies.

In the weeks and days before the wedding, Ugo and I kept telling each other that we had no special feelings about getting married, that it was nice and neutral. It was an affirmation, a celebration of our being together for almost twenty years. I had always thought that wedding parties were celebrating future failed relations, as many marriages end in divorce and hatred. In our case, we already had a successful life together, sharing body and mind, each being a teacher to the other—a great collaboration, and a fulfilling love. It was already accomplished. The fact that two men could get married was still for me a bit bewildering. When I was a teenager in the 1950s, two men having sex was a crime, and marriage was a fantasy, not an aspiration. When Ugo and I were married, gay people had been doing it for years, and it had become quite ordinary; for me, it was still miraculous. We rendezvoused at the city clerk's office with our friends Laura Hoptman and Verne Dawson, who would be our witnesses. We felt good being in the art deco marriage bureau. "Something old, something new," I said. "Something borrowed, something blue." I had two late-nineteenth-century gold stickpins with oriental pearls, which my mother had bought in an antique store in Southampton in the 1950s. I wore one of them, a Tiffany pin, on my lapel, and I pinned on Ugo's lapel the other, a gold dragon claw grasping the pearl, borrowed. After waiting some time, the wedding ceremony took a minute. We celebrated with a splendid lunch at Odeon and drank lots of champagne. As the weeks and months passed, Ugo and I each had an ever growing warmth, subtle joy, and exhilaration that we were married. It changed our minds in a powerful, nonverbal, positive way.

WHEN I DIE, I always imagined I'd like to be buried, blood and bones, in the Giorno family plot in Calvary Cemetery in Queens.

I inherited the grave deed from my father. It is the huge Catholic cemetery everybody passes through on the Long Island Expressway coming and going to JFK Airport. The grave is on the top of a high ridge in the far northeast corner of the cemetery, among old trees, not far from the top of a ninety-foot cliff over a street below. From the Giorno gravestone, there is a magnificent view of the Manhattan skyline—the Chrysler and Empire State Buildings, Citicorp, and now the new super-high-rise condos built for billionaires—and in the foreground are the office towers recently sprouting in Long Island City.

Since childhood, I thought it was a picture-perfect postcard view for a grave. The splendid view makes it worthy as a pilgrimage site. In later years, I have done meditation practice there for my dead mother and father, as well as my grandparents. My grandmother Maria Panevino's brother Vincenzo Panevino is also buried in the plot along with his wife and children. Most important were the family spirits and protectors, who travel from one generation to another, some lingering in the grave. There is also the residue of the subtle energy of each dead person, which stays for quite a long time, before dissolving into the earth. I liked doing meditation there.

But Ugo and I want to be buried together, and we don't know where. I had wanted my blood and bones to be buried in the cemetery, but maybe cremation is the simplest. Ugo suggests both of us be cremated, and half of our ashes put in the Giorno grave, and the other half put somewhere else, but where? Ugo is legally entitled to be buried in my family grave, as we were both born Catholic, and were married in New York. Do we want the New York skyline, which comes with the karmic baggage of an Irish American and Italian American Catholic cemetery?

IN THE 1970S, every year I did a one-month strict solitary meditation retreat in a cabin at Tail of the Tiger, Trungpa Rinpoche's center in Vermont, and in Darjeeling or Kathmandu, trying to realize the Tibetan Buddhist teachings I had received from Dudjom Rinpoche. In everyday life, my preferred habitual time to do meditation, when I am alone and it fits into my schedule, is early in the morning: I wake up at 5:30 a.m., wash my eyes and have tea, and then do mantra and Vipassana practice until 9:00 a.m. Watching my breath and mind, seeing thoughts arising in my mind and not following them. Intrinsic awareness is seeing where no self is found, and the miraculous emptiness display of life. Then I begin the day slowly, writing, making art and poetry projects. When I wake up every day with Ugo, we do a half-hour meditation together, and I meditate again during the day.

Starting in 2016, every year in April, I have done a one-month strict Dzogchen retreat with Khenpo Tsewang Dongyal at Padma Samye Ling monastery in Walton, New York. About fifty of us receive the teachings of Tecu and Togyal from a text written by Lama Shabkar, a great seventeenth-century Tibetan yogi. Doing practice twelve hours a day every day always brings positive results—training the mind, purification, accessing the blessings of the Nyingma lineages of enlightened lamas—the mind rests in clarity and emptiness. Letting it come, letting it go.

I am eighty-two, in relatively good health, but nearing the end of my life, happily. I believe and feel in a soft way that I have lived a failed life because all my accomplishments were based on the force of my ego. I have one more really important thing to do, and that is to die. I hope I do it right, after doing meditation for more than fifty years. Tibetan Buddhists believe that total enlightenment is possible at the moment of death, if the person has trained their mind and done many years of retreat with the teachings and blessings of the great lamas.

Great demon kings are people controlled by their big egos, but sometimes their egos inspire them to aspire to realize the empty true nature of mind; and they become Buddhas.

ILLUSTRATION CREDITS

Page 4: Courtesy of Nancy Giorno and John Giorno

Page 11: Lawrence Ferlinghetti / Wikimedia Commons

Page 12: Library of Congress Prints and Photographs Division / *New York World-Telegram and Sun* Newspaper Photograph Collection / Phyllis Twachtman

Page 18: Tom Palumbo / Wikimedia Commons

Page 29: Lasse Olsson / Pressens Bild

Page 33: Jack Smith

Page 36: Jonas Mekas, *The Brig*, 1964

Page 39: Library of Congress Prints and Photographs Division / *New York World-Telegram and Sun* Newspaper Photograph Collection / Al Ravenna

Page 41: Fred W. McDarrah / Getty Images

Page 45: Heritage Image Partnership Ltd. / Alamy Stock Photo

Page 56: Photograph by Mark Michaelson

Page 57: The Andy Warhol Museum, Pittsburgh; Founding Collection. © 2019 The Andy Warhol Foundation for the Visual Arts, Inc. / Licensed by Artists Rights Society (ARS), New York.

Page 63: Andy Warhol, "John in Hammock," 1963 / 16mm film, black and white, silent, 3 minutes / © 2019 The Andy Warhol Museum, Pittsburgh, PA, a museum of Carnegie Institute. All rights reserved.

Page 68: *Film Culture* no. 31. Jonas Mekas, ed. Courtesy of John Giorno.

Page 80: Bettmann / Getty Images

Page 87: Photograph by Sally Chamberlain

Page 90: Photograph by Gianfranco Mantegna

Page 96: Bettmann / Getty Images

Page 99: Clairol, Inc. / Wikimedia Commons

Page 105: Ron Galella / Getty Images

Page 113: Courtesy of John Giorno

Page 125: Loomis Dean / *LIFE* Pictures Collection / Getty Images

Page 129: Wikimedia Commons

Page 134: Cecil Beaton / Condé Nast / Getty Images

Page 138: Photograph by John Giorno

Page 143: Jack Mitchell / Getty Images

Page 154: Courtesy of John Giorno

Page 157: Wikimedia Commons

Page 161: Courtesy of John Giorno

Page 162: Courtesy of John Giorno

Page 178: Photograph and design © 1967 by Les Levine

Page 181: The Andy Warhol Museum, Pittsburgh; Founding Collection. © 2019 The Andy Warhol Foundation for the Visual Arts, Inc. / Licensed by Artists Rights Society (ARS), New York.

Page 183: Courtesy of John Giorno

Page 188: Photograph and design © 1967 by Les Levine

Page 190: Photograph and design © 1967 by Les Levine

Page 194: Courtesy of John Giorno

Page 200: Photograph by Françoise Janicot

Page 222: Courtesy of John Giorno

Page 224: Design © 1969 by Les Levine

Page 227: Design © 1969 by Les Levine

Page 231: The Estate of David Gahr / Getty Images

Page 233: Photograph by Gianfranco Mantegna

Page 236: Unknown / The Museum of Modern Art

Page 238: Fred W. McDarrah / Getty Images

Page 239: Design by John Perreault / Courtesy of John Giorno

Page 243: Untitled drawing by Joe Brainard is used by permission of the Estate of Joe Brainard and courtesy of Tibor de Nagy Gallery, New York.

Page 248: Photographs and design © 1969 by Les Levine

Page 259: Courtesy of John Giorno

Page 263: Courtesy of John Giorno

Page 268: John Mills / Dhammadipo

Page 270: Courtesy of the estate of Allen Ginsberg

Page 271: Courtesy of John Giorno

Page 280: Photograph by Gianfranco Mantegna

Page 292: Photograph © 1976 by Les Levine

Page 295: Entermedia / Joseph Asaro and David Secter

Page 302: Giorno Poetry Systems

Page 303: Photograph © Kate Simon

Page 305: Photograph © Kate Simon

Page 309: Giorno Poetry Systems / Keith Haring and Mark Michaelson

Page 312: Giorno Poetry Systems / Mark Michaelson

Page 317: Courtesy of John Giorno

Page 331: Courtesy of John Giorno

Page 334: Courtesy of John Giorno

Page 338: Photograph by Peter Ross

Page 347: Photograph by Maru Teppei

A NOTE ABOUT THE AUTHOR

John Giorno (1936–2019) was a New York–based poet and performance artist and the founder of Giorno Poetry Systems. A long-time member of the Lower Manhattan art scene, Giorno was also an AIDS activist and a Tibetan Buddhist whose work has been exhibited at the Museum of Modern Art and other institutions.